WITHDRAWN

YURY OLESHA

THE
COMPLETE
PLAYS

Edited & Translated by

Michael Green & Jerome Katsell

Ardis, Ann Arbor

Yury Olesha, *The Complete Plays*
Copyright © *1983 by Ardis Publishers*

Translated from the original Russian

Ardis Publishers
2901 Heatherway
Ann Arbor, Michigan 48104

ISBN 0-88233-635-5 (cloth)
ISBN 0-88233-636-3 (paper)

CONTENTS

INTRODUCTION

Olesha and the Theater

Although Yury Olesha (1899-1960) lived from the days of Nicholas II to those of Khrushchev, his literary career was essentially limited to the years 1924-34. As V. Pertsov wrote in his introduction to a 1956 edition of Olesha's selected work, [1] "The literary fate of Yury Olesha is an unusual one. Some thirty years ago he wrote *Envy*—a novel which immediately made his name well-known. After this appeared a book for children, *The Three Fat Men*. Between these comparatively large-scale works and after them there was a cycle of short stories. During these same years Yu. Olesha wrote several dramatic works. All this was accomplished in the second half of the 'twenties, in about the space of six years. Then Olesha fell silent."

It was in 1956, the same year as the above passage was written, that the fragments "from a literary diary" began to appear: these were collected posthumously in 1965 under the title *No Day Without a Line*—a title which seems to indicate a decision not to embark on another work of the proportions of *Envy*, or perhaps an incapacity to do so. Apart from this resolute exercise of his craft, Olesha was active in the cinema and the theater after his brief creative blossoming. The scenario of an anti-Nazi film, *Swamp Soldiers*, dates from 1938. In the 1950s Olesha made a dramatic version of Dostoevsky's *The Idiot*, and one of his last works was a stage version of Chekhov's "Late-Blooming Flowers."

Olesha had grown up in Odessa (which he thought of as his native city), and it was here that he wrote lyrical, dreamy poetry in the manner of Blok, a manuscript collection of which (with an epigraph from Blok) still survives. A move to Moscow in 1920 provided pecuniary reason for a change of style. "I shall never write abstract lyric poetry. That's no use to anyone": so runs the inscription to Mikhail Bulgakov on a collection published in 1924 of topical verse satire he wrote for the railway newspaper *Gudok* under the pen name of Zubilo ("Chisel"). Apart from Bulgakov, his colleagues at *Gudok* included Ilf and Petrov and Valentin Kataev.

Why was it that the author of *Envy*, which has some claim to be the most brilliant novel of the Soviet period (he himself considered it to be an "immortal" work), was unable to create a successor to it? Perhaps the speech made by Olesha at the first All-Union Congress of Soviet Writers in 1934 provides an answer to that question:

Six years ago I wrote a novel called *Envy*. The central character of that story was Nikolai Kavalerov. I was then told that there is a lot of myself in Kavalerov, that this personage is autobiographical, that Kavalerov is me. Yes, Kavalerov looks at the world through my eyes. Kavalerov's colors, images, similes, metaphors and conclusions belong to me. And these were the

7

freshest, brightest colors I had seen. Many of them came from childhood, from a cherished corner of the treasure chest of never-to-be-repeated observations. As an artist, I endowed Kavalerov with the purest power, the power of the first thing, the power of conveying the first thing. And then it was said that Kavalerov is a vulgar nonentity. Knowing that there is much of myself in Kavalerov, I felt this accusation of vulgarity and worthlessness to be directed at myself.

It is not, of course, as a writer for the theater that Olesha is primarily remembered. But the theater—and later the cinema—was important to him. He wrote in 1934, "I love the theater, like to write for the theater and dream of one day becoming a co-director of my own work." The plays included in this almost complete collection of Olesha's dramatic work (only the "Little Drama" in rhymed alexandrines, *Play on an Execution Block*, is omitted) mark the beginning and the end of Olesha's brief creative career. The fairy-tale novel *The Three Fat Men*, though published in 1928, after *Envy*, was in fact written before it and is Olesha's first important work. *A Stern Young Man*, a film scenario written in 1934 for a film made two years later, involved Olesha in political trouble which was probably one of the factors leading to his long creative silence.

Olesha made a dramatic version of *Envy, The Conspiracy of Feelings*, in 1928 at the suggestion of the Vakhtangov Theater, where it received its first production on March 23, 1929. As a kind of variation on a brilliant novel it is of special interest. A. D. Popov, the director, later wrote that Sergei Eisenstein had considered the production his most significant work of that period. The losses entailed by dramatization are more immediately obvious than the gains. The first part of *Envy* is written in the form of a diary of the hero (or anti-hero) Kavalerov, and this leads to a brilliance of visual perception—Olesha's forte as a writer—which is largely lost in the dramatic adaptation, although by means of a scene intended to represent a dream of Kavalerov's Olesha does manage to retain a little of the novel's "first-person" vision. On the other hand, Olesha did sometimes feel that *Envy* suffered from an over-abundance of color and imagery which he would curb if he rewrote the novel. In a way, *The Conspiracy of Feelings* may be said to be such a "rewriting."

Structurally, the play may be held to be superior to the novel. A leading character—and perhaps the least successfully realized character in the novel, the "new Soviet man," the soccer player Volodya Makarov—is eliminated, and Valya is involved instead in a love affair with the salami manufacturer Andrei Babichev. While the novel ends with Kavalerov and Ivan Babichev drinking a toast to indifference on the widow Anechka Prokopovich's sumptuous baroque bed, the play, at least in one version, has Kavalerov turning on Ivan, the leader of the "conspiracy of feelings," and cutting his throat with the razor intended for his brother Andrei, thus symbolically annihilating his own past.

8

That Olesha did not succeed in eliminating this past is clear from his only full-length work for the stage that is not an adaptation of earlier narrative fiction. Elena Goncharova, the actress heroine of *A List of Blessings* was described by a Soviet critic as "the sister of Kavalerov." First presented at Meyerhold's theater on May 20, 1931, *A List of Blessings* is one of several attempts made by the embattled director between 1929 and 1933 to stage a tragedy built on contemporary Soviet reality. Olesha was an admirer of Meyerhold, claiming that "he invented everything which others are now assimilating," and Meyerhold seems to have helped Olesha in the shaping of this piece about the fate of a Soviet theatrical figure whose dilemma reflected his own.

There is a theatrical tradition, going back at least as far as Sarah Bernhardt, who played the role *en travestie*, that Hamlet can be played by a leading actress, and this is the part identified with Goncharova. An outstanding Russian Hamlet of the twenties was Mikhail Chekhov, who was in charge of the Second Moscow Art Theater. Chekhov was an actor of disturbing intensity, and in 1924-25 he presented a version of *Hamlet* in which the Danish Prince was driven to the verge of insanity by his own and mankind's problems—a subjective interpretation which infuriated the Communist press. We are told by Konstantin Rudnitsky in his authoritative *Meyerhold the Director* [2] that Mikhail Chekhov was "of paramount importance to both Olesha and Meyerhold," and that when Meyerhold was asked directly whether there was any truth in the rumors linking Olesha's play with Chekhov, who by this time had been in the West for three years, the director "looking mysterious, stated that he had described 'something' of his talks in Berlin with Mikhail Chekhov to Yu. K. Olesha when the play was still in the planning stages, asking him to use this material, polemically sharpening some of the assumptions and situations."

The part of Goncharova-Hamlet was played by Zinaida Raikh, Meyerhold's wife, and, according to Rudnitsky, "Meyerhold used Raikh's lips to answer many people. It was not without reason that he dreamed of staging *Hamlet* in those days." The consistency of Soviet cultural policy may be illustrated by the fact that the passage from *Hamlet* put into Goncharova's mouth by Olesha-Meyerhold also held special significance for Shostakovich, if we are to credit the composer's smuggled memoirs published under the title of *Testimony*: "I'm particularly touched by Hamlet's conversation with Rosenkrantz and Guidenstern, when Hamlet says that he's not a pipe and he won't let people play him. A marvelous passage. It's easy for him, he's a prince, after all. If he weren't, they'd play him so hard he wouldn't know what hit him." [3]

In 1929 Stanislavsky and Nemirovich-Danchenko suggested that Olesha should make a dramatic version of his fairy-tale novel *The Three Fat Men*, which had been published the previous year although written some time before *Envy*. The piece, which ill health prevented Stanislavsky from directing personally, was first performed on May 24, 1930. This "gentle and transparent" reflection of "the complex social process," to use the author's own words, was Olesha's homage to such "amazing poets as the brothers Grimm, Perrault, Hans Andersen and Hoffmann." This fairy-tale world, in which the "revolutionaries" are performers in a travelling circus and the "dictators" three rather jolly stout gentlemen, one of whom sports a blossoming wart, was a treatment of revolution that the authorities found unalarming. It has become a Soviet classic, provided material for an opera and a ballet; a cinematic version was made by Lenfilm in 1961.

Olesha's choice of acrobats and tightrope walkers, the most fantastic figures of the circus, has, as is usual in his work, a personal and autobiographical connection. As a boy his most cherished ambition was to become an acrobat: "Perhaps this dream of being able to do a somersault was also the first stirring of the artist within me."

As Elizabeth Beaujour points out in her study of Olesha, [4] the period of Olesha's major productivity is bounded by Doctor Arneri and the circus performers of *The Three Fat Men* and Doctor Stepanov and the Komsomol athletes of *A Stern Young Man*. Certainly a persistent type in Olesha's work, alongside the poetic dreamer and longer after glory unable to accept the new Communist society, is the type of the new Soviet man—athletic, handsome and dedicated to the new order. In this context we may remember the heady feelings Olesha experienced for Mayakovsky: "I was in love with Mayakovsky. When he arrived I was overcome with confusion, I trembled when, for some reason or other, he turned his attention to me." These figures, alas, are not among Olesha's successes, products of will and social duty rather than of instinctive understanding. The film scenario *A Stern Young Man* was Olesha's last and perhaps most successful attempt to create such a type. In his speech at the All-Union Congress of Writers in 1934, Olesha thus described his conception: "I want to create a type of young man who will represent the best of my own youth. Communism is not only an economic but a moral system as well, and this aspect will be embodied in its young men and young women. I shall try to show that the new socialist attitude to the world is human in the purest sense of the word."

The film, directed by Abram Rohm, was made two years later at the Ukrainfilm studios, [5] only to be banned as "ideologically and artistically defective," its discussion of equality and leveling was dismissed as pretentious, abstract and empty, the notion that in the future classless society the advanced intelligentsia would hold the reins of power was damned as the influence of bourgeois technocracy, and the idea that the human condition was essentially the same under communism as under modern capitalism was dismissed as "philosophical pessimism directed against the Communist ideals of the revolutionary proletariat." Finally, the film was charged with deviations from the style of socialist realism in its use of stylization and formalistic devices. As a result, Rohm's film was removed from Soviet screens, with reprimands to him and the author.

The fragment *The Black Man*, first published in 1932, precedes *A Stern Young Man*, and its author's failure to complete this promising work can perhaps be explained in part by Olesha's discouragement over the *Stern Young Man* affair. In his brief introduction to the fragment, Olesha confesses his inablility to occupy himself with a "new, significant, vigorous, life-affirming 'sunny' theme" and finally crush the "black lizard theme" which haunts him. The theme which obsesses the writer Zand, Olesha's "double" in this play, is that of murder, and it is worth giving some thought to the extent to which violence pervades Olesha's dramatic work. Although, as he observes in "Notes of a Dramatist," murder, a favorite theme of the bourgeois theater, is not a fit subject for a Soviet dramatist, Olesha is unable to reconcile himself to this corpseless situation: *The Conspiracy of Feelings* and *The Black Man* both pivot around crimes of passion, while the heroine of *A List of Blessings* is shot (by a White Guardsman with a Soviet pistol—a final irony) while shielding a French Communist leader with her body.

Olesha is a wonderfully sensitive writer in his reaction to the visual world (not for nothing did the Soviet critic A. Gurevich note in an article of 1934 that "everything near and dear to his heart is immediately associated in his consiousness with an effect of light"). His thought is profoundly ambiguous, even self-contradictory, represented in its most schematic duality by Elena Goncharova with her two lists, one of the blessings, the other of the crimes of the new Soviet order. A genuine wish to reach out a welcoming hand to the changed society brought about by the Revolution is vitiated by an insurmountable sadness. Gurevich observed that Goncharova's list of the crimes of Soviet power "is saturated with emotion. It is put together out of resentment, tribulation, hardships, out of anger, hatred, anguish and despair . . . .And the list of blessings? Written with a cold hand, it is rationalistic, logical, cold."

If *The Conspiracy of Feelings* was relevant to the industrializing USSR of the nineteen twenties, it is not a whit less relevant to the computerized and automated USA of the 1980s—perhaps more so. The "feelings" of Ivan Babichev's "conspiracy," however ignoble and ridiculous, seem human and appealing when set against the impersonal mechanized world of the future. Olesha's career as a writer was stopped in midstream by an inability to produce the kind of thing required by the authorities: not for him a five-year-plan novel of Socialist construction. "I could go to a construction site, live in a factory among workers, describe them in an article, even a novel, but that wasn't my theme, a theme that came out of my bloodstream, out of my respiratory system. I would have lied, fabricated; I wouldn't have had what is known as inspiration. I find it hard to understand the worker type, the type of hero-revolutionary. He is not someone I am capable of being." It was, then, this reluctance to "lie and fabricate" which made life as a writer difficult for Olesha; it also made him a writer who will undoubtedly survive.

NOTES

1. V. Pertsov, Introduction to Yu. Olesha, *Izbrannye proizvedenniia* (Moscow 1956).

2. Konstantin Rudnitsky, *Meyerhold the Director* (Ann Arbor: Ardis, 1981).

3. Dmitri Shostakovich, *Testimony: The Memoirs of Dmitri Shostakovich*, ed. Solomon Volkov, trans. Antonina E. Bouis (New York, 1979).

4. Elizabeth Klosty Beaujour, *The Invisible Land: A Study of the Artistic Imagination of Iurii Olesha* (New York, 1970), p. 127.

5. Beaujour, p. 129.

THE CONSPIRACY OF FEELINGS

A Play in Seven Scenes

CHARACTERS

Andrei Petrovich Babichev—Director of the Food Trust
Ivan—his brother
Valya—Ivan's adopted daughter
Nikolai Kavalerov
Solomon Shapiro
Anechka Prokopovich—a widow
First tenant
Second tenant
Third tenant
Young Man
Elizaveta Ivanovna
Her husband
Doctor (appears in dream sequence only)
Mikhal Mikhalych
Zinochka
Lady in green
Lady of the house
Vitya
Harry
Heavily intoxicated guest
Less intoxicated guest
Venerable old man
Harman—a German

In Scene Two: tenants
In Scene Seven: union representatives, soccer players, spectators

The action takes place in the 1920s in Moscow.

SCENE ONE

The house of Andrei Babichev. Morning. A light, clean room. On the wall in a glass frame the plan of the factory-canteen "Quarter." The huge sign "Quarter" hits you smack in the eye. The first floor. Windows, a glass door; beyond the windows a terrace, greenery and a garden. Everything is light and clear. Doors to the left and to the right. Kavalerov is sitting on an unmade divan-bed. He slowly gets dressed. On the floor in the middle of the room is a mat with a stool on it. Andrei Babichev is pouring water from a pitcher into the wash-basin. Andrei is bare to the waist, wearing knitted underpants.

KAVALEROV. A month ago you picked me up in front of a beer hall. You brought a completely unknown young man into your house. And here I am, a wretched lumpenproletarian, already living a month under the roof of a famous man.

ANDREI. Don't be so sheepish. Everything's turned out terrific. You know English. I'm working on a book and you've been a great help. I'm really thankful.

KAVALEROV. That means I can sleep on this divan until you've finished your book. Yes? And then what?

ANDREI. Then, I don't know.

KAVALEROV. See what I mean. Well, in that case I'll clear out today.

ANDREI. It's not right to leave your work. (*Places the wash-basin on the stool*). That's right . . .yes. An excellent basin. I think water looks much better in a basin than out in the open, free. Just see what a super blue basin it is. A beauty. Take that window over there; if you bend over you can see it dancing in the basin. (*Bends down and looks into the basin, walks around it*). Ah, terrific! (*Jiggles the basin*). Well then . . .(*Admiringly*). A beaut. (*Goes into the bedroom*).

KAVALEROV (*alone*). How much do you weigh?

ANDREI (*from the bedroom*). Two hundred fifteen pounds. (*Comes out carrying a towel*). Yesterday I was going down a flight of stairs. I was going along and then I felt—the Devil knows what—my boobs were bouncing. Got that, Kavalerov? My breasts bouncing away, like a woman. It was a nightmare. There and then I decided to slap on a new set of exercises. (*Proceeds to his exercises. Deep knee bends*). O-o-one . . .two-o . . .o-o-one . . .two-o . . .o-o-one . . .two-o . . .You're really getting fat. How old are you, Kavalerov?

KAVALEROV. Twenty-eight. The same age as our twentieth century.

ANDREI (*throwing out his arms*). And a one-two. And a one-two. And a, and a, and a one-two.

KAVALEROV. I often think about the century. It's an illustrious one.

My youth coincided with that of the century.

ANDREI. And a one-two. And a one-two...Ugh...

KAVALEROV. But, unfortunately, I was born in Russia. I would like to have been born in a little French town, to grow up with dreams...To set myself some sort of high goal...And one beautiful day to leave the little town on foot for the capital and there to reach my goal...But I wasn't born in the West.

ANDREI (*running in place*). Up-down. Hup-hup, up-hup.

KAVALEROV. In Europe a gifted man has room enough to gain fame. They love the famous over there. But here? Nobody likes it when the other fellow's famous. That's true, isn't it?

ANDREI. Sure is true. (*Lies on his back. Raises his legs one after the other*).

KAVALEROV. In our country the roads to fame are blocked as if by railroad crossings. The man of talent here has to decide to lift the crossing with some terrible scandal, or else just fade away.

ANDREI (*raising a leg*). Oo...O-one...My leg is like a railroad crossing. Each weighs eighty-five pounds.

KAVALEROV. You say that personal fame must disappear. You say the human personality is nothing, that the human mass is the only thing. Isn't that what you say?

ANDREI. That's what we say.

KAVALEROV. Nonsense. I want my own glory. I demand recognition.

Andrei gets up from the mat and then down on all fours so that his rear is turned to Kavalerov.

ANDREI (*up on his feet*). U-ugh...That'll do it. Now for some water. How about it.

KAVALEROV. You demand a sober approach to life. That's why I'm going to create something patently ridiculous, on purpose. I'll perpetrate a piece of brilliant mischief. On purpose. You want everything to be useful, but I want to be useless. (*Pause*). For example, I might just finish myself off. (*Pause*). Without any reason; out of mischievousness. To prove that I have the right to deal with myself any way I please. Namely, to commit a stupid suicide. And right at this very time when so many people are talking about clearness of purpose. Yes, hang myself. (*Pause*). I'll just hang myself right here in your doorway.

At this point Andrei goes out carrying the wash-basin through the door on the right, then returns.

ANDREI. It'll be better to hang yourself from the entryway to the

National Economy Department. On Revolution Square. There's a huge archway there. Have you seen it? Over there the whole thing would come off quite effectively. (*Goes out again through the door on the right, carrying the stool*).

KAVALEROV (*alone*). Stupid bureaucrat.

Andrei returns and continues to the bedroom by the door to the left.

I want to tell you about a little incident.

ANDREI (*from the bedroom*). Tell me about it.

KAVALEROV. Once...it was long ago...I was a little high-schooler. My father took me to the wax museum. You know, a waxworks exhibition. There were some glass cases there with various figures in them: Cleopatra, a gorilla abducting a maiden, Robespierre on the guillotine... A handsome man was lying in one of the cases, wearing a frock coat. He was wounded in the chest, a dying man with his eyes rolling up. My father told me that it was the French President Sadi Carnot who had been wounded by an anarchist. (*Pause*). The magnificent man lay there, his beard thrown back. His life ebbed slowly...like the hours...It was incredible. For the first time then I heard the roar of time.

ANDREI (*still from the bedroom*). How's that?

KAVALEROV. The roaring drone of time. Don't you get it? I heard time roaring. Understand? The ages crashed about me. I cried from ecstasy. I decided right then to become famous.

ANDREI. Oh yeah, sure thing.

KAVALEROV. I was still a high-school boy, but I made up my mind that day to become famous. I decided that no matter what I would be so successful that my portrait and wax double, filled with the roaring of the centuries, would adorn the great museum of the future...

Andrei comes back dressed from the bedroom.

There are people things don't like, and there are people things like. Take you, Andrei Petrovich...things like you. Suits you just right. Me, well, things don't like me.

Andrei takes some food from the cupboard and sits at a round table, eats.

The furniture conspires to trip me. Yesterday this corner (*points to corner of the writing desk*) literally hit me. See, I just dropped a cuff-link. Where is it? Where did it disappear? If you'd dropped a cuff-link it would stay somewhere nearby, but for me it goes tumbling under a sideboard. Just look, the sideboard is laughing at me!

17

ANDREI. Kavalerov, you should meet my brother Ivan. You'd find a common language. By the way, he's appeared in Moscow again. Didn't show himself for a whole year. He was always around, my brother Ivan, then — poof and he's gone. Where's Ivan? Nobody knows. Impossible to know; maybe he's in jail, and maybe he's in the nut house . . .(*Pause*). Yesterday he was walking on Petrovich Boulevard. I saw him from the bus stop. He was walking along holding a pillow behind his ear. Children were running after him. A nut, a looney. So there he is, striding along, then he stopped, took off his bowler and bowed in all directions.

KAVALEROV. With a pillow?

ANDREI. Yes, with a pillow. A great nut, my little brother Ivan.

KAVALEROV. Why does he go around carrying a pillow?

ANDREI. Oh, the hell with him.

Pause. Kavalerov sits down to shave and continues shaving throughout the scene.

So, Kavalerov, we're on the verge of great things, eh?

KAVALEROV. Because your brother's back?

ANDREI. The hell with my brother. I mean that in a few days a new type of salami sausage is coming out.

KAVALEROV. I've been hearing about that sausage of yours for a month.

ANDREI. You think it's nothing to make a sausage? And what a sausage! Do you understand something about the salami business?

KAVALEROV. Zero.

ANDREI (*having eaten and in an expansive mood*). It'll be a remarkable sausage. You should respect me, Kavalerov. I've really produced something. It'll be a great triumph. We're sending it to the Milan exhibition. And then we'll build "Quarter." Here, let me show you our "Quarter." (*Walks over to the plan of "Quarter," looks, steps back, approaches with admiration*). Our factory-canteen, a mass production kitchen, is called "Quarter," Kavalerov. Why call it "Quarter," you say? Huh? Because we're going to sell a two-dish dinner there for twenty-five kopecks. A quarter each. Terrific, isn't it? I think both dishes should be meat; good, eh? Have a look at these plans our German drew up. What a beauty! Huge main building, over here a garden. See it? Towers, a patio. Terrific? I think it's just terrific. He's a young German too. Well, that's it, "Quarter." Oh yeah, here's the dining commons. There'll be breakfasts, tea, dinners, home delivery, a children's area with scientifically prepared milk porridge. You know, Kavalerov, we'll be able to put out two thousand dinners. A regular sea of cabbage soup. You've got to write an epic on it, Kavalerov.

KAVALEROV. An epic? About what?

18

ANDREI. About cabbage soup, of course. An epic on mass dining. Two thousand people eat cabbage soup to the music of Wagner. Sounds grand to me. An epic poem on the demolition of cooking pots. (*Pause*). It's just terrific! Terrific! To hell with small portions of this and that; to hell with little bottles and packages. You know, a bit of salt, a little bottle of sunflower oil . . .It's terrible. Strictly amateur. "Quarter" will show them. We'll stock eight hundred pounds of sunflower oil! We'll smash all those frying pans and bottles and pots; to hell with the lot of them.

KAVALEROV. Andrei Petrovich, do you know . . .I think I saw your brother yesterday too . . .Does he look like you?

ANDREI. Yes . . .Only smaller.

KAVALEROV. Wears a bowler.

ANDREI. Yeah, goes around in a bowler. I'd like to smash it flat on his head. The nut, the monkey. It's just not right to go around in a bowler. Only our little old men and ambassadors pull that kind of stuff.

KAVALEROV. That's right, sure. In a bowler . . .I saw him. On Chernyshevsky Lane.

ANDREI (*excited*). Where?

KAVALEROV. He was standing in the middle of the road. His bowler was tilted way back on his head. There he was in the middle of the road, a small, plumpish little man with his head thrown back . . . Doesn't Valya live over there, on the second floor?

ANDREI. That's where you saw him?

KAVALEROV. Yes, there. He had a pillow in a yellow pillow-case. An old one . . .

ANDREI. The bastard. He was standing under Valya's window . . .

KAVALEROV. But Valya *is* his daughter.

ANDREI. Not quite, his adopted daughter. Not natural daughter, adopted daughter. And that's all over with. She left him; he has no rights over her; she's completely independent. (*Pause*). Was he really under her window?

KAVALEROV. No doubt about it.

ANDREI. And Valya? Did you see her? Did she glance out?

KAVALEROV (*after a moment*). No. Her window was empty. There was only a small vase with a single flower in it in the window.

ANDREI. She's finished with all that. He doesn't have any right to her.

KAVALEROV. Andrei Petrovich, it seems to me . . .

ANDREI (*roughly*). What *seems* to you?

KAVALEROV. Let me tell you a strange little tale. Listen . . . A simple scene I saw: a little man in a bowler stood in the road with a pale and good-natured face. He held a pillow pressed to his chest, and that was all.

ANDREI (*roughly again*). And so what?

KAVALEROV. You think that kind of thing is funny. Let me tell you

19

something. Yes, I remember it now. I was struck right away by a certain something. It was your brother's expression; it simply astonished me. Do you know ... I believe your brother is a man of genius.

Andrei is silent.

Why do you hate your brother?

ANDREI. He should be shot. (*Andrei sits at his desk and begins to work, soon wrapped in concentration*).

KAVALEROV (*shaves*). I hate you, Andrei Petrovich. (*Pause*). I hate you. You don't hear me. When you work you don't hear a thing. What are you so damned busy with that you can't hear a thing? (*Pause*). Bureaucrat. Stupid bureaucrat. You're quite the hot shot, Andrei Petrovich.

ANDREI (*tears away suddenly from his work, quickly raises his head*). What? What's that? Someone's calling.

KAVALEROV (*frightened*). Yes?

A telephone on the table; Andrei grabs the receiver, listens.

ANDREI. Yeah, I'm listening. Hello! Who is it? (*into the receiver*). They've already called. (*Goes back to work*).

KAVALEROV. I hate you. Know why? Because you're a man without imagination, a dullard, a sausage-maker ... (*Pause*). Why do you think you're the good child of the century and I'm the bad one? (*Pause*). You're crushing me. Who gave you the right to crush me? (*Pause*). Are you more highly organized? (*Pause*). Stronger? More significant? (*Pause*). Why should I recognize any superiority in you? We're going to have this out, Andrei Petrovich ... You know, I'm only twenty-eight and you're already forty!

ANDREI (*suddenly gets up again; violent and loud*). What? What was that? What did you say? Forty? Ha-ha-ha! (*Overcome with laughter, snarls, snorts*). Forty. He said forty. Raving birdbrain. You're a nut, Kavalerov. A regular comedian. Forty...Just listen...You say —forty; no, it's not forty. We're going to sell them for thirty-five; do you believe it, thirty-five apiece. Get it? Here's the figures...Come over here. (*Pulls Kavalerov to the table and grabs up some papers*). Look. I counted it up. (*Laughter*). Now you just take a look! Seventy percent veal. Terrific? I think it's just terrific. Thirty-five kopecks apiece, Kavalerov, thirty-five, but not forty. You did say forty?

KAVALEROV. Uh-hum, forty.

ANDREI (*laughs*). No, thirty-five. It's fantastic, really terrific. Listen to me, Kavalerov. We're sending this salami of ours to the exhibit in Milan. Don't you understand? We're sending it to Milan, you nut. Thirty-five apiece. It's a real victory...Hooray! Shout hooray, Kavalerov.

Kavalerov is silent.

What does that look on your puss mean?

KAVALEROV. Just that I have no desire to shout hooray.

ANDREI. An eccentric. Why not? Don't you think it's possible to sell seventy percent veal sausage for thirty-five kopecks each? Have a look here; it's the complete tally. It should be clear enough.

KAVALEROV. Oh, it's quite clear.

ANDREI. Well then, shout hooray! Silence . . .he's some kind of comic.

KAVALEROV. It's not your sausage.

ANDREI. Not the sausage, then what? You know all the factories and children's homes will buy our salami; look here (*indicates some papers*); here's the figures on food values . . .Carbohydrates, just look . . .

KAVALEROV (*suddenly*). Bravo! Bravo! All right, I'll shout hooray. Hooray, Andrei Petrovich! Hooray!

ANDREI. It is terrific, isn't it? I think it's simply terrific.

KAVALEROV. Terrific. Imagine: a rocket blasts off . . .

ANDREI. What does a rocket have to do with anything?

KAVALEROV. Just imagine: a rocket blasts off. A blind man listens to the rocket bursting. He hears the explosion of the rocket. Does he understand anything of what's going on?

ANDREI. I don't think he understands anything.

KAVALEROV. I don't understand anything either.

ANDREI. What's not to understand? Here are the figures.

KAVALEROV. I simply can't understand your enthusiasm.

ANDREI. It means you're blind.

KAVALEROV. You're wrong there. To me it means that my eyes are my only real possession. Only the eyes. There's nothing more. I see everything.

ANDREI. Then have a look at these figures.

KAVALEROV. It's you I'm looking at.

ANDREI. A regular comic.

KAVALEROV. And I see a famous man, a man with the mark of fame on him.

ANDREI. Do you really think so?

KAVALEROV. I look at you and see that you simply glow.

ANDREI. Of course. Why not glow when victory is yours.

KAVALEROV. I see that the nature of fame and glory has changed. In this world fame flares up simply because a new type of sausage pops out of a machine. But you were once a student too, Andrei Petrovich; you even lived in Paris; you read biographies, history . . .It's all quite different there. Paris has lots of monuments. They speak of a different sort of glory. I look at you and realize that the nature of fame and glory has changed.

ANDREI. Yes, in my opinion too it has changed.

KAVALEROV. Everywhere? Or just here? Andrei Petrovich, I want fame, I want it too.

ANDREI. So what's your problem?

KAVALEROV. I want my fame right here, right now, next to you.

ANDREI. Then let's shout hooray together.

Kavalerov is silent.

I don't understand a thing.

KAVALEROV. I want to beam and glow in the way you do.

ANDREI. Beam away, old boy, beam away.

KAVALEROV. A new breed of salami does not inspire me to beaming.

ANDREI. Just what the hell is it you want?

KAVALEROV. Fame.

Valya comes in from the terrace.

ANDREI (*to Valya*). See how it is; you've come and I'm leaving.

VALYA. I can go with you.

ANDREI. No, sit here awhile, with Kavalerov.

KAVALEROV. Hello there, Valya.

ANDREI. Do you know that Ivan's popped up?

VALYA. Yes, I know. He was standing under my window yesterday. He called out to me.

ANDREI. What'd you do?

VALYA. I hid myself. I heard him though; he stood there a whole hour. Well, then I took a look anyway. I'm sorry for him.

ANDREI. He's not worth it. You shouldn't have bothered to look.

VALYA. But he called out to me.

ANDREI. The hell with him!

VALYA. Come on, that's cruel.

ANDREI. Cruel. Hell, no, no way it's cruel.

VALYA. He's really humiliating himself. He stood there for a whole hour.

ANDREI. Yeah, humiliating himself. Just think . . . Stood there a whole hour, stood under your window . . .

VALYA. A whole hour . . .

ANDREI. It's all a big show if you ask me. Don't believe him; he just likes standing under windows. I know his tricks; likes walking under my window too.

VALYA. He came with a pillow. "Here, Valya," he said, "I've brought you the pillow you slept on once upon a time."

ANDREI (*laughs loudly*). Really? How did it go? " . . .the pillow you slept on once upon a time!" Can you believe it? And why is that pillow any better than the one you sleep on now? Every pillow has its story to tell. In other words, I have no doubt . . .

VALYA. Did you see him too, Kavalerov?

KAVALEROV. I did.

ANDREI. Why didn't you tell me Valya talked to him?

KAVALEROV. I'm not Valya's keeper.

ANDREI. You're the same type as he, Kavalerov. Don't you think so, Valya? They should really get together. Don't you think, Valya? They'd find lots to talk about. Well, I'd better go . . .Are you coming? No, better stay with Kavalerov. (*Suddenly*). But why do you walk under Valya's window? (*to Valya*). Stay with him here. He likes it under your window.

KAVALEROV. You talk to me as if I were your clown. One thing I don't understand—why did you pick me up? When I was drunk silly in front of the beer hall—you shouldn't have bothered. Why did you, anyway?

ANDREI. A man's heart isn't made of stone.

KAVALEROV. But you, a glorious man of action, and me, a nobody. I mean, why would such a famous man bring a complete unknown into his house?

ANDREI. Valya took pity on you. Remember? (*to Valya*). What was it you said, Valya? You, Kavalerov, were lying spread-eagled. Valya took us in the car. Remember, you said it, Valya. She said, Kavalerov, that you have a tragic face. Does he have a tragic face?

VALYA (*with a smile*). It does seem tragic to me. Why attack Kavalerov; he's a good fellow.

ANDREI. You really think so?

VALYA. Yes, I do.

Pause.

ANDREI (*looks at his watch*). Well, okay. You know how much we're going to sell this sausage for? Thirty-five apiece. Terrific! Well, let's go. You coming?

They go out the glass door.

KAVALEROV (*alone, goes after them a bit, not yet finished with what he has to say*). Valya . . . (*Holds shaving set in his hands. Collects shaving things; the razor glistens in his hand. Addresses himself*). Why did you kill Andrei Babichev? (*Pause*). Out of hatred? (*Pause*). No. No.

(*Pause*). So, why then? (*Pause*). I was living in courtyards. He took me in. He's my benefactor. Then why did I raise my hand against him? (*Pause*). Why did I kill Andrei Babichev?

CURTAIN

SCENE TWO

A kitchen. A gas-stove, faucet above the sink. Entryways, passageways, stairways. Several doors at various heights. An exit door at the top; a long staircase leads to it. Morning. The tenants are in the kitchen. Lizaveta Ivanovna—a pretty woman wearing a robe which keeps coming open. Little shelves, dishes, a primus-stove, steam.

FIRST TENANT (*at the stove over a boiling pot*). You shouldn't pay any attention to rumors. It's just idiotic gossip.

SECOND TENANT (*cleaning his slippers*). My pal at work told me about it. He saw it all with his own eyes. There was this wedding. I even know the address, it's on Yakimanka Street. An ordinary wedding, a bill collector got married. My pal was there. And then some unknown guy came walking in . . .just sauntered in . . .no one knew him . . .understand? A very strange fella . . .wearing a bowler . . .He didn't take off his hat and had a pillow in his hands to boot . . .I can even give you the particulars; a yellow pillow in a yellow pillow-case.

FIRST TENANT. Bull. Absolute bull.

SECOND TENANT. Everything's bull to you. Just listen, and you too, Lizaveta Ivanovna. There're some fantastic things happening these days in Moscow.

LIZAVETA IVANOVNA. You better speak more quietly about it.

SECOND TENANT. Why should I, I'm not speaking about politics. Okay, then . . .So an unknown person in a bowler with a yellow pillow came to this bill collector's wedding. He came and said (*strikes a pose*): "Why are you marrying? Don't marry, you'll only produce your enemy in the world."

LIZAVETA IVANOVNA. What business is it of his?

SECOND TENANT. Amazing. "Don't get married," he said, "no reason to marry. Our children—are our enemies." Listen to what happened next: the bride, of course, fainted, and the groom got ready for a fight. It was then that the unknown man left.

FIRST TENANT. What's so surprising about that? Drunks do all sorts of things.

SECOND TENANT. Wait a second, there's more to come. After the unknown visitor left, the guests sat down to have a good time and to chow down...before they knew what was going on the wine had turned to water in the bottles...

A door opens. The third tenant comes in with his briefcase; he is on his way to work.

Silence.

THIRD TENANT. What are you talking about? About the man with the pillow? I heard about it too...Different incidents are being talked about...A man with a pillow is walking around Moscow...around the apartments, beer joints, word of honor!

Silence.

FIRST TENANT. It's a simple matter, citizens. Very simple. Society, or rather the street, is thirsting for a miracle. You get what I'm saying? People live boring lives. Get that? They're searching for something unusual. But this is all gossip, gossip...Where we live, are miracles really possible? Is it really possible for port wine to turn into water?

Pause.

THIRD TENANT. The Devil knows...Maybe it's some kind of advertisement, maybe a film shooting. Some strange things are happening, anyway.

LIZAVETA IVANOVNA (*to the first tenant*). Your milk is boiling over.

SECOND TENANT. It really is true; we do lead boring lives. Make the milk, go to the toilet, go to work. And, who knows, maybe a real miracle worker has arrived?

FIRST TENANT. Crap.

THIRD TENANT. Why do you say crap? I don't mean a miracle in the direct sense, but possibly there's some kind of a hypnotist; practicing mass hypnosis.

LIZAVETA IVANOVNA. And what do you think he puts into people's heads?

Silence.

SECOND TENANT. It's all very strange.

FIRST TENANT (*hurries to his doorway with a pot*). Don't pay any attention to it, he's probably just off his nut. And the public is always ready for far-out sensations . . . (*Disappears in the doorway*).

THIRD TENANT. They'll arrest him eventually. (*Goes up the stairs and out*).

The second tenant also abandons the kitchen. Lizaveta is alone by the gas stove. A young man looks out from a doorway above.

YOUNG MAN (*leans on a railing at the top of the stairs and looks at Lizaveta Ivanovna*). If you didn't love him you couldn't sleep with him. How can you belong to me and still remain his wife?

LIZAVETA IVANOVNA. What do you want anyway? Go ahead, cut his throat. If I leave him, he'll kill you, and me too.

YOUNG MAN. Are you afraid?

LIZAVETA IVANOVNA. Go ahead, slit his throat.

YOUNG MAN. You really want me to? I'm ready to cut his throat right now.

Lizaveta Ivanovna is silent.

Where is he anyway? He hasn't gone out yet, has he?

LIZAVETA IVANOVNA. No, I'm making his breakfast hash.

YOUNG MAN. Aha, he's still at home. Oh, I can imagine him; he's sitting on the bed in his pants with the footstraps, combing his hair and thinking that you'll be bringing him his breakfast soon.

Lizaveta Ivanovna is silent.

You're a real whore. You can love two at a time and give yourself to both. It's all the same to you; either I'll cut his throat or he'll cut mine. Why do you come out to the kitchen practically naked? I know why. You want everyone to get excited seeing you. You're just a slut.

The third tenant leaves the door at the top of the stairs open as he goes out. The open doorway shimmers; it leads to the out-of-doors and morning. Ivan Babichev appears in the doorway. He is a small rumpled fat fellow in a bowler. Behind his ear he carries a large soiled pillow in a yellow pillow-case. He stops at the head of the stairs and listens.

LIZAVETA IVANOVNA. I love you.

YOUNG MAN. You're a liar. You love your husband just as much as me.

LIZAVETA IVANOVNA. Here's the knife. (*Points; a knife is lying on the stove; pause*). Here's the knife.

The young man is silent.

Coward.

YOUNG MAN. All right. (*Comes down the stairs to her*). What are you smiling about? You don't believe that I can commit a crime for you?

A man's voice behind the door.

Liza!

YOUNG MAN. Go...your master is calling.

VOICE. Liza!

LIZAVETA IVANOVNA. Coward!

YOUNG MAN. Now just you wait. I'm no coward. But if I slice his throat...I'll go right now and cut his throat, but they'll put me away, I'll rot in jail eight or nine years, and you, what about you? You'll live with some others.

VOICE. Liza!

YOUNG MAN. Do you really want me to? Listen, you'll come back in a minute and I'll be dead as a door nail. I'll cut my own throat. Want me to?

LIZAVETA IVANOVNA. You're just saying all that. (*Shouts to the door*). I'm coming! (*Exits*).

YOUNG MAN (*sits on the stairwell in great agitation*). What should I do? What can I do?

IVAN (*from above*). In my opinion, you have to cut the husband's throat.

YOUNG MAN (*jumps up*). What? Who's that? Who said that?

IVAN. In my opinion, you have to cut the husband's throat.

YOUNG MAN. You overheard us? What business is it of yours, anyway?

IVAN. Don't be angry. Yes, my friend, whole days, days and nights I walk about...along strange stairways, I look into strange windows, I catch the sounds of strange words. (*Pause*). What are you waiting for, young man? The knife is gleaming. Why do you hesitate? Right at this very moment the lady you love is kissing someone else. Listen carefully...such silence behind the door. They're kissing.

YOUNG MAN. Jesus, you've got a lot of nerve.

Ivan comes down into the kitchen. He sits on a stool, takes off his bowler and breathes heavily. He places his pillow by his feet.

YOUNG MAN. Get the hell out! Who are you, anyway? Maybe you've come to steal the primus?

IVAN. I've come in search of heroes.

YOUNG MAN (*with irony*). I like that. So, you heard what we were

27

talking about?

IVAN. Yes, I did. I listened to you and I was delighted. Aren't you going to finish the little drama which you have begun so marvelously?

YOUNG MAN. No, just you listen, this is some kind of absurd nonsense. What do you really want, huh?

IVAN. As I told you, I'm searching for heroes.

YOUNG MAN. Stop being such an ass. (*Looks him over*). A pillow. I don't understand any of this . . .some sort of dangerous behavior . . .

IVAN. You are a hero. You're a true hero and don't even have an inkling of it. You should be proud of yourself.

YOUNG MAN. You're making me late for work.

IVAN. I'm speaking of jealousy.

YOUNG MAN (*angrily*). What?

IVAN. I'm thinking of your jealousy.

YOUNG MAN. It's none of your business.

IVAN. It is, indeed. You simply must kill the husband of that pretty woman. She is very pretty, you know. But you're right, she's a bitch. You called her a bitch-whore, a slut. In other words, she is what was called in the old days, in the old world, that is — a demonic woman.

YOUNG MAN. That's right. You can see it at first glance . . .Oh, my God, what can I do?

IVAN. Don't lose courage.

YOUNG MAN. It's hard not to.

IVAN. Why hold yourself back? The feeling of jealousy — is a great and ancient feeling.

YOUNG MAN. But what can I do?

IVAN. Assert yourself. The ancient feelings are wonderful. Love, hate, jealousy, pride, envy, pity.

YOUNG MAN. Are you an actor?

IVAN. I'm a leader, young man.

YOUNG MAN. You're making my head spin.

IVAN. I'm the ruler of these ancient feelings. I'm the leader of a conspiracy.

YOUNG MAN. I'll call the neighbors.

IVAN. I'm putting a troupe together. I need the most shining representatives of various feelings. Lovers of honor, traitors, cowards, jealous lovers . . .

YOUNG MAN. Who the hell knows what this is all about!

IVAN. You are a carrier of one of the great feelings. Jealousy. Therefore you're a participant in my conspiracy.

YOUNG MAN. God help us, some sort of baloney. He walks into a strange house . . .

Pause.

IVAN. Here, take the knife and go in without knocking. She's in his embraces right now.

YOUNG MAN. Get the hell out of here!

IVAN. Look here now, there are two types of lover. You, for example, are jealous. But your jealousy is passive. Consequently, you're an unhappy lover.

YOUNG MAN. Do you really think so? But tell me . . . Oh, get the hell out!

IVAN. Love, like unhappiness, is an ancient concept. The unhappy lover is also a character from the old world. And so I greet you. You will take part in the last parade of human feelings. And you'll be on an equal footing with all the other heroes.

YOUNG MAN. She's beautiful, don't you think? You noticed that immediately.

IVAN. She shines like a vase. But now, at this very moment, your rival is squirting his love into that vase. Quick, take the knife.

YOUNG MAN. I can't, I just can't.

IVAN. Quiet. Listen. Soft rustling. A pillow fell. A pillow fell from their bed because of their love-making. Quiet.

They stand by the door and listen. Suddenly there is a terrible scream inside and the door swings open. Lizaveta comes running out in a terrible state. Neighbors appear; distraught faces, hands in the air, panic. The husband appears in the doorway.

SECOND TENANT. For God's sake! For God's sake! What happened?

HUSBAND. I'm satisfied. Don't interfere please. You're all swine.

SHOUTS. He killed his wife! Hold him!

HUSBAND. Break it up, now . . . Where is he? (*Climbs the stairs*). Where's the little sniveler? (*Knocks on the door from which the young man had come*). Swine! Pig! I'll break it down! Open up! Don't hide. I'll kill the both of you.

SHOUTS. Guard! Police!

IVAN (*to the young man who is hiding behind his back*). Where are you hiding? No, that won't do. Go on now, don't hide, young man. Go to your destiny. You've got to stick up for your lover. (*Cries out to Liza's husband; points to the young man who is hiding*). Here he is! Right over here!

YOUNG MAN. Oh my God, what's happening! Don't let him . . . Help, save me! Aaaaaahh!

The husband comes down the stairs and catches sight of his rival. A moment of intense quiet.

SHOUTS. Grab him!

HUSBAND (*falls at Ivan's feet*). I killed her.

IVAN (*claps his hands*). Long live the ancient human feelings! Long live love!

SHOUTS. He's insane! Help, police!

IVAN. My brother, where are you? Do you see it, Andrei? Andrei, my brother. Come to me, come. Cowards! Jealous lovers! Those struck by love! Heroes! Knights! Come to me! To me, the old world, the old feelings! I'll lead you on your last campaign.

CURTAIN

SCENE THREE

At Andrei Babichev's. Evening. Andrei is working at a table. Ivan.

IVAN. We haven't seen each other for half a year. How are your state farms, apiaries and dining halls coming along?

ANDREI. I've invented a new type of sausage, Vanya.

IVAN. And I've invented a machine.

ANDREI. No kidding? That's great. What kind of machine is it?

IVAN. I've invented an amazing machine, Andrei. You know that my dream has always been to invent the machine of machines, the universal machine. I thought about a perfect piece of technology; I hoped to concentrate in a single piece of apparatus hundreds of different functions. I thought about how to tame the mastodon of technology, to make it tame and domestic.

ANDREI. That's great. I envy you; you have tremendous range. I'm even ashamed, with my sausage . . . And here you are — tackling the mastodon of technology — and me with some sort of miserable salami. True, it is seventy percent veal. But go on, go on . . .

IVAN. And I've succeeded, Andrei. I've invented such a machine.

ANDREI (*suddenly*). Why do you drink, Vanya? You've really puffed up.

IVAN. Don't interrupt me. I've invented a machine which can blow up mountains, which can fly, lift weights, crush ore . . . It's the very essence of engineering . . . (*Suddenly*). Why are you smiling?

ANDREI (*with irony*). From pleasure. I'm savouring your triumphs ahead of time. You'll be rendering the state an unforgettable service.

IVAN. I've invented a machine that knows how to do everything. I gave it hundreds of abilities.

ANDREI. Listen, maybe it could be used in the sausage industry too.

IVAN. She can do anything.

ANDREI. Goddamn! We'll give you the Banner of Labor. What's the time? Eleven. It's late, otherwise I'd call . . .the Committee of Inventions, and the National Economy Department at the Council of People's Commissars.

IVAN. That would be useless.

ANDREI. Why?

IVAN. You didn't let me finish what I was saying. Wait a second . . .I understood the day I built the machine that I had been given the supernatural possibility of taking revenge for my epoch. Neither you, nor the Committee of Inventions, not even our age as a whole — none of you will get my machine.

ANDREI. This is a great blow to us. Just think, we were so far behind and suddenly your machine comes along. Your machine — you would have made us happy, your machine would have propelled us to the forefront, to the very flowering of technology.

IVAN. Don't be a fool, Andrei. I'm speaking very seriously. So please don't be a fool. I can only repeat — I've invented an amazing machine.

Silence.

But you won't get it. You're right, I'm the knight of a dying age. I'm avenging my age, my age which gave me the brain I carry around in my skull, my brain, that invented this amazing machine. Who should I leave it for? You? You and your kind are gobbling us up like food . . .You gobble up the nineteenth century in the way a boa-constrictor digests a rabbit. I don't want to be digested and squeezed out again. You're in the habit of chewing us up, digesting us and then eliminating us. You're sucking up our technology, our feelings. You won't get my machine, you won't use me, you won't suck out my brains. Do you know what my machine is?

ANDREI. I haven't a clue, Vanya.

IVAN. Well, here you are representing the new age, and me the old age. And here's the finger for you. My machine — that's the finger, the fig, a big bright "up-yours" that the dying world shows the age being born. Oh, the machine, it's your idol.

Silence

I took revenge for my epoch. The age that was a mother to me.

ANDREI (*with a smirk*). You really scare me.

IVAN. I've perverted the machine. Do you understand what that means?

ANDREI. No, what are you getting at?

IVAN. You mock our feelings. You think that our soul, the ancient human soul is fated to decline. That's why I, the last Don Quixote on earth, am avenging our feelings. To the greatest creation of technology — my machine — I allotted the most vulgar of human feelings. I've disgraced the machine. From the best of all machines I've made a liar, a vulgar bitch, a sentimental good-for-nothing. On the day of the October Revolution celebrations, I'll show my machine to the people on Soviet Square. You'll see, Andrei, she can destroy mountains, but I've forbidden her. Understand? I taught her to sing romantic ballads, the silly romantic songs of the old century. She sings, she's melancholy, she gathers flowers, the silly flowers of the last century. She falls in love, she's jealous, she cries, she dreams. And that's not all, Andrei. You've got to understand that she's designed to corrupt all your machines. You're building "Quarter," Andrei. You're erecting the structural frame right now. I'm going to set my machine up on your scaffolding. She'll wreck your construction. The screws will come spinning out by themselves, the bolts will simply fall out, the concrete will peel away, like skin from a leper. My machine will teach every beam and girder how to disobey you. She'll turn every one of your calculations into a useless flower. That's how I'll take revenge on you. While you were striving to turn man into a machine, I've turned a machine into a man.

Silence.

Well, what, don't you believe that my machine really exists?

ANDREI. No, not really.

IVAN. You don't believe it?

ANDREI (*softly*). You didn't invent anything, Vanya. It's just an obsession of yours. You're making a bad joke. Aren't you ashamed of yourself? Do you take me for a fool? Well, what sort of machine can it be? Is a machine like that possible, after all?

IVAN. You don't believe me?

ANDREI. Excuse me, but I don't believe you.

IVAN. The machine exists, Andrei. Be careful, Andrei, she exists, I tell you. I gave her the name of Ophelia. You know who Ophelia is? They called a girl who lost her mind for love by that name. I gave the machine the name of a girl who lost her mind for love and from despair. Ophelia. She drowned herself.

ANDREI. She was a smart girl. Now sit down, Vanya. I want to tell you about my invention, about my salami. It's a completely new sort. You spoke of the machine of machines. Now just imagine to yourself the salami of salamis, the universal sausage. A sausage uniting in itself a multitude of various qualities. Food value, aroma, delicate taste, low price, beauty of form, color, proteins, fats, carbohydrates. The only thing I can't figure out is what to name it. How about Ophelia? Why not call it "Ophelia?" But no, Ophelia doesn't fit. Ophelia is a girl who lost her mind for love. Isn't there at least one girl in the classics of literature who ate herself silly on salami?

32

IVAN. I hate you, Andrei. You're an idol. An idol with popping eyes. You know what your head looks like. Like a clay piggy-bank. Oh, I hate you.

Andrei laughs.

Idol. Just you wait, Andrei, we'll settle scores one day.
ANDREI. Why do you hate me so much?
IVAN. You stole away my daughter.

Silence.

Where's my daughter?
ANDREI. She left you on her own account.
IVAN. Give me back my daughter.
ANDREI. She's not your daughter. She's a foundling.
IVAN. Now I'm asking you, where's Valya?
ANDREI. She's living with a girl friend. Come on now, you know about it. You were standing under her window the other day. Don't play the fool. You called to her, but, see, she didn't respond.
IVAN. That was your idea. You put her up to it.
ANDREI. You were systematically driving her out of her mind. If it wasn't me, the law would have dragged her away from you.
IVAN. You bastard.
ANDREI. Don't shout. If you kick up a scandal, I'll throw you out.
IVAN. You're a son-of-a-bitch, a voluptuary.
ANDREI. What was that?
IVAN. You're a voluptuary. You've corrupted Valya.

Silence.

How dare you dream of such a girl, you sausage-maker. I'll choke her with my own hands.

Silence.

I know everything. Oh, the bastard! You want to bring out a new breed of people, just as you bring out a new breed of salami. So you picked my daughter. Well, my daughter is not an incubator. Do you hear me? My daughter will not be your incubator.
ANDREI. Ivan, you know . . .it's difficult to get me really angry. I'm a good person! It's the profession I have. As director of the Food Trust I have to deal with calves, lambs, fishes, bees, herbs and spices, powders, colognes. I'm essentially good-natured and therefore so is my behavior.

You want me to flare up, cause a scandal that will compromise me. You call me a debauchee. You're a liar, Ivan. You've known for a long time that Valya is everything to me.

IVAN. Don't you dare speak of love. People of your epoch don't know about love. You look upon a woman as a reservoir, a vessel. Valya won't be your vessel. Get it?

ANDREI. Now stop it, Ivan. It's all clear. I understand, you hate me because you're a failure, physically and socially.

Pause.

IVAN. I'll kill you.

ANDREI. Be my guest. As far as I'm concerned you can go right ahead and kill me. You're right about one thing; your century is over. There's only one thing left for you to do — scram. You're just a stupid Don Quixote, but I've got news — I'm not your windmill. I'm a real live enemy. Well, go ahead, kill me. Go out with a big bang.

IVAN. Andryusha, I'm sick . . . I'm sick, Andryusha . . .

ANDREI. You're not sick, Vanya. You're a son-of-a-bitch, Vanya.

IVAN. I'm unhappy, Andryusha.

ANDREI. That's not true, Vanya. I don't feel sorry for you. You're simply a charlatan. They just forgot to shoot you, Vanya. That's all. Get the hell out of here.

IVAN. You're chasing me away?

ANDREI. Get the hell out, Ivan Petrovich. I have work to do. Just slide off like a fried sausage.

IVAN. All right, Andrei. I'm going, but remember . . .

ANDREI. What's to remember? We had a talk and basta.

IVAN. Just remember, you're talking to a leader. You're a leader too, but so am I. Watch your step, Andrei.

ANDREI. Okay, okay.

IVAN. Don't play the big shot, Andrei. I've got a great army. I'm the leader of those people you call jerks. People will come running to me from all sides. Those weighted down with grief, the children of a dead age will come to me borne on the wings of a song. They'll hear my summons, those who kill out of jealousy and he who is ready to hang himself. The jerks and the dreamers, fathers of families who cherish their daughters, honest bourgeois, people who are faithful to traditions, who submit to the norms of honor, duty and love — they are the participants in the conspiracy of which I stand at the head. It's a peaceful conspiracy, a peaceful revolt of feelings. It's a new sort of counterrevolution, Andrei. It's a sexual counterrevolution. (*Walks out*).

ANDREI (*alone*). Too bad Kavalerov wasn't here. (*Walks about in thought. Goes over to the table, to the telephone; picks up the receiver*).

Five — sixty — zero two. Yes. Is this Comrade Shapiro? Hello, Solomon Davidovich. Yes, it's me. A bit later? You're not sleeping? Listen, Solomon Davidovich, how's my beauty? Under lock and key? I'm in love with her. What? Yes, yes. When can I see her? Wednesday or Thursday? Give her a deep bow for me. Yes, I dreamed about her. Rosy, beaming, tender. Yes. Do you think we'll be able to sell it for thirty-five kopecks? What will we call it? You don't happen to know if there's a girl somewhere in classical literature who stuffed herself with sausage and went out of her mind for love? What? Yes, yes. You think I'm running off at the mouth. Is it really possible, though, to lose your mind for love? What? Ah, yes, yes . . .and in the new world people won't go out of their minds for love. What? They won't? Love will make them smarter, eh? You deserve a hug for that, Solomon Davidovich. (*Hangs up and sits down in thought. Goes to the phone once more and picks up the receiver*). Five — sixty — zero two. Comrade Shapiro? You're still not sleeping? Now tell me honestly, I do have a right to get married, don't I? Fine, okay, good night.

Valya comes in.

(*Andrei sees Valya*). Another crazy nut. You're in the way of my work. I'll let you stay for ten minutes, not any longer.

VALYA (*sits on the divan*). I could really use some sleep. Do you mind if I sleep on the divan?

ANDREI. Kavalerov sleeps there, and he'll be here soon.

VALYA. Kavalerov told me when he first saw me that when I walked by it was as if a branch filled with blossoms and leaves rustled past him.

Andrei works absorbedly at his table.

Kavalerov says that you don't hear anything around you when you get absorbed in your work . . .Is it true, Andrei Petrovich? Fire! (*Pause*). Kavalerov says you snore at night. There's a volcano called Krakatau. That's how you snore: Krra-ka-taa-u, Krra-ka-taa-u . . .A regular nightmare. (*Pause*). Kavalerov says you sing in the morning in the bathroom. That's very pretty.

Silence. It's impossible to tell whether Andrei is listening.

I love you, Andrei Petrovich. I love you, my darling uncle, more than anything in the world . . .I promise you a wonderful love, my dear, darling uncle. I promise to be a remarkable person . . .I'm very beautiful, I'm better than that sausage you're always dreaming about. Uncle dear! Do you hear me, uncle! You know what, you're a glutton, a hog! Do you hear what I'm saying? Look at me, you idiot!

35

Silence.

We'll go to the soccer match together. A famous German team has arrived. The famous forward Getzke is with them. We'll go to the game together. I'll rustle like a branch filled with blossoms and leaves. But we won't take Kavalerov. Why did you take him in in the first place? I want to sleep here on the divan. I'll get undressed, then I'll sleep, and then you'll see what kind of a branch I am. You'll go out of your mind. Uncle, I'm starting to get undressed. One-two-three! The buttons are flying! He doesn't hear anything, the horrible sausage-maker.

Silence.

(*Sleepily*). Let's go to the lab together. I'll show you some remarkable things. You should study chemistry, uncle . . .It would help you with the canning. Bye-bye, uncle, I'm falling asleep, the springs are singing . . . Listen to the springs sing . . .sprinkling drops . . .down from the divan . . . clusters of grapes . . .

Quiet, Valya drifts off.

I'm already asleep, goodbye . . .bye . . .bye . . .

ANDREI (*goes to the phone, wants to pick the receiver up but changes his mind; speaks, addressing the phone*). It's me again; yes, me, Solomon Davidovich. Wake up. I don't know what to do. What should I do, Solomon Davidovich? She's here sleeping. What should I do, Solomon Davidovich? Wake up, wake up, the Chairman of the Board is talking to you. What should we call it? Isn't there somewhere among the classics of literature a girl who loved a sausage-maker?

CURTAIN

SCENE FOUR

At Andrei Babichev's, early morning. Andrei and Shapiro are at Andrei's work table.

SHAPIRO. I was already getting undressed. I would have been asleep in another five minutes. And then you called: Shapiro, is it okay for me to get married? Well, I got on some things and came over to your place. Hello there, I said. You've brought me to the point of passing nights without a wink of sleep. Don't you sleep yourself?

ANDREI. Oh, I was just thinking, thinking. Then I began to read. Look, it's Kavalerov's book: Shakespeare's plays.

SHAPIRO. And where's this Kavalerov of yours?

ANDREI. I don't know. He may be at that widow's of his place.

SHAPIRO. What widow is that?

ANDREI. It's an awful story. He was almost crying when he told me how he had fallen in—drinking you know—with a forty-year-old matron. She's a cook, gets up meals for a bunch of barbers in the barbers' union. It's over there in that house he lived in before he moved in here. It's terrible you know, really tragic. Those high-falutin' dreams, and then suddenly flop, right into a matron's bed. (*After a short silence*). But I'm sorry for Kavalerov. Maybe he could be given some advertising jingles to scribble. Or let him write an opera about our "Quarter."

SHAPIRO. I really don't like any of this business, Andrei. What kind of a lamebrained idea was it to pick up a drunk in the street and bring him home? Why, it's straight out of Shakespeare.

ANDREI. And now I haven't a clue as to what to do with him.

SHAPIRO. Why not say: "Thank you and good-bye. Take your beloved Shakespeare and get the hell out."

ANDREI. I've just finished "Othello." Do you know who he was?

SHAPIRO. Everyone knows that, a black man.

ANDREI. In the first place, he wasn't a black man, but a Moor, but that's not important. Do you know *who* he was? He was a general. A general and governor of the island of Cyprus. Altogether you might say that "Othello" is a military drama, a regimental tale. Iago is a first lieutenant, Cassio a lieutenant, an officer from headquarters; and Desdemona is a proper regimental lady. And I think it's just terrific! Yeah, really great! General Othello was ugly, a real rogue. He was in fact a monster, all black, everyone hated him; he won over Desdemona with stories about his military triumphs. She fell in love with him for the suffering he'd been through.

Pause.

SHAPIRO. Oho! I see that Kavalerov is beginning to have an influence on you. You're dreaming of heroes already!

ANDREI. I had a brother, Roman. Do you know him, Roman Babichev? There were three of us Babichevs, three brothers. The third, as in a fairy tale, was Ivan. And so there was an eldest brother, Roman. He was a hero. He threw a bomb at the governor. At the governor-general, at some kind of Othello. And then he was hanged. He was a hero who threw a bomb. And I'm a sausage-maker.

SHAPIRO. Well, I'll be damned. And so there was a brother called Roman. Another romantic. But it's harder to make salami and sausage. A bomb can be whatever way it likes, but a sausage has to be nutritious.

ANDREI. Oh, yes, I dream of heroes. I want sausage-makers to be heroes. Do you understand? Ivan looks for heroes, and I'm looking for them too. Please understand. But the way it is...I'm surrounded by workers who almost always take the path of least resistance. But I demand enthusiasm. *(Carried away, he stands and speaks as if in front of an audience).* You know about the business with Prokudin? The other day he produced a red rowanberry lozenge, and what do you think he called it? Would you believe "Rosa Luxemburg?" What do you think of that? Comrade Prokudin repels me because he follows the path of least resistance. If Comrade Prokudin has to think up a new name for a new kind of pie, then he'll call it, for example, "The Legacy of Lenin." Words once written in blood, Comrade Prokudin now decks out in sugar. That's what we call the path of least resistance. Last week he put out twelve kinds of chocolates. He suggested such names as "Pure Music," "Battling Butterflies," and, if I'm not mistaken, "Slave Girl." Comrade Prokudin would like to call a Soviet candy "Slave Girl," can you beat that? It's a straight line in any case; at one end of the line "Rosa Luxemburg" and at the other end, "Slave Girl." That's, as I say, the line of least resistance. So I told him that the name for a Soviet candy should be taken from science, and it should be serious too. Of course, it has to sound attactive. There are after all poetic sciences, don't you think so, Shapiro. Geography, astronomy and so on. We should choose names like "Eskimo," and "Telescope," and "Equator." Comrade Prokudin didn't have a clue, I mean, I don't have to think up names for candies, do I? I don't have the time, but I'm forced into it anyway. If I don't, I'll be tortured by obsessive dreams in which Comrade Prokudin puts out a pie to be called: "This is our Final and Decisive Battle of the Butterflies." I have to get involved in everything. They want me to be as painstaking, petty and wary as a housekeeper. They want me in ten places at once, like a fakir. I'm a member of the Society of Political Prisoners, and not a fakir. *(Pause).* I demand enthusiasm, Shapiro, enthusiasm. Here's a can over here with pickled preserves *(takes a can from the table).* The people who manufactured this can are enthusiasts. It was sent by the Far East Preserves Trust. What do you think is inside it? Crabs. Just look at the light blue color of the can. A beautiful, heavy can, bright and noble, like a flag in an ocean breeze. It was made by enthusiasts.

Pause. Voice from the bedroom.

VALYA. Andrei Petrovich!

Shapiro is taken aback.

Andrei Petrovich! Is that you, uncle? Uncle!
    SHAPIRO. Well hello there. Andrei Petrovich isn't here. I'm Shapiro and I'm here. Andrei Petrovich went out for a walk in the garden. He took a

copy of Shakespeare's plays and went for a turn about the garden. What are you doing there?

VALYA. I'm sleeping here.

Andrei listens silently.

SHAPIRO. But what right have you? You're not married yet, are you?

VALYA. Not yet.

SHAPIRO. Do you love him?

VALYA. Since I was a little girl. It's terrible.

SHAPIRO. What's terrible?

VALYA. That I'm in love.

SHAPIRO. Silly girl. Don't say "terrible"; on the contrary, it's wonderful when a girl falls in love.

VALYA. Who said that?

SHAPIRO. Shakespeare.

VALYA. Who?

SHAPIRO. Boris Shakespeare.

VALYA. No, no, he's called William!

SHAPIRO. Oh sure, I just forgot.

VALYA. You should be ashamed of yourself.

SHAPIRO. Why, because I forgot the name?

VALYA. No, it's shameful that I'm in love. Love—it's a feeling that belongs to the middle ages.

SHAPIRO. Now I'm confused, Valya.

VALYA. Love shouldn't exist. In general, chemistry and technology will make it possible to call forth any feeling by means of a machine. And then comes along an unhappy man, let's say Nikolai Kavalerov. He comes to the Institute of Emotions; we'll have established one by that time. Kavalerov shows up and announces: I'm unhappy.

SHAPIRO. Why is he unhappy?

VALYA. I'm unhappy, he tells us, because I love with an unrequited love.

SHAPIRO. Who says that? Shakespeare?

VALYA. No, Kavalerov, William Kavalerov. Then the professor seats Kavalerov in front of the instrument panel, puts a special headpiece on our friend, turns on a special chemical ray beam and the machine hums— rrrrrr—a minute passes and William Kavalerov, thanks to the action of the ray, receives all the emotions which a person experiencing unrequited love is supposed to feel. That's the whole thing.

SHAPIRO. That's all very beautiful, madam, but very boring. Chemistry should be used mainly in agriculture.

VALYA. You don't understand a thing. The new man must be absoutely rational. Andrei Petrovich doesn't understand it either.

SHAPIRO. Andrei Petrovich is an awful man anyway. I mean, after all, he's a member of the All-Russian Central Executive Committee, a Party man since 1910—and what does he go and do? He lets himself be in love with a girl.

VALYA. Do you think he's in love?

SHAPIRO. Yes, I imagine so. He's acting just like some sort of medieval baron.

VALYA. Did he tell you he was in love?

SHAPIRO. No, he didn't, but it got around that he came to the "Institute of Emotions" and said, "I want to love, slap a headpiece on me." The professor seated him in front of the instrument panel; it starts to hum—hmmmmmm—a minute passes and Andrei Petrovich says, "Thank you, I feel infected with emotions already; I'm in love with a girl."

VALYA. You're acting like a clown.

SHAPIRO. Of course I am. You know what kind of an elephant Andrei Petrovich is. If he came to the Institute of Emotions and they told him love was impossible, why he'd smash all the instrument panels like a bull-elephant.

ANDREI (*suddenly*). I've had about all I can take.

SHAPIRO. Oh, you're here!

VALYA (*from the bedroom*). What are you so fed up about, Andrei?

ANDREI. I'm fed up with Romanticism.

VALYA. You're just irritated that I slept on your bed. And you've spent a sleepless night. Where's Kavalerov?

ANDREI. He's been appointed governor-general of the island of Cyprus.

VALYA. Why are you so angry? I'm already dressed and you can go back to sleep if you like. (*Comes out of the bedroom*).

ANDREI. You're so fresh, as if you'd just had a bath.

VALYA. It's from happiness.

ANDREI. Is it really true?

VALYA. Why are you lisping?

ANDREI. Lisping—I'm not lisping am I?

VALYA. In that case, please say, "Valya, I love you."

ANDREI. There's no lisping sounds in that sentence.

VALYA. Then you can add the word "strongly." Valya, I love you strongly.

ANDREI. Go to hell's kitchen. There's a lisp for you.

SHAPIRO. I've had it with all this crap.

ANDREI. What's eating you, Solomon Davidovich?

SHAPIRO. Romanticism, that's what. In the new world love should be eliminated. Don't you think so, madam? Chemistry and technology in general will enable any emotions to be summoned up by electronic means. An "Institute of Emotions" will be founded.

ANDREI. Who said so?

SHAPIRO. Shakespeare.

ANDREI. That Shakespeare of yours is a jerk.

Kavalerov enters from the terrace.

KAVALEROV *(to Valya)*. You here, Valya? What are you doing here? Did you spend the night?

SHAPIRO. What business is that of yours, Comrade Kavalerov? Does it make any difference where Valya spent the night?

KAVALEROV. Andrei Petrovich, I'm probably going to leave you now, and for good. I want you to listen to me.

ANDREI. Okay, out with what's on your mind.

KAVALEROV. I want to talk about Valya.

ANDREI. Hear that, Valya, he wants to talk about you.

KAVALEROV. You exert a moral pressure on Valya. May I speak?

ANDREI. Go ahead.

KAVALEROV. It's just impossible that a young girl could seriously love a forty-year-old man. It's just your position, it seems to me, that impresses her. You're a famous man, but she doesn't love you. I've given it a lot of thought, so what I'm saying isn't something just on the spur of the moment. She doesn't love you. *(Pause)*. I don't have any right to preach to you, but it seems to me that you are quite close to committing a non-communist act.

ANDREI. Anything you say, old buddy.

KAVALEROV. I don't want to make you angry. I'm talking to you man to man. Listen for a minute. Fate has brought us together in a strange way. I can see that we are headed for a conflict. It's in the natural course of things. See, I'm speaking with perfect calm. I'm not drunk or excited. The conflict is caused, as I see it, by the inequality of our positions, and by Valya.

VALYA. And what?

KAVALEROV. And you, Valya.

VALYA *(to Andrei)*. What did he say?

KAVALEROV. I love you, Valya. I'm saying this to you with all my heart. Answer me.

VALYA. What is he saying? How can I answer?

KAVALEROV. I've waited for you all my life.

VALYA. Andrei Petrovich, what can I do?

KAVALEROV. Valya, answer me, did you spend the night here because you . . .because you are already his wife?

VALYA. Leave me alone.

KAVALEROV. Do you love Andrei Petrovich?

Silence.

Then that means, it means . . . You've taken everything from me, Andrei Petrovich. Dreams of life, dreams of love.

ANDREI. I haven't taken anything from you, Kavalerov.

KAVALEROV. You must be able to see how I've been cheated.

ANDREI. It's not my fault.

KAVALEROV. I haven't got anything to live for. It's clear now, everything belongs to you. And I'm a beggar in this terrible new world. Give me Valya, Andrei Petrovich.

Silence.

Give me Valya. I have a right to demand her of you. You don't need her, you're right at the top of the heap as it is.

ANDREI. You say such strange things, Kavalerov. Valya, I don't really get all this. Shapiro, help us.

KAVALEROV. Don't you dare to get Shapiro involved in this. (*To Shapiro*). Get out of here. You're a pimp. Valya, why don't you say something?

VALYA. I don't care to. You're most likely drunk. It would be better if you left.

KAVALEROV. I don't have anywhere to go. Where would I? To the garbage dump? But you . . . you can stay here . . . to, to carry out your, er, function.

VALYA. What function?

KAVALEROV. You know what kind, the function of a reservoir.

SHAPIRO. He's flipped his lid.

VALYA. I don't understand any of this, uncle.

ANDREI. How did he put it, reservoir? That's perfectly clear and not hard to understand. He's using the words of my brother, Ivan. Ivan called you a reservoir. So that means you've already met Ivan. I'm quite pleased. I congratulate you, Kavalerov. You remember, Valya, I told you they would meet and find a lot in common.

KAVALEROV. Yes! I'm assuming the defence of your brother and his daughter. I'll go to war with you for his sake, and for the sake of this girl who has been deceived by you, and for the sake of tenderness, feeling, for the human personality, for everything you're suppressing in life. Valya, you can't believe him! You're simply a dainty morsel as far as he's concerned. (*Suddenly Kavalerov notices how threatening Andrei's silence has become*). No, you wait a minute now, don't be angry. I swear to God, I'm only joking, I'm drunk. Why don't you say something? Don't act like that. Comrades, on my honor, it's all a misunderstanding, it's absolute nonsense. You're not going to give any significance to the ravings of a drunk. Andrei

Petrovich, for God's sake don't be angry. You're an intelligent man; you've got to understand. My nerves are shot; I'm all worn out and on the verge of breaking. I need to take showers like you. We could exercise together. Why don't we? How about it, can we? Why don't you say something, Andrei? Believe me, I'm sorry. I didn't know what I was saying. Please, my God, what's the matter?

Silence.

I didn't mean to insult you. Have pity on me. I lead a bad life, I get drunk, I'm conceited, I boast, I hate everybody, I envy everybody. There's a lot I want to do and I don't do a thing. It's very hard for me to live in this world of ours.

Silence. Everyone is silent: Andrei, Valya, Shapiro.

Valya, tell him.

Silence. Ivan appears at the window looking out on the terrace. The assembled group doesn't see him. He listens, smiles. Kavalerov fidgets uneasily.

All right, then, you don't want to talk to me. What should I do? Go away, clear out, is that it? But how can I leave like that, thrown out like a dog? I just don't know anything. Okay, I'll get out, slink away like a beaten dog. Where to? To the widow Prokopovich, to her matronly bed? And Valya, she'll stay here? That means I'll never see her again. Clear out, that's what you want?

Silence.

How can I simply clear out after what's happened? I've got to make amends. If I've insulted you, you can hit me.

Silence.

Don't you want to say something? Are you pretending not to understand me? Or are we speaking different languages? Yes, that's it, different languages. You're a communist, a builder, and I'm just a pathetic intellectual. Well, I'll challenge you to a duel.

Silence.

Hear me? Get your weapon and we'll fight. Give me a pistol. I won't just go away. Hear me! I won't go away!

Silence.

I'll insult you so badly that you'll have to fight me. Hear me! You're a sausage-maker, a damn sausage-maker who seduces this girl and . . . You rapist!

Silence. Valya appears to be agitated.

VALYA (*to Andrei*). Why don't you say something?
ANDREI. He's having one of his fits. There's nothing to be done about it.
VALYA. Well, I'm leaving. (*Quickly goes out of the terrace door*).
ANDREI (*after her*). Valya!

Valya rushes back and slaps Kavalerov's face.

SHAPIRO. Well done!
KAVALEROV. All right, I'll be going then. Where are my things? (*Looks around and takes a book from the table*). This is my book, and here's my razor (*picks it up*), yes (*catches sight of Ivan at the window*).
IVAN (*removing his bowler*). Good day to you, Andryusha. Do you know what this business you're engaged in is called? It's called the sexual counterrevolution! Come here, Kavalerov my poor friend! Come here. Oh, without doubt you've got to be the leader of my troupe!

Kavalerov goes out onto the terrace, and through the window he can be seen leaning on Ivan's shoulder.

IVAN (*loudly*). Did you notice, Andryusha, he took his razor with him.
ANDREI (*seizes a pillow lying on the divan and threatens Ivan with it*). Get the hell away from here!
IVAN (*catches the pillow and raises it aloft; he stands still and then with one arm he embraces Kavalerov. The other hand still holds the pillow, but he throws it down and raises his own greasy yellow pillow lying nearby*). Thank you, but I have my own.

CURTAIN

SCENE FIVE

At Anechka Prokopovich's. A small room stuffed with furniture.

There is little room to move about in the stale and stuffy room. It is dominated by a huge bed. The bed's shadow rises like a temple, like a gothic cathedral. It is evening. Ivan, Anechka, Kavalerov.

IVAN. I see, so that's it. Yes, I see, I see. So that's the place Kavalerov used to live. Anna Mikhailovna, you know that from this day forward your room will become a historical monument. After all, you are, one way or the other, the, well, wife, or ladyfriend of Nikolai Kavalerov.

KAVALEROV. Don't put on a show, Ivan Petrovich!

ANECHKA. Kolya hates me.

IVAN. That's not good, Kavalerov, to hate such a sweet lady. After all, Anna Mikhailovna allowed us to lie on her remarkable bed. Just look at it—mahogany arches lined with mirrors, dancing cupids, apples tumbling out of horns of plenty.

ANECHKA. My late husband won this bed in a lottery.

IVAN. There you go, a family heirloom. And you reject all this. You've been offered love, a family, an heirloom, a legend, but you turn up your nose. And Anna Mikhailovna herself...Look at her, would you: how wide she is, how soft, how kind. Did you ever dream, Anna Mikhailovna, that you'd be transformed into a bed? I'm surprised at you, Kavalerov. You're taken in homeless by kind people, Anna Mikhailovna and then by my brother Andrei, and everywhere you carry on disgracefully. You seem to hate everybody.

Kavalerov is silent.

ANECHKA. A movie house opened next door. It's very elegant. It's called "The Phantom." And it's just around the corner. Why don't we take in a show?

IVAN. Why not? Excellent idea. But you know, Kavalerov, we've talked a good deal about feelings, but we've forgotten the main thing...indifference. Right. I believe indifference is the best of all states of the human mind. We should be indifferent, Kavalerov. It's the way to true peace, just look! *(points, first at Anechka, then at the bed).* Let's have a toast to indifference; to indifference, Kavalerov.

Silence.

Listen to me, Kavalerov. Woman was the best, the most beautiful, the purest light of our culture. I looked for someone of the female sex who would unite all the feminine qualities; I was looking for the very essence, the very ovary as it were of feminine qualities. The feminine was the glory of the old century. I wanted to shine with this feminine quality. We're dying, Kavalerov. I'd like to carry a woman above my head like a torch! I thought

45

woman as such would fade away with our era. The millenium lies like a burial pit, and in the pit machines, scraps of cast iron, tin-plates, propellers and springs are scattered about. It's a dark dreary pit, and rotten pieces of wood, phosphorescent fungi, mould can be seen to glimmer. Those are our feelings, all that remains of the blossoming of the human soul. The new man comes to the pit, gropes about, climbs into it, chooses what he likes . . .maybe a machine part will come in handy, a nut or a bolt, and the stuff that's falling apart he'll dispose of. I dreamed of finding a woman who would blossom in that pit with unheard-of feeling. Like the marvelous blooming of a fern. So that the new man who came to pilfer our steel would be frightened, draw back his hand, cover his eyes and be blinded by the light of what appeared to him to be rotting wood. And I found such a person, close to me, Valya. I thought that Valya would flare above the dying century, that she would light the way to the great cemetery. But I was mistaken. She darted away; she threw away the old century's bed headboard. I thought that woman was ours, that tenderness and love belong to us alone, but, as you see, I was mistaken. Valya went to him. You've got to calm down after that, Kavalerov. It just isn't worth fighting any more, is it? She loves him, doesn't she? Nobody stole her away, she went on her own, didn't she?

KAVALEROV. I'll tear her away from him.

IVAN. Oh no, Kavalerov, you won't tear Valya away. She won't go with you because your youth is past.

KAVALEROV. That's not true, I'm only twenty-eight. He's older than me, and she doesn't, can't love him.

IVAN. You're a thousand years old, Kavalerov. Don't giggle, Anna Mikhailovna. He's old, your Kavalerov, he's ancient. He carries within himself the entire age, all the sclerosis of the present century. But the other one, my brother—he's young, youthful, he struts about, he's a cupid hovering with a quiver at the gates of the new world; sticking his nose in the air, he doesn't see you any more. See, Kavalerov, this is your lot in life; a grubby but quiet courtyard, a bed, a warm sty, and warm Anna Mikhailovna. What's to dream about? See what you've become, a clown in shortening pants. You keep thinking you're young, so that life's not over, but that's it, there won't be anymore; you've been served up on a platter, you're finished. That's it, my friend, and what can we do about it, eh? Of course it's a bitter pill, very sad, yes, I know, somewhere on Chernyshevsky Lane, windows on the second floor, clouds pass through the sky and across the windowpane, and in the pane their paths cross. And in the window a girl is leaning on her elbows, and she's as slender as a flute. Forget about all that, it's not for you, you old Russian potato nose. Your youth is past. You won't be either handsome or famous. You won't fulfill that dream of going from your provincial town to success in the capital, you won't be a general or a scholar or a runner or an explorer—everything is over. You're a papa already, and you should have had a son.

ANECHKA. See, I told you, Kolya. Ivan Petrovich is repeating my very words. I told you you'd calm down when you had a child.

IVAN. So what are you waiting for? You've got the charms, Anna Mikhailovna. So take him to your bosom. Open your embraces to the aging, doddering century. Hooray! Bear him a child, Anna Mikhailovna. We'll lay him on my pillow. We'll arrange an October Revolution day. If a son is born, we'll call him Quarter, and if it's a girl, she'll be called Ophelia. Let's drink to that! Drink up, Kavalerov! To departed youth, to the conspiracy of feelings that has come to nothing, to the machine, Ophelia, which does not and will not exist!

KAVALEROV. You're a son-of-a-bitch, Ivan Petrovich! My youth is not over! No! (*Grasps Ivan by the collar*). Do you hear me? It's not true and I'll prove it to you, do you hear!

ANECHKA. Don't shout, Kolya, don't make a scandal!

KAVALEROV. Shut up, you, you . . . old hag! I'm no match for you, reptile! Do you hear me? You got me in your clutches when I was drunk. Get it straight, it was by chance, an accident, and that's that.

ANECHKA. But you kissed me so passionately that night. Kolya, you said, "Oh what sweetness this is after the embraces of a prostitute—the love of a pure woman."

KAVALEROV. Ugh, how awful, how terrible. Don't forget she's a foolish woman, Ivan Petrovich, she's a fool, but you, why are you laughing at me? Tell her, will you, tell her that she's old and run-down, that she can be squashed like liver pâté. Leave me alone. Get out! Go away! (*Pause. He staggers, exhausted*). What can I do, Ivan Petrovich, what can I do?

IVAN. You've got to kill my brother Andrei.

Silence.

KAVALEROV. It's you, you're the provocateur, who ought to be killed.

Silence.

ANECHKA. God knows what you're talking about.

IVAN. You wanted fame. Well, that can be your fame, to leave an honorable memory after yourself as the hired killer of the century. I give you my blessing.

KAVALEROV. Leave me alone. Get out. Get out of here and leave me alone. (*He staggers to the bed and falls into a sprawl on it*).

Silence.

IVAN. Well okay, Anna Mikhailovna, we can go to the "Phantom" now. We'll let Kavalerov sleep.

ANECHKA. It's just around the corner. Can I go without a hat? I'll take a scarf.

KAVALEROV (*getting up*). Ivan Petrovich, for some reason it seems to me that Valya will come here. Word of honor. We might run into each other on the street, or at the gate. You tell her how to find her way; it's easy to get lost here in the corridor. She might come to make up for being so cruel to me. She must understand how miserable I am.

IVAN. There's no reason to make Anna Mikhailovna jealous by talking that way. Don't worry, Anna Mikhailovna, no one will come to see him. Ah, you look like Carmen in that scarf. I would gladly carry you over my head like a torch, but alas you're not a torch, but an entire projector. (*Ivan and Anechka go out*).

Kavalerov lies on the bed. Silence. He begins to dream. The stage appears to tremble, shadows line up next to each other and an invisible source of light seems to come from somewhere in the middle of the furniture. An unpleasant yellowish light. A knocking at the door. Kavalerov sits up in bed.

KAVALEROV. Come in.

Enter Valya. She is like that tender, airy and elegant being known as a "peri."

KAVALEROV (*sitting up in bed*). There, I knew it. I was waiting.

Andrei Babichev enters and Kavalerov gives a start. Andrei and Valya sit at a table without noticing Kavalerov. He is in sight, but they do not see him; it is a dream.

ANDREI. Yes, yes. Well, that's good. That's very good indeed.

KAVALEROV (*from the bed*). Hello, Andrei Petrovich.

ANDREI. So we'll get married. It's pleasant here, don't you think so?

VALYA. Go away.

KAVALEROV. Valya, I'm here.

VALYA (*not seeing, not hearing*). Why have you brought me here?

ANDREI. Don't you like it here? Just look at the bed, it's mahogany, made by enthusiasts.

KAVALEROV (*gripped by fear*). Andrei Petrovich!

ANDREI (*not seeing, not hearing*). You're uncomfortable, feeling ashamed? Do you love me?

VALYA. I don't know.

Andrei guffaws. In the dream looks as Kavalerov had imagined him—a terrifying idol, a scarecrow.

ANDREI. You can't be embarrassed? Ha-ha-ha!

KAVALEROV. You're not alone, Andrei Petrovich. I'm here, Nikolai Kavalerov; you can see me, can't you? Here I am!

ANDREI. I'll take your clothes off now.

KAVALEROV (*shouting*). Valya!

ANDREI. What made you jump like that?

VALYA. Is someone calling me?

KAVALEROV. Valya, I'm here!

ANDREI. Calling you! Nonsense. That's some kind of silly mysticism. It's all very simple. You and I will lie down on the bed. And then, what's the point of mysticism?

KAVALEROV (*shouts unseen and unheard*). I won't allow this. Do you hear, you bastard! Why can't he hear me?

VALYA. I don't feel right.

ANDREI. Ivan taught you that one, silly girl. Do you want me to sigh or something?

VALYA. I want to see Kavalerov.

KAVALEROV. Valya! Valya! Look, I'm here, I'm here! What's going on? I'm screaming Valya! Valya! I can't be invisible, can I? Here I am, my hands are here, here I am standing right next to you.

VALYA. I want to see Kavalerov. He told me I was lighter than a shadow, lighter than the brightest of shadows, the shadows of falling snow.

ANDREI. I'll just have to pack him off to the nut house.

VALYA. You're a tyrant.

KAVALEROV. Don't act so stupid, Andrei Petrovich. You're pretending not to see me because you're ashamed of yourself. You didn't expect me here. Valya, you can see me, I'm sure of it. It's just that you're afraid of him. Don't be afraid, Valya! Don't be afraid! Look at me, I'm with you, I'll save you, I've waited all my life for you. Valya, Valya . . .They want to marry me off to Anechka. Valya, have pity on me. (*He kneels before her and clasps her knees*). Have pity on me. I'm here, don't you see? Don't you feel that I'm touching your knees?

VALYA (*not seeing, not hearing*). Kavalerov saw me on the soccer field. I was wearing shorts. He told me my knees were like oranges. You never say things like that to me.

ANDREI. That's how dead men talk. It's the language of the dead.

KAVALEROV. I'm not dead! Why can't you see me? Valya, don't you see me either?

ANDREI. You're a reservoir, Valya. Do you understand? You're an incubator. We'll lie on that comfortable bed, you and I, and then you'll give birth to a child. We need descendants. All the rest is mysticism.

KAVALEROV. Valya, don't go to bed with him, don't sacrifice your youth to him. Didn't you hear what he said? He said you're a reservoir. Valya, he's an ass, a monster, a lousy machine!

VALYA. I don't want to lie on the bed with you.

ANDREI. But you will.

VALYA. I'll scream . . . Kavalerov! Kavalerov!

KAVALEROV. Here I am! I'm here! Yes, here I am!

VALYA. Save me, Kavalerov!

KAVALEROV. What can I do? She doesn't see me.

Kavalerov grabs a bottle lying on the table. He can't move it. It is a dream. The bottle stands as if riveted.

A-a-a-a!

ANDREI. Don't shout. Forget the word "love." Everything is over. What are you carrying on for? A giant building is going up, a mammoth of a building, a dormitory-factory. And what are you looking for while all this is going on? Your own individualized portions? Little kisses? Little caresses? Sighs? The hell with all that! It's so primitive, I spit on your little kisses. Now get the hell out! I'll build that factory-dormitory. It'll be terrific, huh?

VALYA. You've completely crushed me! Let me go to Kavalerov. He told me I brushed past him like a branch full of flowers and leaves. Where are you, Kavalerov? (*She speaks without seeing or hearing Kavalerov*). Where are you? You won't live in courtyards any more. I want to come to you. It's me, it's me, come here, it's me, the one you've waited for all your life. Here is my hand, as slender as a reed. Your youth has not vanished in mid-air, no . . . I love you, I'll save you. My dearest, my dear one. Where are you?

KAVALEROV. I'm here.

ANDREI (*screams in a terrible rage as if all at once catching sight of Kavalerov*). Doctor!

A doctor appears in a dressing gown, glasses and with a yellow bald spot. He is a skinny, bony man.

KAVALEROV (*in the horrified voice of a man screaming in his sleep*). A-a-a!

DOCTOR (*jerkily, as if he doesn't know how to speak and had to be taught*). Where's the patient?

ANDREI. Here he is.

DOCTOR. Ah! (*Squeals with pleasure*).

KAVALEROV. Valya!

DOCTOR. Take off your jacket. (*To Andrei*). Help me. That's it,

50

that's it.

Andrei helps undress Kavalerov.

Just take your shirt off.

KAVALEROV. I don't want to. I'm ashamed, Valya, I'm ashamed. Don't, don't . . .

ANDREI. Come on, take it off. That's it; my what a handsome fellow.

They have undressed the pitiful Kavalerov.

DOCTOR. That's it . . . that's it . . . Just a moment, hm, yes, muscles, yes, flabby musculature, hmmm, yes, horny, clearly horny, hmm, yes. Come on, look at the light, show your pupils. Let's see how they react . . . . Get over to the light. (*Drags Kavalerov*). Ah, that's it, that's it, to the light, come on. A-a-a . . . (*Raises his voice several tones and shouts*). He's out of his mind!

Everyone flees.

KAVALEROV. Let me go! Let me go! (*Falls on the bed, wakes up*).

Kavalerov's dream comes to an end and the stage looks as it had previously.

Let me go! Let me go! I'm going. I'll save her. Let me go! (*Shouts*). Valya! Valya!

The cry continues until the curtain falls.

CURTAIN

SCENE SIX

A small room in a middle-class apartment. It's the owner's name day. A table is set with things to eat. There is a hanging lamp beneath a broad orange shade. Guests. Nikolai Kavalerov and Ivan Babichev led by Mikhal Mikhalych (the life of the party) enter to the applause of those assembled. Ivan has his pillow and Kavalerov has the air of a sleepwalker. He is reddish and tousled.

GUESTS. Bravo! Bravo! Bravo!

IVAN. Good evening, my friends, good evening!

VENERABLE OLD MAN. Please have a seat. Make yourselves at

home!

IVAN. Thank you. Sit down, Kavalerov.

KAVALEROV. If you say so. It's all the same to me. I've gone mad. Do whatever you like.

IVAN. This is Nikolai Kavalerov. A young man with a highsounding but really rather vulgar last name.

VENERABLE OLD MAN. Bravo! Bravo!

KAVALEROV (*fidgets uncomfortably*). What's happening to me? What have you done to me, Ivan Petrovich?

MIKHAL MIKHALYCH (*winking conspiritorially*). Quiet. Shh...Listen!

KAVALEROV. You've made a fool out of me. I wind up in strangers' homes. It all seems like a dream to me. There are such dreams, special ones, when you have a dream and you know it's a dream. Tell me, is this a dream? Will I wake up?

Silence.

I want to wake up! Citizens, help me to wake up!

Silence.

LADY OF THE HOUSE. My God ...(*sighs*).

MIKHAL MIKHALYCH (*bustling about, he is the life of the party, he wants everyone to be happy and interested, he shows off Ivan to all the guests*). Shh...Shh...Listen to what's coming next.

ZINOCHKA (*trim young girl*). I'm terrified.

HARRY (*a positive young man*). Nonsense. We are witnessing the end of an era. Legends are being created at this very moment. Legends about me. I'm the hero of a legend. You, of course, want to be a hero of a legend, don't you, Kavalerov?

VENERABLE OLD MAN. Bravo! Bravo!

HEAVILY INTOXICATED GUEST (*to Ivan*). Let's drink up, dad, what's the point of wasting time.

MIKHAL MIKHALYCH (*raises himself high above the table and prepares to explain what is going on*). Allow me, citizens.

LESS INTOXICATED GUEST. Don't stub out your cigarette butt in the jam.

MIKHAL MIKHALYCH. Allow me, gentlemen. Today, on Elena Pavlovna's name day, I decided ...it's a kind of present. I've arranged as a present to have a remarkable man about whom you've all heard so much. I invited him to join us, here (*indicating with a broad gesture*) is Ivan Petrovich Babichev. We met on the street, then we went to a beerhouse, and in the beerhouse Ivan Petrovich urged all far and wide to take part in an uprising against his brother.

LADY IN GREEN. But who's his brother?

MIKHAL MIKHALYCH. Please don't interrupt. Ladies and gentlemen, before anything else we must greet Ivan Petrovich, a man, if I may put it that way, who is a prophet of the twentieth century.

HEAVILY INTOXICATED GUEST. That's exactly right.

MIKHAL MIKHALYCH. How shall I put it, he . . .(*searches for words but fails to find them*).

LADY OF THE HOUSE. I'm delighted, delighted, make yourselves at home. Can I pour you some wine?

IVAN. Thank you. (*Pause*). Can everyone see me clearly? Do me a favor, move back a little bit. I want everyone to see me.

VENERABLE OLD MAN. Bravo.

MIKHAL MIKHALYCH. Quiet. Shh . . .it's beginning.

A general tensing of the atmosphere.

IVAN (*raising his wineglass*). I drink your health, my friends. (*Pause*). Look at me, everyone. I am your king. Look me over.

Pause.

KAVALEROV (*with irritation*). He's not crazy, not at all. You think he's out of his mind? No, he's a confidence man!

HEAVILY INTOXICATED GUEST. That's exactly right.

Pause.

IVAN. I am your king, look me over. I'm quite plump and I have a bald spot. The bags hang down beneath my eyes like purple stockings. Look. Memorize those features. It's Ivan Babichev who is sitting in front of you. Some day they'll ask you—what was he like, Ivan Babichev? And you'll be able to talk about me . . . . See my bowler? It has a rusty color. My bowler has begun to look like a glazed Danish pastry. (*Pause*). Look at me. A king is sitting in front of you. I'm the king of the vulgarians.

VITYA (*an enthusiastic young man, with puzzlement, surprise*). And the pillow?

IVAN. That's my coat of arms, my dear ladies and gentlemen. An old deserving pillow, slept on by many heads.

VENERABLE OLD MAN. Bravo, bravo!

IVAN. Here, I'll put it down by your feet. See how it settles down comfortably like a sow.

HEAVILY INTOXICATED GUEST. That's exactly right.

ZINOCHKA (*in a hush*). Tell us, is it true that you are able to work miracles?

IVAN (*amid silence*). It's true.

Pause.

LADY OF THE HOUSE. Mikhal Mikhalych, ask your friend to perform some miracles.

KAVALEROV. Show them a miracle, Ivan Petrovich.

From this point Kavalerov puts his head down on the table and remains a non-participant in what is happening. It is possible that he is asleep.

LESS INTOXICATED GUEST. Goddamm it!

IVAN. All right, I'll do it, my friends.

VENERABLE OLD MAN. Bravo! Bravo!

MIKHAL MIKHALYCH. Comrade Babichev, miracle worker of the twentieth century!

IVAN. I agree to perform a miracle, but in order to do it it's necessary first that each person confess in turn his deepest desires.

HEAVILY INTOXICATED GUEST. That's right.

Silence descends.

HARRY. It's not so easy to confess your deepest desires.

LESS INTOXICATED GUEST. Some desires are not quite proper.

Pause.

IVAN. I'm waiting. Who will be the first to confess?

Laughter, pushing, giggling.

ZINOCHKA. All right, I would like to . . .(*breaks off*). Oh no!

MIKHAL MIKHALYCH. Don't be shy, Zinaida Mikhailovna. The most interesting part is just beginning.

ZINOCHKA. Let somebody else . . .

Pause.

VENERABLE OLD MAN (*suddenly and out of character*). Well, all right. There's nothing to be afraid of, you know. Well, a simple human desire, a desire for peace and quiet. Well, there it is. I'm sixty years old, I would like a place of my own. A little house, a country cottage. And I'd like to have a garden and a flowering hedge, with jasmine blooming. And also a verandah that looks out into the garden. Trailer rugs would be nice too, and a grand piano with a cover, plus a sundial sticking out of the window. Peace and quiet. Every Sunday the whole family will visit me: my brother— he's an old man, my hundred-year-old uncle, my engineer sons, and my grandsons and granddaughters. We'll all sit on the verandah and eat strawberries. My granddaughter plays Drigo's serenade on the grand piano. We eat strawberries. And the littlest baby crawls on the grass, his nose stained with crushed berry juice.

LADY OF THE HOUSE. Oh how lovely!

A hush.

VITYA (*suddenly, abruptly*). And I would like . . .I would like, wait a minute. I dream of a special love.

LESS INTOXICATED GUEST. Goddammit!

VITYA (*passionately*). I dream of a special love. Can I? This is what I wanted to say . . .I'm an electro-technician by profession. I often have to be in people's apartments. And what do I see? Quarrels, eternal fights, hatred, the children torn apart. It stinks. The heart should burst from happiness.

HEAVILY INTOXICATED GUEST. That's right.

VITYA. And so, this is what I say: I have one sacred longing—to love a woman with a great, boundless love.

IVAN. Excellent!

LADY OF THE HOUSE. Well, and I . . .I have a daughter Zina . . .

ZINOCHKA. Oh mom, don't.

LADY OF THE HOUSE. Wait a second, Zinochka, and don't interrupt. If someone can be of help, why not explain what it's all about? So here's my Zinochka. She's very talented.

ZINOCHKA. Oh mom . . .you don't have to . . .

LADY OF THE HOUSE. She sings beautifully. I would like . . .oh, it's so easy to justify my dreams. After all, I am a mother, and I want the girl's happiness. I so much want Zina to become famous throughout the world. And it's possible; she sings like an angel. It's not a sin to wish your child riches and glory, is it?

LESS INTOXICATED GUEST (*with sudden fierce inspiration*). A man wants to rule the world. The main desire must be—to rule the world, in order that every last being, every Chinaman should know you.

HEAVILY INTOXICATED GUEST. Don't be downhearted, Volodya.

Pause.

LESS INTOXICATED GUEST. We had a cashier who wanted to

have a really good time. Ran through forty thousand of our roubles. Cards and racing, anything that caught his fancy, stuffed himself with food, drank, fulfilled all his desires!

HEAVILY INTOXICATED GUEST. Don't let it get you down, Volodya.

Pause.

LESS INTOXICATED GUEST (*in a fit of frankness*). Let's tell them why a man tears his heart out, shall we? Why does he hate his neighbor? Because of a lousy room.

VENERABLE OLD MAN (*excitedly*). What do you mean?

LESS INTOXICATED GUEST. This is how I understand it—a worthy old man, respected by everyone. But there's one thing—I live next door to you, only a thin wall separates us, and I listen hard at night, hoping you'll die. One foot in the grave, but here he is still kicking. That's what my greatest desire really is. Just ask me, what is your deepest longing, and I'll answer—I desire your death, old man, the death of my neighbor Sergei Nikolayevich Mikulitsky. That's the truth! I want you dead so that your room will become vacant.

VITYA. This is terrible!

VENERABLE OLD MAN. The hell with it. How can you allow, Elena Pavlovna . . .(*cries*).

General indignation.

ELENA PAVLOVNA. Disgusting! You're drunk, Nikitin.

LESS INTOXICATED GUEST. I apologize, of course . . .

HEAVILY INTOXICATED GUEST. Don't be downhearted, Volodya!

IVAN. Bravo, my friends, bravo!

HARRY. So we agree.

LADY IN GREEN. Well then. Can you realize our desires?

VITYA. We live such poor and boring lives. Nothing but sadness, hatred and fighting.

IVAN. All right, I've listened to you.

MIKHAL MIKHALYCH. Let me, let me also . . .Of course it's an extremely intimate thing, and perhaps everyone will think it's funny to listen to, but if you'll let me, I'd like to say something too. My wife is pregnant, in the eighth month. And so I have one little wish, little, of course, but vitally important, a fatherly dream, in a manner of speaking. Couldn't it be arranged that the child should look like me?

IVAN. Bravo. (*Pause*). That's very good. I've listened to everything. Now all that's left is to make your dreams come true.

HEAVILY INTOXICATED GUEST. Go to it, daddy-o, go to it!
ZINOCHKA. Mom, will I really be a great singer?

Pause.

IVAN. It's impossible to fulfill your desires. I am king of the dead.
LADY IN GREEN. In other words, you've tricked us?
HARRY. What's this?
IVAN. Dead men cannot have desires and dreams. I am king of the dead.
ZINOCHKA. It's not true! It's not true! I *will* be a famous singer.
IVAN. My dear girl, they won't let you become famous.
LADY OF THE HOUSE. Who won't?
IVAN. My brother, Andrei Babichev.

Silence.

My brother, Andrei Babichev, the builder of the new world, is annihilating vanity, love, the family and cruelty.
VENERABLE OLD MAN. What does that mean?
IVAN. Our century is finished, that's what it means. The old human feelings are condemned to destruction.
HARRY. Phrasemonger.
IVAN. My friends, the new man will teach himself to despise the old feelings. The poets have glorified them, the muse of history has glorified them, but now it's all over and done with.
VITYA (*sadly*). All done with.
IVAN. You spoke of the family, old man. There will be no family. You (*to the less intoxicated guest*) wished death on your neighbor. There'll be no cruelty in the new world. There won't be lovers or humanitarians or brave men or loyal friends or prodigal sons.
VENERABLE OLD MAN. Then what can we do?
IVAN. The great human feelings are now pronounced worthless and vulgar. You want to know what we can do? Well, you, electrotechnician, listen to what I have to say. You know what happens when an electric light bulb unexpectedly goes out—it's burnt out, right . . .
HARRY. Right, burnt out . . .
IVAN. But if this burnt-out light bulb is refitted, charged up again?
HARRY (*joyfully*). It will light up again.
HEAVILY INTOXICATED GUEST. That's exactly right.
IVAN. It'll light up and burn for some time yet. Eventually the filaments break . . . what are they called?
VITYA. Tungsten.
IVAN. The tungsten filaments collapse and melt together, and from

57

their contact life returns to the bulb . . .a brief, unnatural life.

VITYA (*enchanted*). Unnatural.

IVAN. A life clearly doomed. It's a fever, a too white heat. Then darkness. Life will not return. The dead burnt-out filaments can only rustle in the darkness. Do you understand what I'm saying? But the shortlived glow of light and life is beautiful. (*Pause*). You ask what we can do. And I'm telling you. The bulb must be charged up, the heart of a burnt-out age must be recharged. The bulb (that is the human heart) must be charged up so that the filaments will contact each other and burn with a momentary but beautiful glow.

VITYA (*enthralled*). Beautiful glow.

ZINOCHKA (*together with him*). Beautiful glow.

IVAN. Yes, we are dying. History! We are dying, the nineteenth century is dying. History. But we are still alive! Our death-agony will be terrible. History, I want to show you something—here is a man in love, here is a fool, here is a mother cherishing her daughter. Here is a proud man, here a fool—here they are, the carriers of great feelings.

Pause.

I want to gather a large group so we can have a choice. I've come to you looking for heroes. For the last time before disappearing, before being subjected to mockery, let the feelings of the world come forward. I've been going from house to house searching. Love, where are you?

VITYA. Here I am, here . . .It's me. I'm the one who wants to love!

IVAN. Where are you, vanity?

ZINOCHKA. That's me, mom, it's me he's calling. I want fame . . . I . . .

IVAN. Come to me. Love! Be jealous, be proud! Be cruel and tender. Let's go! I'll show you to my brother. He's making fun of you, of your saucepans and pots, of your peace and quiet, of your right to give your children a candy sucker. What is he trying to squeeze from your heart? Your own homes, that's what, your beloved homes. He wants to make you wanderers through the wild fields of history. Chase him to hell. Here's a pillow, I'm king of the pillows. Tell my brother that you each want to sleep on your own pillow. Tell him to leave our pillows alone. Don't touch our pillows, don't call us, don't tempt us! What can you possibly offer us in exchange for our ability to love, hate, hope, weep, feel pity and forgive?

HEAVILY INTOXICATED GUEST. Guys like that should be killed!

Kavalerov raises his head.

IVAN. He will be killed.

LADY IN GREEN (*squeals*). Hee-hee-hee!

Silence.

IVAN. I went around searching for a hired killer in the name of the century. I found him. (*Kisses Kavalerov on the forehead*).

Silence.

Nikolai Kavalerov will kill my brother Andrei. Tomorrow at the soccer match. Kavalerov, tell us that tomorrow at the soccer match you'll kill my brother Andrei.

Kavalerov is silent.

(*Taking a razor out of the side pocket of Kavalerov's jacket*). Do you see this? He's held on to his razor. And with this razor he's going to cut the throat of our brother Andrei Babichev.

VITYA. Cut his throat!

MIKHAL MIKHALYCH (*rejoicing*). The evening has been a great success! Fantastic! Quite right, of course, his throat must be slit!

IVAN. Hear that, Kavalerov? They're giving you the freedom to do it. The children of the dying century entrust you with their highest mission. This may be the very purpose for which you were put on earth. (*Embraces Kavalerov and caresses him tenderly*). Oh my restless friend, my dearest, how weary with dreaming you are! Perhaps now the hour has arrived of that glory of which you have been dreaming since childhood! Don't turn back, don't let the opportunity slip away; millions of hearts are beating in time with yours. Accomplish this mighty deed and you can be sure that the great century, the nineteenth century, will give you its blessing.

KAVALEROV. I'm afraid. I don't know. Maybe I've made a mistake. Maybe I've let something else slip past. I think, I think . . .oh, I'm feeling sick, help me . . . . Maybe fate has sent me undreamed-of happiness . . .the opportunity to be near him, and I've let it slip away. You tell me the century gives me its blessing, but what if the new century curses me? I'm terrified, I'll fall to my knees before him, before your brother. I'll beg him to forgive me, but he won't hear, as in a dream.

Unexpectedly, the bulb beneath the shade goes out. Panic.

VITYA. It's nothing, don't worry, it's just burnt out. I'll fix it . . .its nothing. Burnt out.

LADY OF THE HOUSE (*screams*). Shake it! Shake it!

The door opens. Andrei Babichev appears against a lighted background. He is enormous, like a stone guest. General shouting and then silence.

ANDREI. Excuse me, does Citizen Shapiro live here? Solomon Davidovich Shapiro?

LADY OF THE HOUSE (*with relief, almost with a moan*). No, that's upstairs, on the third floor.

The door closes. Darkness.

KAVALEROV (*rushes toward the door, plates are smashed*). Andrei Petrovich! Don't chase me away. I understand everything. Trust me as you trust in Valya. I'm young too. I'll be a great scientist too, I'll pray for you too! How could I let it happen, how could I have stayed blind and not done everything in my power to make you like me. Forgive me, forgive me!

IVAN. Stop it, Kavalerov. He doesn't hear or see you.

KAVALEROV. Oh you're gone? You don't want to? Well, all right. My own fault. You wanted this . . .(*quiets down*).

Pause.

IVAN. All right, my friends, remember, tomorrow at the stadium.

CURTAIN

SCENE SEVEN

The stadium. The soccer match is beginning. A bright, sunny day. Posters in enormous letters, greenery, flags. Buffet tables, wooden partitions, walkways. At the buffet tables: Mikhal Mikhalych, Zinochka and the venerable old man, all from Scene Six.

ZINOCHKA. He won't really kill him?

MIKHAL MIKHALYCH. He will so. We've talked about it so much. If he doesn't kill him, then he's a pig.

VENERABLE OLD MAN. Listen . . .Won't it be dangerous? How shall I put it? Won't we be arrested as accomplices?

MIKHAL MIKHALYCH. On what grounds? After all, it's not a criminal murder, but a historical one—one man kills another for no reason whatsoever.

VENERABLE OLD MAN. How does he plan to do it? I guess he'll put on some disguise, stick on a moustache?

ZINOCHKA. And suppose the moustache suddenly fell off! How embarrassing that would be!

Ivan Babichev with his pillow and Kavalerov appear.

MIKHAL MIKHALYCH. Shhh...here they are. Shh...no disguise at all. Ivan Petrovich, come over here. (*To a waiter*). Citizen, bring us two orders of ice cream. (*To Ivan*). What kind would you like? Strawberry?
IVAN. Strawberry.
ZINOCHKA. I'll have some too!
MIKHAL MIKHALYCH. And mineral water too, get a move on!

Silence.

ZINOCHKA (*to Kavalerov*). Aren't you afraid?
MIKHAL MIKHALYCH. Don't interfere, Zinaida Mikhailovna! Don't intefere or you'll spoil everything.
IVAN. We need more spectators.
VENERABLE OLD MAN. There are plenty of them, and they keep on coming.
MIKHAL MIKHALYCH. The weather's just right today. The sun is shining brightly. The whole world can see us.
IVAN. Have you read Shakespeare, Kavalerov? Do you remember how "Hamlet" ends? Corpses, passion, grief and suddenly Fortinbras enters. The conqueror enters, and that's it. Passion is over, enough. Enter Fortinbras who doesn't give a damn about passion and torment. The soliloquies are over. Shouting, flutes and trumpets begin...(*Pause*). So that's it...Look, Kavalerov...(*Points to the stands with a sweeping gesture*). The soccer players are coming out soon, and they don't give a damn for your passions and torments. You'll have to hurry, Kavalerov.

Andrei appears together with the German Harman, representative of the Union of Workers in the Food Industry, and Valya. They sit above the first group, separated by a partition. The staircase unites them. The first group becomes frightened, dispirited.

KAVALEROV.They don't see me. It's like a dream.
IVAN. He doesn't give a damn about your passions and torments. In a moment he'll give the soccer players a shout, and you'll be wiped off the face of the earth.
MIKHAL MIKHALYCH. Hurry, Comrade Kavalerov.
VENERABLE OLD MAN. Maybe you ought to go. For God's sake, let's get out of here.

They look at the others and listen.

ANDREI. Today's soccer match is organized by the Union of Workers in the Food Industry in honor of the production of a new kind of sausage. Here are the representatives of the Union of Workers in the Food Industry (*indicates*), over there is Mr. Harman from Berlin, a government man who studies the question of public nourishment.

They exchange bows.

Mr. Harman knows Russian, so if you start making digs about his being a capitalist—well, it would be awkward. (*To Harman*). Now our employee Solomon Shapiro will present a specimen of our salami sausage.

HARMAN (*speaking painstakingly*). Oh please, cut a piece for me.

ANDREI. We'll make you a sandwich. Unfortunately there's been a slight delay. You see, today's soccer match is not only a sports event, but an advertising gimmick too.

HARMAN. Yes, I heard about it just before. A man went to the referee's box and shouted through a megaphone that tomorrow the sausage will be on sale in all the shops and kiosks.

ANDREI. Well, see how it is. And we're upset about being behind our production schedule. By the way, I was thinking it'd be a good idea to present today's winning team with a few pounds of salami. What are you smiling at, Fesenkov? You should be ashamed in front of a foreign representative. Mr. Harman, as you can see here in the Soviet Union we have not yet overcome the tradition of knightly jousting. For example, trade-union official Fesenkov here insists that the winning team be presented not with salami but with roses.

HARMAN. Very bad, Mr. Fesenkov.

ANDREI. Es ist nicht gut, Herr Fesenkov. Our salami-sausage is as good as roses any day. Herr Harman, we'll make us up a rose sandwich.

HARMAN. Oh Citizen Babichev, you're a real poet!

ANDREI. Hear that, Safronov. You think I'm a sausage-maker, but it turns out I'm a poet. All right, tomorrow we'll visit the "Quarter" construction site with Mr. Harman. "Quarter" will be opening in November. Mr. Harman, we are getting ready for a great relocation of people. There's Fesenkov grinning again. Don't grin there, I'm a poet, I'm obliged to express myself in this way. Yes, we are getting ready for a great relocation of people.

HARMAN. But where are the people migrating to?

ANDREI. To the beautiful land of public nutrition. It's called "Quarter." We're attempting to build a tempting road to the new land. The new migrants will be met with messengers calling: "Quarter" Cigarettes, "Quarter" Soap, "Quarter" Fruit Drops. We're quite sad that we won't be able to sell our sausage cheaper than thirty-five kopecks a kilo. If we could lower the price to twenty-five kopecks, that is a quarter, then we could call our sausage "Quarter," and that would make a terrific logo for the new territories. (*Suddenly becoming angry*). Where the hell is Shapiro? He should be here. He's walking around somewhere along the warm streets carrying our sausage with him. He could be attacked by dogs, couldn't he? Mr. Harman, there'll be a schnitzel conveyer in the "Quarter" building. If a thousand people smack their lips over sausage at once, you'll be able to hear it as far as Germany.

HARMAN. Mr. Babichev, you are a great poet. (*Catching sight of the approaching Shapiro*). But here apparently comes the man you call Shapiro. He's carrying a package.

ANDREI (*roaring*). He's the one! Get over here, Shapiro, quickly! We're waiting! Hurry up. We're waiting!

SHAPIRO (*coming closer*). I'm sweating, Andrei Petrovich. I hurried and brought it. (*Puts the package on the table*).

ANDREI. Attention please. Fesenkov! Mr. Fesenkov, Mr. Safronov, Mr. Stein, look, this is it. Mr. Harman, this is it. This is our sausage. Der Wurst. Oh Shapiro, come here! I could just hug you. You weren't attacked by a dog, were you? Quiet, comrades!

Everyone is quiet, only Andrei is bellowing.

Mr. Harman, get your notebook out and take this down. (*Dictates*). Solomon Shapiro has brought us the sausage. Solomon Shapiro brachte Wurst. Write it down. Got it? Further, it seemed to me at first that he had brought a rose or a rainbow shell . . .

SHAPIRO. Or a peacock.

HARMAN. But it was a sausage. Oh Mr. Babichev, you look like a little boy.

ANDREI. Note down further . . .and then I smelled the aroma. It can probably be smelled in Germany too . . .(*Changing his tone*). Let me tell you something, Mr. Harman. This is a Shakespearean sausage.

SHAPIRO. Seventy percent romanticism. In other words, veal.

HARMAN. Veal and romanticism can't be the same in Russian? I don't know how I can write that down.

ANDREI. Write—I saw a sausage made of romanticism, and romanticism made of sausage.

HARMAN. I'll write that I don't understand anything.

ANDREI. And write this too—I saw a crazy sausage-maker. How would that go in German?

SHAPIRO. In German it'd be—you're terrific, tovarish Babichev!

HARMAN (*speaking German*). Ach ja . . .

ANDREI. Shapiro, give me a knife.

SHAPIRO. Not an easy trick since I don't have one.

Enter Ivan and Kavalerov followed by a crowd.

IVAN (*sees Andrei*). There he is. Kavalerov, you've got to smash the door shut, you've got to cut an ugly scar into history's ugly puss . . .

VALYA (*runs in on the upper platform*). Andrei Petrovich, the game's about to begin.

KAVALEROV. Right . . . coming. I'll probably get shot.

Valya runs down to Kavalerov, who rushes to meet her.

VALYA. Hello, Kavalerov.

KAVALEROV. Hello . . .

VALYA. What's the matter? Are you mad at me for the slap?

KAVALEROV. No, not mad, Valya. Are you, tell me, are you the wife of Andrei Petrovich?

VALYA. No, not yet.

KAVALEROV. I'm going to cut his throat with my razor.

VALYA. You what? Well, go on then, go ahead and cut away. Andrei Petrovich . . .

KAVALEROV. Valya.

VALYA. Andrei Petrovich, Kavalerov's here to slit your throat.

ANDREI. What, me? Right now . . . here? Okay, the hell with it. What should I do, pray tell. Lie down? Open my collar?

SHAPIRO. A little bit of Shakespearean theater is about to commence.

ANDREI. And what do you intend to use in order to slit my throat?

VALYA. He's going to use a razor.

ANDREI. Okay, cut away, cut away, Kavalerov. (*Swipes the razor from Kavalerov and begins cutting a large chunk of salami*). Here's the way to slice it up—can you smell the aroma?

IVAN. Slit his throat! Let's finish off the sausage-makers. Go on, slit his throat!

KAVALEROV. That's not the way, give me the razor. (*Kavalerov grabs the razor out of Andrei's hands and heads for Ivan*).

ZINOCHKA. Stop him!

IVAN. I see, yes, now I see. (*The crowd of Ivan's followers moves back in horror. Ivan rushes offstage. A moment later he rends the air with a terrific scream*).

KAVALEROV (*runs in*). I've killed him. Murdered my past, but I can explain everything.

ANDREI. The old passions are over and done with. A new world is beginning! (*A whistle blows. The soccer players come*

64

out onto the playing field).

CURTAIN

THE END

———

Alternate ending, first published in *P'esy*, Moscow, 1968. Begin reading with Andrei's speech, bottom of page 63.

ANDREI. Fesenkov seems shocked. What do you find so shocking, my admirer of chivalry? Are you worried that there are too many spectators here, gathered in a crowd? What a strange man! The more the merrier. It helps advertise our product. Unwrap it, Shapiro! Here it is, just look at that color!

HARMAN. I'll write down: when I first saw it I thought it was a violin or a melon.

ANDREI. Or Desdemona! That's right! Write this down—but it was a sausage. And get this down too—I saw a sausage-maker off his nut. What would that be in German?

SHAPIRO. In German it would be—You're the tops, Mr. Babichev.

HARMAN. Ach ja.

Ivan moves toward the spectators.

Who is this gentleman? Why does he have a pillow? Perhaps he wishes to emigrate to the land of public nourishment?

IVAN. Andryusha, treat me to some sausage.

Silence.

Mr. Harman, write this down—the insane sausage-maker stole his brother's daughter.

HARMAN. Mr. Babichev, is this what you call advertising too?

Silence.

ANDREI. If you don't get out of here right now I'll order you arrested.

IVAN. They won't hold me, I'm harmless. I'm not a magician, Andryusha, I'm a trickster. And here's my latest trick—a flying sausage. (*Grabs the sausage and waves it about—panic all around; he throws the sausage in Andrei's face, becomes frightened himself*).Bravo, bravo! War is

65

declared. Down with the sausage-maker! How's that! Terrific, eh? All right then—take me, execute me.

Attempts are made to seize him. Ivan runs, holding the pillow as an instrument of defense.

Kavalerov! Kavalerov! Cut his throat! Long live the conspiracy of feelings! Get him! Get him!

Ivan is caught and the pillow tumbles away. Kavalerov moves close to Ivan and his followers. Valya appears.

IVAN (*struggling in the hands of his captors*). Here he comes, the avenger! Don't you see, he'll slit your throat for you. Aha . . .you're turning pale? You're terrified, Andryusha?

Kavalerov lifts himself on his toes. He has the razor in his hands. He catches sight of Valya.

VALYA. It's not true. We're not afraid. Don't be afraid! Don't be afraid!

Kavalerov drops the razor, looks around, makes an attempt to pick it up but can't, sits down on the stairs.

KAVALEROV. Please, your attention for a moment. Andrei Petrovich, I tried to kill you . . .but I can't . . .put me on trial . . .punish me, poke out my eyes . . .I want to be blind. I have to be blind so I don't see you, your vacation land, your world.
VALYA. Andrei Petrovich, it's time this was over, the soccer players are waiting.

In run Vitya, the lady in green, the heavily intoxicated guest, all from Scene Six.

VITYA (*catching sight of Kavalerov lying on the stairs*). Oh we're too late. He's killed himself!
IVAN. He's alive, have no fear. He's a coward, a little doll. Carry Kavalerov to the museum where the other dolls are on display. Carry this man whose life has been stolen from him to the museum.
ANDREI. Take them away. It's time to begin the match!

A march. The soccer players come down to the playing fields.

66

Twenty-two men in brightly colored uniforms. Applause.

CURTAIN

THE END

A LIST OF BLESSINGS

A Play in Eight Scenes

Dedicated to Olga Gustavovna Suok

CHARACTERS

Yelena Goncharova (Lyolya)—a Soviet actress
Orlovsky—a theatrical manager
Nikolai Ilin (Guildenstern)—an actor in the company
Ekaterina Semyonova (Katya)—an actress in the company
Dunya Denisova—a beggar, Lyolya's neighbor
Peter Ivanovich—Lyolya's neighbor
Baronsky—Lyolya's neighbor
Tregubova—a dressmaker
Madame Macedon—a landlady
Fedotov ⎫
Lakhtin ⎬ Soviet representatives abroad
Dyakonov ⎭
Tatarov—publisher of a Russian émigré newspaper in Paris
Three men with guns
Dmitri Kizevetter—son of a Russian émigré
Margeret—manager of a music hall
Ulalum—popular singer
Henri Santillant—member of the French Communist Party
Lamplighter
A little man resembling Charlie Chaplin
Two French policemen
A crowd of workers
An elderly gentlemen with bodyguard
A secret agent
An adolescent
A weaver
His wife
Police chief and detachment of policemen
A messenger
Actors and music hall performers

SCENE ONE

PROLOGUE

After a performance of "Hamlet" a public discussion of the play is underway. On stage are King Claudius, Queen Gertrude, Horatio, Laertes and Hamlet. Hamlet is played by Yelena Goncharova (Lyolya). She is wearing riding boots and has a rapier in her hand. In the foreground, an ordinary little table covered with a red cloth. Orlovsky, the manager, presides.

ORLOVSKY (*ringing a bell*). The discussion of "Hamlet" is over. Now Goncharova, the play's producer and main performer, will respond to your written questions. Comrade Goncharova, please.

LYOLYA (*reads the first questions*). "Are you going abroad? For how long?" Yes, I'm going away for a month. "The play that we have seen, 'Hamlet,' is obviously written for the intelligentsia. The workers can't understand it, it's foreign and belongs to ancient history. Why show it, anyway?" "Hamlet" is the finest work created by the art of the past. That's my opinion. In all probability, Russian audiences will never see "Hamlet" again, so I decided to show it here for the last time. (*Sorting out the notes*). All right, let's read on. "You play the part of Hamlet, that is to say, of a man. But from your legs it's clear that you are a woman." Judging by the emphasis here on externals, this note's writer is not a Party member.

Orlovsky rings his bell.

"You're a famous actress, you earn good money. What else do you need? Why do photographs show you with such a worried look in your eyes?" Because I find it very difficult to be a citizen of the new world.

Orlovsky jingles his bell.

What's the matter? Have I said something wrong?

ORLOVSKY (*to the audience*). Comrade Goncharova is expressing herself in the spirit of Hamlet's monologues. (*To Lyolya*). Answer more simply, please.

LYOLYA. You accompany my every sentence with a ringing of your bell. You'd think my remarks were a flock of sheep. I don't bleat, do I?

ORLOVSKY. Please carry on.

LYOLYA. "What are you going to be doing abroad?" Well, all right then . . . in connection with my profession . . . visit theaters, get to know the performers . . . look at outstanding films that we'll never get to see here.

71

ORLOVSKY (*ringing his bell*). Comrade Goncharova has too high an opinion of foreign films. Our own films, such as "The Battleship Potemkin," "Turksib," "Heir of Ghengis Khan," have won general acclaim in Europe.

LYOLYA. May I continue? (*Reads*). "Why put on 'Hamlet'? Surely there are plays written these days." Contemporary plays are schematic, false, devoid of imagination and obvious. Acting in them means to lose one's skills. (*To Orlovsky*). You don't have to ring your bell, Comrade Orlovsky, I know what you want to say. Yes, it is my personal opinion.

ORLOVSKY. I wasn't ringing. Please go on.

LYOLYA (*reads*). "How can someone become an actor?" To become an actor takes talent.

ORLOVSKY (*nervously*). How many questions are left?

LYOLYA. Not many. (*Glances at one note, tears it up, reads another*). "In this era of reconstruction, when everyone is gripped by the furious tempo of national development, it's revolting to hear the tedious snivelling of your Hamlet." Comrade Orlovsky, grab your bell. I will now say something terribly seditious. (*To the audience*). Honored comrades! It seems to me that in an era of quick tempos the artist must think slowly.

ORLOVSKY (*ringing his bell*). One moment, comrades . . . The things said by Comrade Goncharova are her personal opinion . . . . As far as our theater is concerned, we are not completely in agreement with Comrade Goncharova. This might be called a matter for discussion. Carry on please . . .

LYOLYA. The last question. (*Reads*). "We request that you repeat Hamlet's monologue about the flute." Well I don't know what to do about that.

ORLOVSKY. Read it.

LYOLYA. But where is Ilin, who played Guildenstern? He hasn't removed his make-up yet, has he? Kolya!

GUILDENSTERN. Here I am.

LYOLYA. Well then, shall we do it again to please the audience?

GUILDENSTERN. Yes, let's.

They act.

LYOLYA-HAMLET. O, the recorders! Let me see one.—To withdraw with you:—why do you go about to recover the wind of me, as if you would drive me into a toil?

GUILDENSTERN. O, my lord, if my duty be too bold, my love is too unmannerly.

LYOLYA-HAMLET. I do not well understand that. Will you play upon this pipe?

GUILDENSTERN. My lord, I cannot.

LYOLYA-HAMLET. I pray you.

GUILDENSTERN. Believe me, I cannot.

LYOLYA-HAMLET. I do beseech you.

GUILDENSTERN. I know no touch of it, my lord.

LYOLYA-HAMLET. 'Tis as easy as lying; govern these vantages with your finger and thumb, give it breath with your mouth, and it will discourse most eloquent music. Look you, these are the stops.

GUILDENSTERN. But these cannot I command to any utterance of harmony; I have not the skill.

LYOLYA-HAMLET. Why, look you now, how unworthy a thing you make of me! You would play upon me, you would seem to know my stops, you would pluck out the heart of my mystery, you would sound me from my lowest note to the top of my compass; and there is much music, excellent voice in this little organ, yet cannot you make it speak. 'Sblood, do you think I am easier to be played on than a pipe? Call me what instrument you will, though you can fret me, you cannot play upon me.

LYOLYA. Well, that's all. Nobody's applauding. Well then, close the discussion, Comrade Orlovsky.

A note falls at her feet. She picks it up and reads it.

"What was written in the note you tore up? Answer honestly." It asked whether I would return from abroad. I'll give you an honest answer—I will.

CURTAIN

SCENE TWO

THE SECRET

Lyolya Goncharova's room. That evening there will be a party. Lyolya's friend Katerina Semyonova (an actress in the same company, ten years older than Lyolya) has brought refreshments. Both busy themselves preparing the party.

LYOLYA. I'm going away tomorrow, and I'll leave the key with you, Katya. Drop in occasionally to wipe the cobwebs off my Chaplin. (*On the wall is a large portrait of Chaplin. Addressing the portrait*). Ah, Chaplin, Chaplin! Little man in baggy trousers. I will be seeing your wonderful films. Katya, I'll be seeing "The Circus" and "The Goldrush." Everyone was wild about them . . . Years have gone by . . . and we still haven't seen them.

SEMYONOVA. Cut the apples. We'll make a wine punch with them.

LYOLYA. I'll go to Paris . . . Rain . . . I know there'll be rain . . . a glittering evening . . .slush . . .Maupassant slush. Can you imagine? Gleaming sidewalks, umbrellas, raincoats. Ah, Paris, Paris! All those wonderful books about it! And I'll walk along alone, unknown to anyone, under the walls, under the fences—happy, free . . .And somewhere on the edge of town, one autumn evening, in a little moviehouse I'll watch Chaplin and cry. (*Pause*). It's a journey to my youth. What shall I take with me? This suitcase. And this little one. No, wait a moment. (*Pulls out a drawer*). Here is the notebook I told you about.

SEMYONOVA. The diary.

LYOLYA. It must be hidden better. We'll stow it here under these things. You'll have the key. Or perhaps I should take it abroad with me?

SEMYONOVA. Why drag it around with you?

LYOLYA. Well, I may sell it.

SEMYONOVA. As the diary of an actress?

LYOLYA. No, it isn't the diary of an actress. It's the secret of the Russian intelligentsia. I'll show it to you, if you like.

SEMYONOVA. I'm really not interested.

LYOLYA. It depends on who reads it.

SEMYONOVA. What's the secret? Some sort of stories?

LYOLYA. The complete truth about the Soviet world.

SEMYONOVA. About standing in line for things?

LYOLYA. Idiot! Let me explain it to you.

SEMYONOVA. I don't have the time.

LYOLYA. Look, the notebook is divided into two parts. Here's the first part—a list of the revolution's crimes.

SEMYONOVA. In that case you'd better hide it.

LYOLYA. Don't be afraid. You think perhaps that these are vulgar complaints about food shortages? Don't worry, it's quite another thing. I speak about the crimes against the individual. There's a lot in our government's policies that I simply can't accept. Come here. Look, and here in the other half is a list of blessings. You think I can't see and can't understand the blessings of Soviet power? Now we'll put the two halves together. That's me. Do you understand? Those are my fears, my anxieties. Two halves of a single conscience, a muddle that's driving me out of my mind. I'll hide it in this suitcase. It can't be left here. Anything could happen. Somebody could find it. That'd be awful. They'd interpret it stupidly and say I'm a counterrevolutionary. (*Hides the notebook in the smaller suitcase*). And that's all then. There won't be any more things to arrange, Katya.

SEMYONOVA. You're right, you should sell it abroad.

LYOLYA. How? Tear it apart? Sell just the list of crimes? It's certain they wouldn't give a kopeck for a list of the blessings of Soviet power. Do you expect me to show just the negative side and to say nothing about the positive? No! This notebook can't be divided. I'm not a counterrevolutionary. I'm a woman of the old world who is having a debate with herself. Well, let's forget it. All right. We'll make a wine punch.

SEMYONOVA. When all's said and done, I have the feeling you'll stay abroad.

LYOLYA. I'll come back very soon, and I'll bring you a present.

SEMYONOVA. But what if someone falls in love with you and you get married?

LYOLYA. Who should I marry? I loathe them, those petty, vulgar feelings! The revolution has freed us from petty sentiments. There's one of the revolution's blessings for you.

SEMYONOVA. Do you have a can opener?

LYOLYA. Look in the drawer. No, no, in that one. I'm a terrible housekeeper, as you can see.

SEMYONOVA. No one's stopping you from living comfortably.

LYOLYA. I don't own anything. No books. No furniture.

SEMYONOVA. All you need to do is to buy some.

LYOLYA. No dresses. And the house . . .I've been living in this hole for five years. I'm almost a beggar.

SEMYONOVA. It's in your character.

LYOLYA. Homelessness.

SEMYONOVA. It's your own fault.

LYOLYA. There are people among us who carry in their heart only one list. It's a list of crimes; if those people hate the Soviet regime—they are happy. Some of them, the bold ones, either rebel or run away abroad. The others—the cowards and yes-men—tell lies and write nasty anecdotes. Those I detest. But if a man has the other list, the list of blessings, in him, he will build the new world with enthusiasm. It's his native land, his home. But I have two lists in my heart and so I can't either run away or rebel, or lie, or build. I can only try to understand and be silent. A home, furniture, things . . .Do you call this living? I drift . . .drift . . .drift . . .I can't accept the new world as my homeland, and that's why I can't make a home. Everyone knows how people live in their homeland. They have things, words, concepts. (*Pause*). Jasmine.

SEMYONOVA. What?

LYOLYA. A few days ago we put on a show for the communal farmers. They took me to the gardens, where I saw jasmine bushes in the greenhouse. And I thought, what strange jasmine. No, it was ordinary jasmine. But I suddenly thought: jasmine found in a different dimension is not a thing but an idea. Because it's the jasmine of a new world. Whose is it? Mine? I don't know. There's no private property. Yes, yes, yes—that's the root cause. There are no gardens belonging to others into which beggars peer, dreaming of riches . . .And it's all connected: the meaning of the jasmine with the meaning of the order in which it exists. The scent and color of jasmine are lost, it becomes a loose conception because its usual

75

associations have been destroyed. Many concepts are lost, slip away from eye and ear without reaching consciousness. For example, bride, groom, guest, friendship, reward, virginity, glory . . . To win glory means to stand above everyone. That's why I'll sit watching Chaplin's films. I'll be thinking of the fate of the little man, of the sweetness of finding vengeance for past humiliations, of glory.

SEMYONOVA. Who are you to be crying about glory?

LYOLYA. What is glory if you can't boast about it? I don't have the right to feel better than other people. And that's the Soviet regime's main crime against me.

A knock at the door.
Enter Dunya Denisova, a neighbor; a faded lady in a faded dress.

Oh . . . Dunya Denisova. (*To Katya*). You haven't met her, have you? My new neighbor. She's poor, and she makes a profession of scrounging. Scum, if you ask me.

SEMYONOVA (*in horror, embarrassed*). Lyolya!

LYOLYA (*to Dunya*). What can I do for you, Dunya?

DUNYA. Someone's stolen my apples.

LYOLYA. What apples?

DUNYA. Five of them. (*Pause*). I brought five apples home. I'd just gone out—and they were stolen.

LYOLYA. Who stole them?

DUNYA. How should I know?

SEMYONOVA. Surely she doesn't think we stole her apples?

DUNYA. I don't think anything. I can see there are some apples lying here. (*Gets up and goes*).

LYOLYA. Did you hear that? Isn't that a crime? I'll note that down right away. (*Gets out her notebook*). The actress who played Hamlet for the new man lived next to a scrounger in a dirty hovel.

Enter Dunya and Peter Ivanovich, an educated neighbor.

PETER IVANOVICH (*to Lyolya, immediately stern*). Why do you steal apples? (*Pause. To Dunya*). Do you recognize your apples?

DUNYA. She's cut them up in pieces.

PETER IVANOVICH. You should recognize the pieces.

LYOLYA. Yes, I must confess. We really did steal your apples.

PETER IVANOVICH. That's obvious enough.

DUNYA. Why did you cut them up? You didn't have any right to!

PETER IVANOVICH. She needs whole apples. She wanted to bake them.

DUNYA. I wanted to bake them.

76

LYOLYA. And now you'll just have to stew them.

PETER IVANOVICH. Don't tell her what to do.

SEMYONOVA. Listen here, I don't get it . . . How can you accuse us of stealing apples?

DUNYA. The door was open. If the door was locked, it would have been impossible to steal them.

PETER IVANOVICH (*to Katya*). Was the door open?

SEMYONOVA (*at a loss*). I don't know.

DUNYA. What's the point of asking? You can't steal through a locked door.

SEMYONOVA. But don't you know who we are? This is Yelena Goncharova, the famous actress! She's going abroad.

PETER IVANOVICH. It's different abroad.

DUNYA. Who is she to tell me to stew my apples. I get apples only once a year, and she . . .

LYOLYA (*hysterically*). Get out of here!

A knock at the door. A man bursts in—Baronsky, a neighbor.

BARONSKY (*loudly, waving his arms*). I hear everything the other side of the wall. Disgraceful! A fine lady talking with plebeians.

SEMYONOVA (*defending herself*). She's accusing us of stealing apples.

BARONSKY. What an outrageous tone! Simply outrageous! (*Advancing on Lyolya*). What are you? What? An aristocrat of the spirit, is that it?

LYOLYA (*calmly*). You burst into a room without permission.

BARONSKY. Come off it! Don't try those tricks on me! They won't work with me! Who gave you the right to make fun of these people? They're ignorant folk, yes. And you? An actress, yes. But why don't you say anything? They are no better than animals—is that it? Is that what you think: no better than animals? But you, you're an actress. I spit on that! Acting is the lowest form of parasitism. You don't like that? Of course you don't! Well, calm down. You're no better than they are, do you hear, no better! In the face of the future, you're no better than Dunya Denisova. Don't be afraid of her, Dunya: she drinks water supplied by the communal waterpipe, the same as you do. Do you drink water? And bread? You eat bread? Shops are for everybody. You use the electric light? Dunya, don't be afraid of her. The consumer's needs, do you hear, the consumer's needs—that's the formula that makes everyone equal.

SEMYONOVA. Why don't you say something, Lyolya?

LYOLYA. It's a matter of absolute indifference to me. He jumps about in front of me, grimaces, strikes poses. And it's a matter of complete indifference to me. I see you through the mist of a journey, Baronsky, and already I can't make out your features or hear your voice . . .

BARONSKY. You can't hear! But we heard you!

LYOLYA. What did you hear?

BARONSKY. That you want to run away abroad. (*Pause*). Are you frightened?

LYOLYA (*deliberately*). I spit on you.

BARONSKY. Oh, you spit! Do you hear, Dunya? Run, Dunya, and shout it to the whole house: the actress Goncharova is running away abroad.

The door opens. Enter the theatrical manager Orlovsky and with him a young man with a large bunch of jasmine.

ORLOVSKY. Here she is.

YOUNG MAN. Good day, Comrade Goncharova.

ORLOVSKY. This is a present from the communal farm workers to you. From the garden.

YOUNG MAN. You liked the jasmine. You wanted a bush. But you're going away. A bush would wilt—but here's some jasmine for your journey.

LYOLYA. Who from?

YOUNG MAN. From the workers. For the performance.

LYOLYA. How nice! Thank you.

YOUNG MAN. Think of us when you smell it.

LYOLYA. I'd like to write a few lines. Shouldn't I, Orlovsky? (*To the young man*). You'll pass it on?

YOUNG MAN. Certainly.

LYOLYA. Only my things are in such a mess . . . I can't even find any paper . . . (*Searches*).

YOUNG MAN (*picking up the notebook*). You can take a page from here.

LYOLYA. No, no.

YOUNG MAN (*holding up the notebook*). Is this a part? It's interesting to see how an actress works.

LYOLYA. Give it to me. Yes, yes, it's a part.

ORLOVSKY (*professionally*). What part?

LYOLYA. A very difficult one, Orlovsky. All right, then, pass it on by word of mouth. You could put it like this: I thank them, I'll be back soon and I'm very proud to be an actress in the land of the Soviets.

CURTAIN

SCENE THREE

INVITATION TO A BALL

*Paris. The living room of Mrs. Macedon's boarding-house. Tregu-
bova appears. She is a forty-five-year-old woman who tries to appear
younger than her years. She deals in dresses and has with her a large
cardboard box.*

TREGUBOVA. Good afternoon, Mrs. Macedon!

MRS. MACEDON. Have you brought the dresses?

TREGUBOVA. I have an enchanting thing for you in my box today.
Such a dress it is that if . . .

MRS. MACEDON. You're late. The American woman has gone.

TREGUBOVA. It was the Russian one I had in mind.

MRS. MACEDON. Miss Goncharova?

TREGUBOVA. Yes.

MRS. MACEDON. You want to offer her the dress?

TREGUBOVA. Is she young?

MRS. MACEDON. Oh yes.

TREGUBOVA. And beautiful?

MRS. MACEDON. Oh yes.

TREGUBOVA. I saw her picture in the paper. But that's not enough if
we're talking about a dress for her. A picture in the newspaper reflects the
original as remotely as a glove reflects a living hand. Isn't that true. The
complexion, the color of the hair and the way the eyes smoulder or
sparkle . . .

MRS. MACEDON. Do you know she's a well-known actress?

TREGUBOVA. My friend showed me the papers. She's been getting
headlines: "Russian Actress Goncharova Arrives In Paris." (*Pause*). Will
she be at the ball?

MRS. MACEDON. Miss Goncharova? I don't know.

TREGUBOVA. Probably!

MRS. MACEDON. The whole town is talking about the ball.

TREGUBOVA. It's to be held on Sunday. A great International
Artists' Ball. The seamstresses are working non-stop. What an event! All
the celebrities will be there, all the stars.

Lyolya appears.

MRS. MACEDON. Here comes Miss Goncharova. Miss Goncharova, the dressmaker would like to see you.

LYOLYA. What?

TREGUBOVA. Good afternoon, Miss Goncharova.

79

LYOLYA. Good afternoon.

TREGUBOVA. I've come with some dresses.

LYOLYA. To see me?

TREGUBOVA. If you're interested.

MRS. MACEDON. This is Miss Tregubova. She has been serving the clients of my boardinghouse for many years now.

TREGUBOVA. Here's my showcase. (*Indicates showcase with dresses*).

LYOLYA. Yes, but now . . . I simply don't need any now.

TREGUBOVA. But why not have a look?

LYOLYA. You're Russian?

TREGUBOVA. Yes.

Lyolya is silent.

Is something wrong?

LYOLYA. The point is that in Paris there are Russians with whom . . .

TREGUBOVA. I understand. Émigrés? No, I've been living in Paris for twenty years. Mrs. Macedon can confirm that.

MRS. MACEDON. Oh yes, I certainly can.

TREGUBOVA. And so, madam. A beautiful ball gown.

LYOLYA. I'm not worth your trouble, really.

TREGUBOVA. Oh, it's really nothing. (*Opens the box*).

LYOLYA. Oho . . . What luxury, it's beautiful!

TREGUBOVA. And with your hair . . .

LYOLYA. But it must be very expensive.

TREGUBOVA. A model like this from a fashion house famous throughout the world costs ten thousand francs. At Poiret's. At Lelondbas's. At Armand's. There you pay for the label. They'll say it's inimitable, unique, it's the only one of its kind. And in actual fact the design is destroyed. But there are ways of copying designs considered destroyed. We put in a few variations . . .

LYOLYA. One of them is silver.

TREGUBOVA. And as a result, an outfit that costs ten thousand at Poiret's, we can let you have it for four.

LYOLYA. Four thousand francs?

TREGUBOVA. That's all.

LYOLYA. Shut the box.

TREGUBOVA. You didn't like it?

LYOLYA. No, it's just that it's expensive.

TREGUBOVA. It isn't expensive, if you want to shine.

LYOLYA. But I'm not planning to be a sensation anywhere.

TREGUBOVA. Not even at the ball?

LYOLYA. What ball is that?

TREGUBOVA. The International Artists' Ball.

Fedotov enters. The landlady rushes to him and they exchange a few words.

Just think, it isn't an ordinary ball. Paris is organizing an artists' festival.

MRS. MACEDON. Someone to see you, Miss Goncharova.

LYOLYA (*to Tregubova*). Excuse me . . .

TREGUBOVA. Please. (*Does not close the box*).

LYOLYA. No, no, I don't want it.

TREGUBOVA. All right then, madam . . .(*Closes the box, withdraws*).

FEDOTOV (*approaching*). Good afternoon, Comrade Goncharova. You're called Yelena Nikolayevna, aren't you? My name is Fedotov.

LYOLYA. Pleased to meet you. Are you from Moscow?

FEDOTOV. No, on the contrary, I'm going to Moscow. I'm returning from America. I was just passing through Paris and I found out that you were here. So I came to pay my respects.

They shake hands.

LYOLYA. Thank you, please sit down. So you're coming from America?

FEDOTOV. I was on tractor business. Our commission was travelling, Comrade Lakhtin's delegation. Three of us: Lakhtin, Dyakonov and me. So there you are. If you're not busy, shall we get acquainted? Perhaps you're in a hurry?

LYOLYA. No . . . I'm delighted.

FEDOTOV. You know I'm a great fan of your theater company.

LYOLYA. Really?

FEDOTOV. Yes, really. So you understand it's particularly pleasant for me to meet a fellow countryman like you abroad.

LYOLYA. How did you find out I was here?

FEDOTOV. From the papers. Your arrival is a sensation in Paris. The International Artists' Ball is soon, and they write about you, you know. They write that the Soviet star Yelena Goncharova will shine at the ball.

LYOLYA What nonsense. I haven't even been invited.

FEDOTOV. All the better. But do you know what kind of ball it is?

LYOLYA. An International Artists' Ball.

FEDOTOV. And who's organizing it?

LYOLYA. Probably the local actors' society.

FEDOTOV. And who's pulling the strings?

LYOLYA. I don't know.

FEDOTOV. Well I'll explain it to you. This ball is being organized by

81

the banker Lepeltier, you know, an old man, a textile manufacturer, Balthazar Lepeltier. A crisis is hanging over him. He's closing his factories, but when the game's going badly you have to put a good face on things, and so he's hit on the idea of a ball. You understand? It's a phoney demonstration of prosperity. There'll be all kinds of swine there, Russian émigré celebrities, well-known fascists . . . . But at the same time a more serious demonstration is in preparation . . .a march on Paris by the unemployed.

LYOLYA. The unemployed?

FEDOTOV. A hunger march by the unemployed. And you talk about a ball!

LYOLYA. I'm not saying that, you are.

FEDOTOV. Yes, please forgive me; I got rather carried away, it's a long time since I spoke at a meeting. But in case you do get an invitation, I advise you to decline and to publish your refusal in the Communist press.

Pause.

Yesterday I was at the Soviet Embassy. They're expecting you there.

LYOLYA. I keep meaning to go.

FEDOTOV. Let's go there together.

LYOLYA. Let's.

FEDOTOV. The day after tomorrow; we'll meet at my place.

LYOLYA. Where is your place?

FEDOTOV. Lakhtin, Dyakonov and I, we are staying in a boardinghouse on the rue Lanterne. It's not far from the Embassy. I'll write down the address for you. The day after tomorrow at 7 p.m. All right? (*Writes*). Well, how are you spending your time here? Looking at the museums, I imagine?

LYOLYA. I'm not doing anything. Mostly I walk around.

FEDOTOV. Just walk around?

LYOLYA. Sometimes I stop and look; I see my shadow lying before me. I look at it and think: my shadow is lying on the stones of Europe. (*Pause*). I have lived in a new world, and now tears come to my eyes when I see my shadow on the stones of the old world. I remember what my life was like in the world that you call "new." It was only in what I thought. The Revolution deprived me of my past and didn't show me a future. And so my thoughts became my present. To think . . .I thought, only thought—by means of thought I wanted to attain what I couldn't attain by feeling. A man's life is natural when thought and feeling form a harmony. I was deprived of that harmony, and so my life in the new world was unnatural. By means of thought I completely understood the idea of Communism. With my brain I believed that the triumph of the proletariat was natural and in the order of things. But my feelings were against it. I was torn in two.

82

I ran away here from that divided life, and if I hadn't run away then I would have gone mad. In the new world I lay about like a fragment of broken glass. Now I have returned, and the two halves have united. I live a natural existence, and I have regained my present tense verbs. I eat, I touch, I look, I walk...A grain of dust of the old world settled on the stones of Europe. Those ancient, powerful stones, laid down by the Romans. No one will move them.

FEDOTOV (*heatedly*). Those stones will soon be blown out of the earth and barricades will be built from them. You say that your shadow is lying on the stones of Europe? You only saw your own shadow? But I see other shadows...I see people who have turned into shadows...people crushed by the stones of Europe...

LYOLYA. That may be, that may be! I don't know. I've been resting from thinking about the Revolution for three weeks now.

FEDOTOV. You're resting from thinking about the Revolution? But what do you think about now if you're not thinking of the Revolution? It's possible to think either about the Revolution or about the counter-revolution. There are no other thoughts now.

LYOLYA. Everyone wants to think only about himself.

FEDOTOV. This is a bourgeois conversation.

LYOLYA. In other words, human. I am an actress, and my essence must be humanity.

FEDOTOV. There is no such thing as being human.

LYOLYA. That's boring. You want to say that man doesn't exist in general, that there is only class? That's boring. I've listened. I've thought, thought hard. It isn't true. In that case an actress will only become great when she embodies a democratic, generally comprehensible idea that moves everyone...

FEDOTOV. That idea is socialism.

LYOLYA. Not true.

FEDOTOV. What is it then?

LYOLYA. The theme of human fate. Chaplin's idea. The monster wants to be handsome. The beggar, rich. The lazybones wants to receive an inheritance. The mother wants to come to her son...

FEDOTOV. It's the theme of individual happiness? A kulak theme.

LYOLYA. A kulak theme, if you like.

FEDOTOV. At least you understand that.

LYOLYA. I understand everything. That's where my misfortune lies. Help me. I don't know what's happening to me. I'm all alone in the world. All this is in my heart: the struggle of two worlds, old and new. And it's not you I'm arguing with; I'm arguing with myself...I'm carrying on a long, agonizing argument with myself, an argument that's drying up my brain. Just look what's happening to me; my hair is turning gray. I was a highschool girl, and on the day I finished school the acacia was in bloom,

83

the petals fell on book pages, on the windowsill, on the bend of my elbow . . . I saw my life before me and it was beautiful. And the Revolution took place that very day. Since then I've stood like a beggar, on my knees, like an idol, stretching out arms as rough as sand.

Silence.

FEDOTOV. Why didn't you go to the Soviet Embassy?
LYOLYA. There's no one there I want to see.
FEDOTOV. You are officially required to appear.
LYOLYA. I don't know. (*Silence*). Listen . . .
FEDOTOV. What?
LYOLYA. Listen, I want to ask you something.
FEDOTOV. Certainly. What is it?
LYOLYA. Give me some money. (*Silence*). Forgive me, I was joking of course. Pay no attention.
FEDOTOV. Yelena Nikolayevna, you seem to be confused.
LYOLYA. You're only just noticing that, you subtle observer? Incidentally, I asked you for the money seriously. I don't want to return to Russia.
FEDOTOV. What you're saying is terrible. Stop it now, Yelena Nikolayevna. You should be ashamed of yourself. What's happening to you? You're stumbling? You're dividing into two? You're hanging in the air? You're hesitating? Enough. Think of it: unemployment, starvation . . . The blind have regained their sight, fangs are bared . . . What kind of philosophy can there be abroad? A struggle for markets, for rubber, for oil . . . Guns are being invented, war is approaching . . . And here you go talking about your personality. What are you complaining about? That it's been suppressed, that personality of yours? You think that your intellectual complaints are in any way different from the complaints of a kulak that collectivization has deprived him of his farm? Not in the least. It comes to the same thing. What are you talking about? You don't want to return home? You want to stay here, is that it? And you say that . . . you who have already been there, in the land of the Soviets, already with the proletariat laid the first stones of the New World, already lifted on your shoulders huge glory, the glory of the proletarian Revolution. You lower yourself even to thinking of staying here, or running away from the finest world, from the most intelligent, the most advanced, the only thinking environment—that of the workers of our Union. It's a bad dream, a dream, you're delirious, Yelena Nikolayevna, and I don't believe you. Paris, Paris! Well, so we're here in Paris . . . yes! But that Paris which is in your dreams, that Paris doesn't exist now, it's just a ghost. Culture is condemned to death. You think that bourgeois Europe is as young as you are. But its temple is collapsing, and you bow to the fragments of its columns. If you want to

remain here, then be consistent. If you want to remain in the camp of the shopkeepers, the kulaks, the petty property-owners, then go and shoot at the unemployed together with the police. Yes, yes, yes! It's one and the same thing. Anybody who complains about the Soviet regime sympathizes with the police shooting the unemployed in Europe. There's no point in pretending, no point in wrapping yourself up in a philosophy; your exquisite philosophy is simply that of the shopkeeper or the policeman. It means you're with them! It's perfectly clear that you can hold no other position—either here or there. What are you then? With us or with them?

LYOLYA. Kiss me on the forehead. Officially. In the name of the Embassy.

FEDOTOV. Well there you are . . . That's just fine.

Pause.

But don't you very much want to go to the ball?

LYOLYA. Only don't tell the ambassador. I do want to.

FEDOTOV. Is it from vanity?

LYOLYA. Yes.

FEDOTOV. Then it would be more interesting to annoy them. They'll want you to go to the ball, and you'll refuse.

LYOLYA. You're a dear.

FEDOTOV. So are you.

LYOLYA. Goodbye then.

Fedotov takes a revolver out of his trouser pocket.

LYOLYA. What's that?

FEDOTOV. Military habit. I always keep a revolver ready.

Hides the revolver in the pocket of his overcoat and moves in the direction of the exit. At this moment Tatarov emerges from behind the restaurant's glass screen into the living room. Fedotov holds back.

TATAROV. If I'm not mistaken, you are Miss Goncharova?

LYOLYA. Yes, that's right. (*Responds to his bow in silence*).

TATAROV. Pleased to meet you. (*Extends his hand*).

FEDOTOV (*calls out from the distance.*). Yelena Nikolayevna, don't speak to that person. (*He draws nearer*). What do want?

TATAROV. Excuse me . . . I came to have a talk with the actress Goncharova who has defected from Moscow.

LYOLYA. I don't know you.

FEDOTOV. Not a word, Yelena Nikolayevna!

TATAROV. Is that your husband? Did you run away together?

LYOLYA. I didn't run away at all.

FEDOTOV. Who are you?

TATAROV. My name is Tatarov.

FEDOTOV. The editor of the émigré newspaper, "Russia?"

TATAROV. Yes.

FEDOTOV. What have you come here for?

TATAROV. To fight for her soul. You are an angel; I, of course, am a devil. And Miss Goncharova is a righteous woman.

FEDOTOV. Get out of here immediately.

TATAROV. My dear sir...

FEDOTOV. Do you want to provoke her?

TATAROV. I didn't come here to talk to you.

FEDOTOV. Get out or I...(*Puts his hand in his pocket*).

TATAROV. Or you'll shoot me? I don't think so. You wouldn't risk it. They don't like murderers here. Human life is not an abstract but an extremely concrete concept here. First of all two moustached policemen will appear in black capes, they will seize you by the arms, make a little run and hit your back against the wall several times—until they knock out your kidneys. Then, with your kidneys knocked out and spitting blood, they'll take you away.

FEDOTOV. My fingers are itching. I was a brigade commander once, Yelena Nikolayevna.

LYOLYA. But you know, Fedotov, it's interesting. A real live émigré! Let him talk. Then I'll be able to tell them in Moscow how I saw a real live émigré. A pity I'm shortsighted. Well turn round then. What are you like from the back? Or let him walk a little bit. Good afternoon. I recognize you. You are a caricature. I've often seen you on the front page of "Izvestia." You are a flat drawing of a man. How dare you hold out your hand to me! You are a two-dimensional man! You are a shadow, but I am a sculpture. To shake your hand goes against the physical laws.

Pause. Tatarov is motionless.

Let's go, Fedotov. I'll see you off. Let him fly away like a shadow. (*Goes out with Fedotov*).

TATAROV (*alone*). A shadow? Excellent! But whose shadow? Yours.

The landlady appears.

MRS. MACEDON. Mr. Tatarov.

Tatarov is silent.

What has happened, Mr. Tatarov?

Tatarov is silent.

Your friend Mrs. Tregubova was here a moment ago. She brought some dresses. Did you come for her? She left ten minutes ago. Have you quarrelled with her?

A messenger boy enters.

MESSENGER. Does Miss Goncharova live here?
MRS. MACEDON. Yes.
MESSENGER. Letter for her. (*Hands over a packet. Goes out*).
MRS. MACEDON (*reads the stamped inscription on the envelope*). "International Actors' Association." Oh Mr. Tatarov, she's a Russian. If you had seen her! A Russian visitor with a room in my place. She'd be to your taste, I'm sure. Tregubova told me you like blonds.
TATAROV. Give me the envelope. I'll give it to the Russian lady and that will be my excuse to get acquainted.
MRS. MACEDON. Poor Madame Tregubova! You probably betray her at every step!

Enter Lyolya. The landlady exits to the side.

TATAROV. Yelena Nikolayevna.

Lyolya stops. She says nothing.

That young man interrupted me in carrying out a task entrusted to me by the International Actors' Association . . .

Lyolya stands at an angle, saying nothing.

I have come to give you an invitation to the ball.
LYOLYA. Give it to me. (*She takes the envelope and tears it to pieces*).

Tatarov goes out. Lyolya is alone. The landlady returns.

MRS. MACEDON. Well then. Did you take the dress? You know, she's a first-class tailor and apart from that takes credit.

A man who has apparently been running bursts in from behind the glass door. He fidgets uneasily; he is clearly being pursued.

Help! Help!

87

Panic. Three men with guns come running in. They seize the escapee.

LYOLYA. What are you doing? What are you doing?
ARMED MAN. Take her away.

Lyolya is pushed behind the glass door. The landlady runs up the staircase. Silence falls. The glass door is slammed shut. Weak with horror, Lyolya sees the pursuers grip the unknown man by the arms behind the glass door, they hit his back against the wall. Lyolya strikes the glass barrier with her fists. The captive is badly beaten. He crumples to the floor. He doesn't shout, doesn't groan. The entire scene takes place in complete silence. The unknown man is dragged to the exit. The landlady comes downstairs, half dead with fright.

MRS. MACEDON. What is it, gentlemen? Who is this?

Lyolya is almost in hysterics behind the glass door. She shouts almost inaudibly behind the door.

LYOLYA. Let him go! Let him go! How dare you! What have you done to this man!
FIRST MAN WITH GUN (*to the landlady*). Who is this? . . .Does she live here with you?
MRS. MACEDON. She's a Russian actress.
CAPTIVE (*lying against the arms of those who have beaten him, his arms extended, his legs dragging along the floor, half-conscious, hoarsely*). A Russian? Long live Moscow!

CURTAIN

SCENE FOUR

THE SILVER GOWN

At the dressmaker's. Evening. Tatarov and Tregubova.

TATAROV. I went to see her shortly after you. But it turned out that the Soviet Embassy had already attached a Chekhist to her. Before I could say two words to her he began threatening me. (*Tregubova gestures with her hands. Insulted, with anger and at the same time with a certain envy*). The bandit!
TREGUBOVA. My God, you frighten me so.
TATAROV. I left without anything. But if there hadn't been a

88

Chekhist with her, I would have made her talk. She's very careful. She said that she wouldn't want to talk with just any Russian in Paris.

TREGUBOVA. With émigrés, isn't that what she meant?

TATAROV. Yes. That pride will last a week. We've seen a great many of the righteous ones from the Soviet paradise who lost their faith forever after sniffing the scents of Paris.

TREGUBOVA. I had the impression that she was very proud.

TATAROV. A saint in the land of temptation. I don't believe that. We'll juggle her. What? We won't manage it? Or—what? I don't understand, simply don't understand that stare of yours. Turn away those darkening turquoises of yours.

TREGUBOVA. I was thinking about something else.

TATAROV. About what?

TREGUBOVA. If you are now capable of hating so strongly, it means you can love with equal strength.

Tatarov is silent.

But you don't love me, and never did.

Tatarov is silent.

Well it doesn't matter. Don't be cross. I won't mention it again.

TATAROV. So as to gaze right into her very soul, they've attached a sailor with a revolver to her. I should be with her, not a Chekhist; then all her secrets would be revealed.

TREGUBOVA. She was just a young girl when you ran away from Russia. Surely you didn't know her there?

TATAROV. Yes I did.

TREGUBOVA. Everything is possible. Your past is unknown to me. Tell me, could this actress perhaps be your daughter?

TATAROV. It's possible.

TREGUBOVA (*with great emotion*). Is it true?

TATAROV. Or perhaps my niece.

TREGUBOVA. Your niece?

TATAROV. Or perhaps not mine, but the niece of a lawyer who looks like me.

TREGUBOVA. What lawyer, Nikolai?

TATAROV. Or not a lawyer. Perhaps a bank manager. Or a member of the land board, or a professor . . . Doesn't it all come to the same thing? What is there here that can be understood? Russian intellectuals, we're all from the same tribe as her. But it so happens that I am a pitiful fugitive, while she is a big-shot visitor from the fatherland. I don't believe in her pride. I know she's unhappy. And she can be as silent as a mirror, I'll hear her all the same. I'll force her to cry out in her misery.

TREGUBOVA. It could turn out that your suspicions are unfounded.

TATAROV. Do you think she's honest?

TREGUBOVA. Yes. You read me an article about her yourself. The Bolsheviks value her.

TATAROV. But she lies to them all the same. I'll prove it.

TREGUBOVA. She was in favor.

TATAROV. That makes the experiment all the more interesting. She was permitted a great deal. She put on "Hamlet." Just think of it, "Hamlet" in a country where art has been lowered to propaganda for the breeding of pigs, for the digging of silo pits . . . The Soviet authorities have spoiled her, a brilliant example, I will prove once more, unnecessarily but utterly convincingly, that in Russia there is slavery. The whole world is talking about it. But what does the world hear? It hears the complaints of woodcutters, the obscure muttering of slaves who can neither think nor make themselves heard. But now I can draw complaints from someone with the highest gifts . . . And the world will be twice as terrified. A famous actress from the land of the slaves cries out to the world: don't believe in my glory, don't believe in it! I got it for refusing to think . . . Don't believe in my freedom. In spite of everything, I was a slave.

TREGUBOVA. But surely slaves aren't like that. She's a happy woman by the look of her.

TATAROV. Happy? Proud? Incorruptible?

TREGUBOVA. So it seems to me.

TATAROV. One of the righteous? Without sin?

TREGUBOVA. Yes.

TATAROV. I'm convinced that she has sins, and if not, I'll invent some for her. (*Pause*). She's been invited to that notorious ball. For us, it's already a feather in our cap.

TREGUBOVA. She refused the gown.

TATAROV. Because the gown came first and then the invitation. But if the reverse . . .

TREGUBOVA. She hasn't got the money.

TATAROV. That's a second feather in our cap. Let her have the gown on credit. It's very easy to get entangled and fall in a gown that's lined with credit.

TREGUBOVA. You know I can't refuse you anything. But I'm afraid.

TATAROV. Of what?

TREGUBOVA. You said she was "a beauty in the land of beggars." Have you fallen in love with her?

Enter Dmitri Kizevetter, a thin fairheaded young man of twenty-five.

What have you come for, Dmitri?

KIZEVETTER. I was looking for you, Nikolai.

TREGUBOVA. Nikolai Ivanovich, I asked you not to have meetings with this person in my house.

TATAROV. He lives with me because he's an orphan and poor. His father, Pavel Kizevetter, was my friend.

TREGUBOVA. You have your own house.

TATAROV. But can't I receive someone dear to me in your house?

TREGUBOVA. I'm afraid of him.

TATAROV. You reject my friendship?

TREGUBOVA. You've worn me out . . .

KIZEVETTER. She's frightened of me? Why?

TREGUBOVA (*to Tatarov*). Don't you see he's insane?

TATAROV. Nonsense.

KIZEVETTER. Why do you think I'm crazy?

TREGUBOVA. I don't want you here.

KIZEVETTER. Why do you think I'm crazy?

TREGUBOVA. Leave me alone! (*Weeps*).

Silence.

TATAROV. Drop it, Lidochka. Well, give me your hand. (*Takes her hand and kisses it. He lifts her head and kisses her on the lips*). Treat Dima more gently. He's unemployed. Have you thought of that? They fired five thousand of them.

KIZEVETTER. Should I shoot through the window because I was fired?

TATAROV. Shoot the Soviet ambassador.

TREGUBOVA. Why are you saying such a thing to a madman?

TATAROV. Europe has gone blind. Give me a platform. I'll shout it in the face of Europe: the Bolsheviks are attacking you! Cheap bread. Every grain of Soviet corn is a cancer bacillus. Every grain is another unemployed. Give me a platform, like the Pope in Rome! Hm . . .Dress me in the tiara and robe of the Pope in Rome! . . .Ah! Me not him, a plump Italian in spectacles. I must call Europe to the struggle against the Bolsheviks.

KIZEVETTER. You'd look good in a tiara. But the lady is looking at me with horror. She's surprised—Dima's making jokes. I'm fairheaded, dear lady, very fairheaded, a member of the cadet corps. And I'm good— that's the main thing. I don't want to kill anyone. My word of honor. And why must I think such serious thoughts? Eh?

Silence.

Do you hear, Nikolai Ivanovich?

TATAROV. Well?

KIZEVETTER. Because I'm young, eh?

TATAROV. Well?

KIZEVETTER. Surely the young didn't always have to think such difficult, bloody thoughts?

TATAROV. He fled here with his father when he was twelve years old.

KIZEVETTER. What? Because I'm young? Was it always like this with the young, or different? Chopin. The young Chopin, did he have such a strange life?

TATAROV. The young Chopin lived on the island of Majorca; he had consumption.

KIZEVETTER. Marvelous! I'm for it. Blood pours from my throat. But why must I suck somebody else's blood from somebody else's throat? Eh?

TREGUBOVA. He's delirious!...Surely you realize that!

KIZEVETTER. By the way, I haven't once looked at the starry sky through a telescope. Why not? Why wasn't I meant to look through a telescope when I was young?

TREGUBOVA. I can't bear to listen to him!

KIZEVETTER. I don't have a necktie! And there are as many ties as you like for sale. I don't have any money. And who does? Give money to everyone, eh? The population is too big and the amount of money is too small. If the population increases it will have to be destroyed. We can have a war.

Silence.

Or, for example, I never had a fiancée. Eh? I want to have a fiancée!

TATAROV. You will never have a fiancée.

KIZEVETTER. Why not?

TATAROV. Because you're out of step with the times.

KIZEVETTER. Who should I shoot because of that?

TATAROV. Shoot yourself.

TREGUBOVA. Get out! Do you hear? Get out!...I can't bear it...

TATAROV. Well, all right, Dima. Get going. Wait for me on the bench.

Exit Kizevetter. Silence.

TREGUBOVA. You're leaving? I thought you'd spend the night.

TATAROV. Listen carefully. Tomorrow you'll go to her boarding-house. Take your best gown.

TREGUBOVA. I showed her one that she called "the silver dress." (*Drags the box to the middle of the room*).

TATAROV. It's a magic box. You don't know how to think in symbols, Lida. These gleams and threads, this trembling air—do you know what it is? It's what it is forbidden to think about in Russia, it is the desire to live for oneself, for one's own wealth and glory, it's the human essence, and it's called light industry. It's a waltz that sounds through other people's windows, it's a ball you'd very much like to attend. It's the tale of Cinderella.

TREGUBOVA. You kissed me so tenderly just now. I want to return the debt. (*Kisses him*).

TATAROV. You say: one of the righteous, honesty, loyalty, incorruptibility. You saw her in clothes and shiny baubles that aren't there at all. The Bolsheviks, who can make use of it, see this outfit on her as a sign of honesty and incorruptibility. But I can see that the queen is naked. And only now will we show her to the world as she really is when we dress her in your gown.

TREGUBOVA. You kissed me very tenderly and I want to return the debt with interest. (*Kisses him*).

TATAROV. Let her look into your box a second time, tell her it's all free and she'll go into ecstasies.

A knock at the door. Tatarov comes upstage. He sits in an armchair with his back to the stage. He puts on his glasses.

LYOLYA. Do you recognize me?

TREGUBOVA. Miss Goncharova.

LYOLYA. I found out your address from the landlady of the boardinghouse.

TREGUBOVA. Sit down, please.

LYOLYA. I need a gown.

TREGUBOVA. I'm glad to be of service, madam.

LYOLYA. But the thing is that ...(*Hesitates*). The landlady told me that you allow credit.

TREGUBOVA. Yes, madam.

LYOLYA. I would like that ...

TREGUBOVA. This silver dress?

LYOLYA. Yes.

TATAROV. Who are you talking to, Lida?

TREGUBOVA. A lady has come for a dress.

TATAROV. I was dozing.

Lyolya is embarrassed by the presence of a third party.

TREGUBOVA (*soothingly*). That's my husband.

TATAROV. Forgive me for sitting with my back to you like this.

You've taken a spot near the lamp and the light hurts my eyes.

LYOLYA. That's all right.

Pause.

TREGUBOVA. Very well, madam, let's try it on.

LYOLYA. By all means, let's.

TREGUBOVA. Over here. (*Points to the chest of drawers*). I've blocked myself off a little studio.

Lyolya, carrying the small chest, and Tregubova go to a screened-off place where the fitting begins.

Are you going to the ball, madam?

LYOLYA. Yes, I intend to.

TREGUBOVA. They don't give balls in Russia?

LYOLYA. No.

TREGUBOVA. And now you'll attend a ball.

LYOLYA. When a waltz sounds behind other people's windows, a person thinks about his life.

Pause.

What does your husband do?

TATAROV. I write fairytales.

LYOLYA. Did you leave Russia long ago?

TATAROV (*lies*). Before the war, when the world was exceedingly big and reachable. (*Pause*). Do Soviet children read fairytales?

LYOLYA. It depends what kind.

TATAROV. About the ugly duckling, for example?

LYOLYA. They don't read that.

TATAROV. Why not? It's a beautiful fairytale. Do you remember? They pecked him but he was silent, remember? He was humiliated, but he didn't lose hope. He had a secret. He knew that he was better than the others. He waited; the time will come and I will be avenged. And it turned out that he was a swan, that proud, lonely duckling. And when the swans flew by he flew away together with them, his silver wings gleaming.

LYOLYA. That's typical petty-bourgeois propaganda.

TATAROV. What makes you say that?

LYOLYA. The petty-bourgeois Andersen embodies the dream of the petty bourgeois. To become a swan—that means to get wealthy. Isn't that true? To raise yourself above the rest. That's the dream of the petty bourgeois; to endure want, to accumulate cash, hide, be cunning and then, having become wealthy, to attain might and power—that is, become a capitalist. That's the fairytale of capitalist Europe.

TATAROV. In Europe every ugly duckling can turn into a swan. But what happens to ugly ducklings in Russia?

LYOLYA. In the first place, in Russia they try to ensure that there aren't any ugly ducklings. They are well cared for. They don't turn into swans. On the contrary, they turn into beautiful ducks. And then they are exported. And that's where a new fairytale of the capitalist world begins.

TATAROV. What fairytale is that?

LYOLYA. The fairytale about Soviet exports.

Tatarov is silent.

TREGUBOVA. What kind of dresses are made in Russia these days? Short or long?

LYOLYA. Somewhere in the middle, I think.

TATAROV. And what materials are fashionable?

LYOLYA. Where?

TATAROV. In Russia, madam.

LYOLYA. In Russia, cast iron is in fashion.

Silence.

TREGUBOVA. And what dresses are worn in the evening?

LYOLYA. Morning ones, I think.

TREGUBOVA. And at the theater?

LYOLYA. They go to the theater in felt boots.

TREGUBOVA. What? In a tailcoat and felt boots?

LYOLYA. No, just in felt boots.

TREGUBOVA. Why? Because they don't like tailcoats?

LYOLYA. No, because they like the theater.

TATAROV. Is it true that in Russia they are exterminating the intelligentsia?

LYOLYA. Exterminating in what way?

TATAROV. Physically.

LYOLYA. Shooting them?

TATAROV. Yes.

LYOLYA. They shoot those who hinder the building of the state.

TATAROV. I stand to one side of political arguments, but I've heard it said that the Bolsheviks are shooting the best people of Russia.

LYOLYA. But there's no Russia now.

TATAROV. What do you mean, there's no Russia?!

LYOLYA. There is the Union of Soviet Socialist Republics.

TATAROV. Well yes, a new name.

LYOLYA. No, something different. If tomorrow there's a revolution in Europe . . . let's say in Poland or Germany . . . then that part of Europe will become part of the Soviet Union. What kind of Russia is that, if it's Poland or Germany? So Soviet territory is not a geographical concept.

TATAROV. What kind, then.

LYOLYA. A dialectical one. That's why the qualities of people must be estimated dialectically. Do you understand? And from a dialectical viewpoint the best person can turn out to be a scoundrel.

TATAROV. Ah. I'm satisfied. Consequently you justify some shooting?

LYOLYA. Yes.

TATAROV. And don't consider them to be crimes of the Soviet regime?

LYOLYA. In general I'm not aware of any crimes of the Soviet regime. On the contrary, I could read you a long list of its blessings.

TATAROV. Name at least one.

LYOLYA. As soon as I came here I understood a lot. I shall return home with a list of the capitalist regime's crimes. Concerning the children, say, we've just been talking about . . . Do you know that in Russia the rock of the marriage laws has been broken? . . . We Russians are already used to it and don't think about it . . . But in your country there are illegitimate children. That is, religion and authority severely punish the children begotten by a couple without the aid of the church. That's why you have so many ugly ducklings. We don't have any ugly ducklings. All our children are swans.

Tatarov is silent.

(*To Tregubova*). I think everything is in order. I like the gown very much. But now the main thing; the price . . .

TREGUBOVA. Four thousand francs.

LYOLYA. I'll pay you in a few days.

TATAROV. Are you expecting money from Russia?

LYOLYA. Yes. Apart from that, I'm thinking of making an appearance at the "Globe" music hall.

TATAROV. In what kind of play?

LYOLYA. I'll play a scene from "Hamlet."

TREGUBOVA. Sign this little note, if you would be so kind.

LYOLYA. Yes, yes, of course.

TATAROV. You're looking for a sheet of paper, Lida? Your office is badly organized. Here's a sheet for you. (*Takes a pad from his pocket, tears off a sheet and gives it to Tregubova*). Write. On the other side. (*Dictates, Tregubova writes*). "I received from the dressmaker, Miss Tregubova, a gown at the price of four thousand francs . . ." Put in "ball"; "a ballgown at the price of four thousand francs. I guarantee to pay the sum mentioned..." When?

LYOLYA. In three days time.

TATAROV. Well then, write, "on Wednesday the eighth," Year and signature.

LYOLYA (*signs*). Yelena Goncharova.

TREGUBOVA. Thank you so much.

LYOLYA. That's it then. Goodbye.

TREGUBOVA. Goodbye, madam.

TATAROV. My greetings to the Russian lady.

Lyolya goes out with a bundle, but without her suitcase.

TREGUBOVA. What about that, my friend. You've made a mistake in your calculations. As you can see, she's a patriot of her new homeland. She even justifies executions.

TATAROV. And at the same time smoothes the folds of a Parisian gown.

TREGUBOVA. Her cheeks glowed when she spoke about illegitimate children.

TATAROV. If a Soviet citizen attacks the bourgeoisie and at the same time dreams of making an appearance at a bourgeois ball, I'm not too convinced of her sincerity.

TREGUBOVA. She looks divine in that dress.

TATAROV. Swan's feathers sprouted on a duckling.

TREGUBOVA. And she flies away.

TATAROV. Leaving a little feather in my hand. Take a look at what's printed on the reverse side of her note.

TREGUBOVA (*reads*). "Russia, a daily newspaper, organ of the United Committee of Russian Industrialists."

TATAROV. Consequently, your incorruptible one has signed the subscription form of an émigré newspaper to acknowledge the receipt of a ballgown. Piquant, isn't it? In any case quite a nice sensation for tomorrow's edition: "Saint Readies Self for Ball."

TREGUBOVA. She forgot her suitcase.

TATAROV. Interesting. (*Takes hold of the suitcase*).

TREGUBOVA. She'll come back right away.

Tatarov opens the suitcase, digs in it hurriedly, finds the notebook, leafs through it. A knock at the door. Pause. Tatarov hides the notebook inside his jacket and returns to hs armchair.

TREGUBOVA (*slamming suitcase shut*). Come in.

Lyolya enters.

97

LYOLYA. Please excuse me.

TREGUBOVA. You forgot your suitcase?

LYOLYA. Yes.

TREGUBOVA. It was nothing to worry about. I would have sent it to the boardinghouse.

LYOLYA. Really? Thank you.

Lyolya heads for the exit. Going out, she encounters Kizevetter coming in. For a moment they stand facing each other. She is knocked back by his haste. He is transfixed, shaken by her sudden appearance. She disappears at once. Silence.

TATAROV (*with the notebook*). I've discovered her secret, Lida.

TREGUBOVA. Is that a diary?

TATAROV. I've found the sin I was talking about.

KIZEVETTER (*firmly*). Please tell me, who is that woman who just ran out of here?

TATAROV. A beauty from the land of the poor.

KIZEVETTER. Please, please tell me, who is that woman?

TATAROV. Your fiancée.

CURTAIN

SCENE FIVE

THE FLUTE

In the wings of the "Globe" Music Hall. Evening. Margeret and Lyolya in the costume of Hamlet. On Margeret's table is a glass of milk and a bun.

LYOLYA. I've put my costume on so that you would get the whole effect.

Margeret is silent.

Perhaps you're too busy?

MARGERET. Why busy?

LYOLYA. Well you could be. You have such a big act.

MARGERET. Why big?

LYOLYA. Well, I mean . . . the music hall . . . so many artists . . . It's difficult.

MARGERET. Why difficult?

98

LYOLYA. What an odd way you have of expressing yourself.
MARGERET. Why odd?
LYOLYA. You keep asking "why."
MARGERET. Because I'm busy.
LYOLYA. There you are. That's what I was afraid of.
MARGERET. Why afraid?

Pause.

LYOLYA. Perhaps I should go.
MARGERET. Go then.

Pause.

LYOLYA. Don't you want to try me out?
MARGERET. Yes.
LYOLYA. I can perform a scene from "Hamlet."
MARGERET. Why "Hamlet"?
LYOLYA. I suggested doing it this way, you know. "Well-known Russian actress..." on the poster: "Yelena Goncharova...Selections from *Hamlet.*"

Margeret is silent.

All right then. I'll perform now. Yes, what would be best? Of course the exchange with Guildenstern. (*Moves between two places as she acts, taking two parts*). "O, the recorders! Let me see one.—To withdraw with you:— why do you go about to recover the wind of me, as if you would drive me into a toil?"
Guildenstern speaks now. You must know this scene. I won't explain.
"O, my lord, if my duty be too bold, my love is too unmannerly."
Hamlet: "I do not well understand that. Will you play upon the pipe?"
"My lord, I cannot."
"I pray you."
"Believe me, I cannot."
"I do beseech you."
"I know not the touch of it, my lord."
" 'Tis as easy as lying: govern these ventages with your finger and thumb, give it breath with your mouth, and it will discourse you most eloquent music. Look you, these are the stops."
MARGERET (*waving his hand*). No no no, it won't do.
LYOLYA (*shocked*). Why not?
MARGERET. It's uninteresting. The flute, yes. Are you a flutist?
LYOLYA. Why a flutist?

MARGERET. Now you're the one who's starting to ask "why." To be blunt, it won't do. What is it? An eccentric prank on the flute? You need to be shocking here, you understand! "A flute starts playing"—that's not enough.

LYOLYA. You didn't listen, you didn't understand . . . It's something quite different . . .

MARGERET. Well, if it's different, then tell me what's different. Perhaps different is interesting. An interesting business with a flute could be like this—first you play the flute . . .

LYOLYA. But I don't know how.

MARGERET. But you said yourself that it was very easy.

LYOLYA. But I didn't say that.

MARGERET. You even expressed it very vividly; you said it was as easy as lying.

LYOLYA. You weren't listening, you're too busy.

MARGERET. Yes, I'm busy, I don't even have time to drink a glass of milk, and you're taking up my time. Let's finish what we have to say. I say that an interesting piece of business with a flute could be like this—first you play the flute. Something to get the public into a melancholy mood. Yes. Then you swallow the flute. The public gasps in amazement. A reversal of mood—surprise, alarm. Then you turn your back to the public and it turns out that the flute is protruding from you, from a place from which flutes are not known to protrude. The fact that you're a woman makes it even more piquant. You see. Listen, it's a great idea. Then you begin to blow the flute, you might, with your other end—and this time not a minuet, but something more cheerful, "Tommy, Tommy, let's meet Tuesday." Get it? The public is full of enthusiasm, laughter, a storm of applause.

LYOLYA. You say that I'm taking up your time, but you're wasting it on jokes yourself.

A telephone rings.

MARGERET. Hello! What? He's arrived? It can't be true. I've got a weak heart. I may not be able to stand the shock. He's arrived! Hoorah! Hurry up! Hurry up! (*Flings down the telephone, to Lyolya*). He's arrived! Did you hear that! He's arrived! (*Runs down the passageway*). He's arrived! He's arrived!

LYOLYA. Mr. Margeret, I beg you to listen to me seriously.

MARGERET (*coming back, as if catching sight of Lyolya for the first time*). What? Oh it's you. Yes . . . yes, yes, excuse me. I was talking to you, wasn't I. I've got a horrible trait. When my thoughts are occupied, I listen without understanding anything . . . and I can get into a conversation . . . My thoughts have been occupied for a whole week now, I've been writing all the time, get it, I kept thinking: will he come or won't he? Will he or won't he? And he's arrived! He's going to be dancing at the International Artists' Ball. So I'm free to think my thoughts. Yes. And so what is it you want? You're a flutist.

LYOLYA. I'm a tragic actress.

MARGERET. Why tragic?

LYOLYA. There you go again asking why.

MARGERET. Yes, I'm afraid that's so, stop me. Again my thoughts are occupied.

LYOLYA. You're a funny man. What are your thoughts occupied with this time?

MARGERET. Wait a moment . . .yes yes yes . . .Let me free my mind of the thoughts occupying it. Yes. Ready. So now they're busy with you, devil take it! What do you want from me?

LYOLYA. In my country, I was well known . . .if you like . . .a famous actress. I don't have to start from the beginning, you know.

MARGERET. Yes yes yes! I understand everything. Excellent! What's that you're saying? Why from the beginning? That's right. That's right. That's right.

LYOLYA. Or have you no idea to whom you're speaking?

MARGERET Excellent. An excellent plan. At first, nobody suspects anything . . .Yes, as if it isn't a celebrity, but just something ordinary, some kind of nonsense, a routine number, and no posters. I'll order the posters to be destroyed. We'll do it like this: today—the first appearance. We'll put an international star on in the middle of the program, as a substitute for another act. Unannounced, without advertising. Bravo! Bravo! It's more effective than any advertisement.

LYOLYA. Today? But there has to be rehearsal.

MARGERET. What for? Who needs rehearsal? Him?

LYOLYA. Oh I misunderstood. I thought you were talking about me. Your way of thinking and talking tires me out. (*Pause*). Oh . . .(*Pause*). Surely that can't be true? Tell me, who's come?

MARGERET. Him. He's come to the ball. Ah! And he's agreed to perform for me.

LYOLYA. I know! I know!

MARGERET. If you know, not a word. You'll ruin the whole plan. The public doesn't suspect a thing . . .Keep it a secret. (*Seizes her hand and presses it*). Yes yes, it's him.

LYOLYA. Him! I can't believe it. He'll come right here? Now? Let me stay here, I beg you. I'll agree to any conditions . . .

MARGERET. The conditions are ten dollars a week.

LYOLYA. For what?

MARGERET. What do you mean, for what? For your work.

LYOLYA. What work?

MARGERET. For the flute, of course, devil take it! It's so difficult to talk to you.

LYOLYA. Aren't you ashamed of yourself?

MARGERET. Ashamed? Isn't it enough? Surely it isn't hard to bare your ass and play minuets?

LYOLYA. When he comes, I'll tell him that you, a European impresario, made a mockery of a foreign actress. I needed money. That can happen to anyone. I lowered myself. He'll understand. He is cultured, he is humanity itself, he'll understand and be offended with you, you hear! He'll be on my side, because he is better than all of you, he is the finest man in your world.

MARGERET. Who's the finest man in our world? You should be ashamed of yourself. He's an insignificant, greedy little man.

LYOLYA. That isn't true. That can't be true.

MARGERET. All right then, of course you are willing to forgive him everything. People have made a god of him. The world has gone mad on sexuality. And beyond all doubt, he's a champion of sexuality. For men he is a man, for women he is a woman. Perhaps he really is a god? When I listen to his singing, I feel as if a woman destined for me were taking off her clothes before my eyes. Then I start looking into women's faces. It's phenomenal! He sings and the eyelids of each of them droop like a chicken's, they turn to glass, they're dead. It's ecstasy. And what does he sing? Idiotic ditties! But he has some secret hidden in the erogenous zones.

LYOLYA. I thought you were talking about someone else.

MARGERET. No one else can compare with him. He's a god.

LYOLYA. I thought Chaplin was coming.

MARGERET. Why Chaplin?

Noise, excitement, Ulalum is approaching.

Ulalum. The great Ulalum.

Ulalum enters. Actors on all sides. Ulalum looks at Lyolya. Everyone sees that Ulalum is looking at Lyolya and prepares to slip away.

ULALUM. Who is that, Margeret?

MARGERET. I prepared her for you.

ULALUM. Who are you?

Lyolya is silent.

I am Ulalum.

LYOLYA. I don't know you.

ULALUM. But who are you? A negro? No, you're not a negro. You have golden hair and a face of Persian whiteness. Who are you then? A

Gaul? Are you an ancient Gaul?

LYOLYA. I don't know you. Why are you talking to me in this way?

ULALUM. I am Ulalum.

LYOLYA. I don't know you.

MARGERET. She's pretending so as to entertain you.

ULALUM. Why are you wearing pants?

LYOLYA. Leave me alone.

ULALUM. Wonderful! Today I dreamed of my childhood. A garden, wooden bannisters. I went down the old staircase, sliding my hand along the bannisters, warmed a little by the sun. You are a living metaphor. Take off your jacket, please. You have young arms like bannisters.

LYOLYA. You're a strange man.

ULALUM. People have made me a god. I, too, was a boy. There were green hills. You've come from my childhood, from the town of Nimes, built by the Romans. Come here.

LYOLYA. For a while now life has seemed to me like a dream.

MARGERET. Go. Fortune is smiling on you.

ULALUM. Come to me.

LYOLYA. Don't be ridiculous.

ULALUM. All right, I'll come to you. (*Goes up to her*). I'll kiss you.

LYOLYA. I've remembered. I know. I've heard your little song, on a record, in Moscow, in winter, when I was dreaming of Europe.

ULALUM. May I kiss you?

LYOLYA. You may.

Ulalum kisses Lyolya. Pause. General rapt silence.

ULALUM. Who are you? (*To Margeret*). Where did you get hold of her, Margeret?

MARGERET. She plays the flute with her asshole.

ULALUM. Ugh! And supposing she suddenly started to blow the flute with her lips without washing it.

Laughter.

LYOLYA. But that just isn't true. And you, Mr. Margeret, have invented all this yourself.

ULALUM (*paying her no attention*). Margeret, do you want me to go on now?

MARGERET. Yes. You've got to appear like a streak of lightning.

LYOLYA. Mr. Ulalum!

ULALUM. What do you want?

LYOLYA. You have insulted me.

ULALUM. In what way?

103

LYOLYA. You don't know me. You might think that I really am . . .I came to the theater on business, I thought that the theater . . .but this is a torture chamber. I liked the way you spoke of your childhood . . .

ULALUM. Childhood memories fly away like dandelion fluff.

LYOLYA. You are a strange man.

ULALUM. There isn't a woman who wouldn't come to love me.

LYOLYA. I know, of course . . .

Ulalum is silent. Pause.

I dreamed so much about Europe. I wouldn't want you to have a bad impression of me . . . . In my country I was considered beautiful . . . . You yourself noticed me.

ULALUM. Come tomorrow.

LYOLYA. You don't understand me properly. I'm going out of my mind.

Pause. Applause somewhere. The end of a number. People come running up to Margeret.

MARGERET. Now . . .now it's your turn, Ulalum. Are you ready?

ULALUM. Let's go.

They go out. Lyolya is left alone. Noise in the auditorium, applause, shouts, stamping. Quiet for a second—and again a storm. Then again silence, and in the silence come the sounds of a grand piano—the introduction to the song; Ulalum begins to sing. Lyolya abandons the music hall. Passageways, corridors. Lyolya descends the staircase. The singing fades. Lyolya stops and listens. Now, humiliated and alone, she hears the sound of a party behind shuttered windows. And, listening to it, she thinks about her own life.

LYOLYA. I want to go home. Where are you, my friends? What's new with you? A new world . . .people in rags . . .my youth . . .I wanted to sell my youth . . .I dreamed of you, Paris. I sought your glory. But I know, and how could I forget, that there is no higher glory than the glory of those who are reconstructing the world. Every woman, the mother of children born in the new world, waiting bowed in line, shines with a greater glory than all the stars of Europe. What did I want? A ballgown? Why do I need it? Wasn't I beautiful in a gown made of rags? I want to go home. What are the shows there like without me? My country, I want to listen to the noise of your arguments. Workers, only now do I understand your wisdom and generosity, your faces lifted toward the starry sky of science. I looked down at you and was afraid of you, as a foolish bird is afraid of the man who gives it food. Forgive me, land of the Soviets, I am coming to you. I don't want to go to the ball. I want to go home. I want to stand in line and weep.

A street. Autumn. Leaves. The asphalt gleams. A bench. On it sits a little man. A lamplighter approaches.

LAMPLIGHTER. Hey little fellow, what are you up to?

MAN. I'm eating my supper.

LAMPLIGHTER. In your sleep?

MAN. No, I had lunch in my sleep. I wanted to leave a little onion soup for my supper, but I didn't manage it, you see—I woke up.

LAMPLIGHTER. So that's how it is. I see you're unemployed.

MAN. One can't deny your perception.

LAMPLIGHTER. I'll give you something for supper.

MAN. Don't worry, please. Can't you see that I'm having supper?

LAMPLIGHTER. Cheerful little fellow. What are you eating?

MAN. A tree. Over there, you see, stands a tree. When you come down to it, it looks like an eel. If it weren't for the leaves.

LAMPLIGHTER. There's an oddball for you! If I ever have to eat a tree, I'll certainly eat it with leaves. Surely it's not a bad thing if the eel is served with salad?

MAN. You're right. But I've already eaten my fill. Now I want some dessert. I'll eat some fence. See it? Very tasty. Reminds you of waffles. Only something has gotten into my food, devil take it. Ah, a woman.

Lyolya approaches.

A woman's coming. It's an actress from the music hall.

LAMPLIGHTER. Madam, you've spoiled his dessert for him!

MAN. Margeret chased me out. Tell him that the unemployed will burn down his theater.

LYOLYA. Why did he dismiss you?

MAN. For sympathizing with the unemployed. Apart from that, he doesn't like members of trade unions. I'm a flutist from the orchestra. And you?

LYOLYA. I'm also a member of a trade union.

LAMPLIGHTER. Give him something for his supper. Otherwise he'll feel like eating pork and end up eating a policeman.

LYOLYA. Of course, of course, I know...(*Gives him money*).

MAN. Tell me your address and I'll return the debt.

LYOLYA. I'm leaving tomorrow. (*Goes away*).

LAMPLIGHTER. Just be careful you don't wake up.

MAN. I was wrong. That actress is not from our theater.

LAMPLIGHTER. Add it up, it will do for a bowl of soup.

MAN. It's dark.

105

LAMPLIGHTER. I'll light the lantern. (*Raises his pole*).

The lantern lights above their heads. And in its light a strong resemblance is revealed between the man and Chaplin. The bowler, the haircut, the moustache, the large rough boots, the walking stick. The lamplighter helps him count, gazing into his palm.

Oho! That's a whole ocean of soup.

MAN. But I was only thinking of a little onion the size of an almond.

LAMPLIGHTER. Well, now you can eat an onion at least the size of this lantern. (*Extinguishes lantern*).

CURTAIN

SCENE SIX
LOGIC

A cafe on Lantern Street. At a table Fedotov and Lakhtin.

LAKHTIN (*reading a newspaper*). The White Guard newspaper "Russia" has an article where it says that yesterday in a certain boarding-house you, the Soviet citizen Fedotov, killed a member of the "Russia" editorial staff, Tatarov, with a revolver. Bearing in mind that this article is published in a White émigré rag, allowing that you only scratched this Tatarnikov . . .

FEDOTOV. Tatarov.

LAKHTIN. That doesn't matter. I imagine that you didn't really kill this Tatarnikov. I don't even suppose that you wounded him. I am prepared to believe that you didn't shoot at him at all. It could even be maintained that you weren't even about to fire at him. I even believe that you didn't have the faintest idea of taking a shot at this Tatarnikovsky.

FEDOTOV. That's not true.

LAKHTIN. Surely you didn't wave a revolver about in a dive like that?

A waiter enters.

WAITER. There's a lady asking for you.

FEDOTOV. That's Goncharova. (*Gets up, goes out, returns with Goncharova, draws a chair up for her*).

Lakhtin bows.

LYOLYA. How do you do.

They shake hands.

LAKHTIN. Please call me Sergei Mikhailovich.

FEDOTOV. We'll go to the Embassy soon. Comrade Dyakonov is there now; he'll call us and let us know when to leave.

LYOLYA. Very good.

LAKHTIN. Do you remember me? No? We were introduced once in Moscow, after a performance. In your theater. Don't you remember, I wore sideburns then.

FEDOTOV. You really wore sideburns?

LAKHTIN. Longish sideburns. Like cutlet-chops.

FEDOTOV. Why did you grow them?

LAKHTIN. I don't know why. It was really a silly idea.

FEDOTOV. To get a laugh. And so we've really been introduced in Paris. What part are you performing now?

LYOLYA. Hamlet.

LAKHTIN. You mean Ophelia?

LYOLYA. No, Hamlet himself.

LAKHTIN. Really? A woman playing a man's role?

LYOLYA. Well, yes.

LAKHTIN. But you only have to look at your legs to know you're a woman.

LYOLYA. Women must think like men now. The Revolution. Men's accounts are being settled.

LAKHTIN. I'll pour you some tea.

LYOLYA. I'm really ashamed to be putting you to so much trouble. You seem to really enjoy life.

LAKHTIN. You know I think I've got gout.

FEDOTOV. Maybe it isn't really gout?

LAKHTIN. No, perhaps it isn't gout, but homesickness.

FEDOTOV. Or more likely chronic influenza.

LAKHTIN. Yes, I've got a cold. Well listen then, eat up, drink up, help yourself to sandwiches. Is this your first visit to Paris?

LYOLYA. Yes.

LAKHTIN. Are you here for long?

LYOLYA. I want to leave.

LAKHTIN. Where for? Are you going to Nice?

LYOLYA. No, I want to go home, to Moscow.

LAKHTIN. Really? When?

LYOLYA. As soon as possible.

FEDOTOV. Let's travel together.

LYOLYA. Thank you. I'd like that.

LAKHTIN. Well that's wonderful.

LYOLYA. Well tell me what it's like in America.

FEDOTOV. Not bad, there's lots of everything . . .except that some-how it's unorganized. No ration cards. (*Pause*). Yelena Nikolayevna is going to the ball.

LYOLYA. Forget it, Fedotov. I'm not going anywhere.

LAKHTIN. What ball?

FEDOTOV. The International Artists' Ball.

LAKHTIN. Have you been invited?

LYOLYA. Yes.

LAKHTIN. What impertinence. To invite a Soviet actress to a ball of dressed-up monkeys. You refused, of course?

LYOLYA. Yes.

LAKHTIN. I should think so. Just think what your comrades would have said in Moscow if it suddenly became known that you agreed to dance at a ball given by Balthasar Lepeltier, who condemns his workers to death by starvation.

Enter Dyakonov.

FEDOTOV. Let me introduce you; Dyakonov, Yelena Nikolayevna Goncharova.

DYAKONOV. Who?

FEDOTOV. What's wrong with you?

DYAKONOV. Who?

FEDOTOV. What's the matter with you?

DYAKONOV. You are Goncharova?

LYOLYA. Yes.

DYAKONOV. What have you come here for?

FEDOTOV. Are you drunk?

DYAKONOV. Wait a moment. Have you looked at today's papers, Sergei Mikhailovich?

LAKHTIN. No, I haven't had a chance yet. What's in them?

DYAKONOV (*taking a seat beside him*). I was just at the Embassy, I informed them that we were coming to a reception together with the actress Goncharova. They handed me these newspapers in order to inform you. Here are three French papers and two émigré White ones: "Russia" and "Return."

LAKHTIN. The bit that's outlined in blue?

DYAKONOV. Yes.

LAKHTIN. I did start reading "Russia." Yes, yes. There is something about you here, about you.

LYOLYA. About me? What exactly?

LAKHTIN. This is what it has here: "The actress Goncharova who fled Russia spoke with a reporter from "Russia." She has with her denunciatory material of absolutely unique cultural and historical significance . . ."

FEDOTOV. Don't be upset, Yelena Nikolayevna, they're specialists in libel. They'll publish worse than that yet.

DYAKONOV. This time they wrote the truth.

LYOLYA. What are you sayng?

LAKHTIN. Now be quiet.

FEDOTOV. Don't make a scandal, Dyakonov.

DYAKONOV. But what do you say to this, Sergei Mikhailovich? (*Holds out a page*).

FEDOTOV. Did you write that?

LYOLYA. I can't see. Yes, that's my signature, when I signed for the gown.

LAKHTIN. How did you get hold of an émigré newspaper letterhead?

LYOLYA. I don't know.

LAKHTIN. That makes it worse.

DYAKONOV. Now read a bit in "Return" and in the French papers.

LYOLYA. What nonsense.

LAKHTIN. Quieter, quieter. So. The article has the headline: "Secret of the Soviet Intelligentsia in Exchange for Paris Gown." Did you sell your diary to the émigrés?

LYOLYA. What diary?

LAKHTIN. "Every line of this document is washed in tears. This is the confession of an unfortunate being, of a highly gifted nature which has been worn out by the yoke of Bolshevik enslavement. This is the shining truth about how the dictatorship of the proletariat deals with what we consider to be the most precious treasure in the world, free human thought." On the first page we read: "A List of the Crimes of the Soviet Regime."

FEDOTOV. Is that true?

LYOLYA. Yes. But it isn't like that. I have a notebook, it consists of two parts. Listen to me . . .This is terrible! I'll explain it to you at once. In this notebook there are two lists. One of crimes, the other of blessings.

LAKHTIN. I don't understand anything.

LYOLYA. And I didn't sell it. That's some sort of libel. I don't know how it got into print, but let's go to my boardinghouse, I'll show you this notebook and you'll understand. I'll bring it right away, all right?

DYAKONOV (*takes Lyolya's notebook out of his briefcase*). This notebook?

LYOLYA. Yes.

LAKHTIN. How is it that you have it, Dyakonov?

DYAKONOV. This diary and note accompanied by an insolent letter were sent to the Embassy by the émigré journalist Tatarov, with whom Miss Goncharova has had dealings.

FEDOTOV. What, the same Tatarov who was with you that morning at the boardinghouse?

LAKHTIN. Give it to me. (*Reads*). "List of Crimes."

LYOLYA. Look on ahead, ahead, there's a "List of Blessings" there.

LAKHTIN. No, there's no other list.

LYOLYA. What? Half of it torn off? Who can have torn it off?

DYAKONOV. You tore it off yourself in order to sell it more profitably.

LYOLYA. I didn't sell it.

LAKHTIN. Wait a minute, Dyakonov. Tell us how it all happened.

LYOLYA. I wanted to go to the ball, yes yes, I did. I went to the dressmaker's, chose a gown and they asked for a signed note. I signed, and her husband—I didn't know—turned out to be this very Tatarov. He tricked me into taking the form.

DYAKONOV. A gown costs four thousand francs. Where did you hope to get such a sum?

LYOLYA. I wanted to earn it.

DYAKONOV. Where? It's clear that you got these four thousand francs for the diary. And that's what they say in a French newspaper.

LAKHTIN. Wait a moment, Dyakonov, newspapers can tell lies, I don't trust newspapers.

LYOLYA. Comrades, my word of honor, I didn't sell anything to anyone.

LAKHTIN. I believe you. Did you want to dance a bit at the ball?

LYOLYA. Is that a terrible crime?

LAKHTIN. But you knew that this ball was fascist in nature, even if that wasn't clearly expressed.

LYOLYA. But I hadn't yet decided definitely whether I would go or not. I was hesitant.

LAKHTIN. All right, but you bought a gown anyway? The eagerness for a gown led you to the émigrés.

LYOLYA. Into a trap.

LAKHTIN. Yes, and you got caught in the claws.

DYAKONOV. But were there any claws?

LAKHTIN. You say that your diary was stolen and printed without your knowledge. But if it hadn't existed it would have been impossible to steal it. Your crime was that you secretly hated us. Perhaps because we don't have balls and luxurious gowns.

LYOLYA. I loved you, I swear it.

DYAKONOV. I don't believe you.

LYOLYA. I don't know how I can prove it to you.

DYAKONOV. Since your libel has been made public, you have to prove it not to us, but to Paris and Moscow. We may believe you, but the proletariat won't.

LYOLYA. Yes, I understand. What am I to do?

FEDOTOV. It's essential that you go to the Embassy straight away.

DYAKONOV. I don't know whether the Embassy will want to receive her. There's a general rule that applies here. A Soviet citizen who goes over to the émigré camp puts himself outside the law.

LAKHTIN. It's not your affair. They'll settle it in Moscow.

LYOLYA. I am outside the law.

DYAKONOV. Judicially, yes.

LYOLYA. A traitress? In that case all intellectuals are traitors! All of them ought to be shot!

LAKHTIN. Why are you slandering the intelligentsia?

FEDOTOV. Calm down, Yelena Nikolayevna.

LAKHTIN. I'll call the Embassy now.

Dyakonov and Lakhtin go toward the exit.

DYAKONOV. I'd put the reprobate up against the wall.

Exit.

LYOLYA. Fedotov, what's going to happen now, my dear?

FEDOTOV. Yelena Nikolayevna, please calm down.

LYOLYA. If I go on foot over all of Europe with my head bare, and come to the theater at the Arc de triomphe, go down on my knees in front of the entire gathering . . .

FEDOTOV. You don't have to go on foot over the whole of Europe. Let's take a train along a fixed route: Paris, Berlin, Warsaw, Negorelov . . . And that'll be enough philosophizing You see what it has led to. Your philosophy came in handy for someone. But that doesn't matter, to hell with it. You're not a criminal. That's Dyakonov getting carried away. Put it off till Moscow, and we'll settle it there. Moscow has forgiven more serious criminals; absolute enemies.

LYOLYA. You judge me? But I condemn myself. I've long condemned myself. Is this living? (*Pause*). I feel ill, Fedotov.

FEDOTOV. I'll bring you some . . .(*Goes out*).

Lyolya goes to Fedotov's overcoat, which he took off at the beginning of the scene, takes the revolver from the pocket. Lakhtin returns.

LAKHTIN. The ambassador will receive you.

FEDOTOV. But where is Yelena Nikolayevna?

LAKHTIN. What does this mean?

FEDOTOV. I don't know.

LAKHTIN. But where is she? What were you up to?

FEDOTOV. All this is very unpleasant.

LAKHTIN. Do you trust her?

FEDOTOV. Yes, but I'm afraid she'll do something silly. Perhaps we spoke too sharply to her. I think she's with us, one of us . . .isn't that true?

LAKHTIN. But why has she hidden? What shall we say to the ambassador?

FEDOTOV. You go to the Embassy and I'll go after her . . .to search. Maybe she's at the boardinghouse.

LAKHTIN. If you do see her, tell her it's all nonsense.

FEDOTOV. That's what I'll say.

LAKHTIN. Tell her that everything will be settled.

FEDOTOV. I'll tell her.

LAKHTIN. Tell her that we'll go to Moscow together.

LAKHTIN. Put it to her in her style, that the proletariat is generous.

FEDOTOV. Yes, I'll put it to her in her style; yes, that the proletariat is generous.

CURTAIN

SCENE SEVEN

THE BOUQUET

At Tatarov's house. The silver gown lies in an open box. Lyolya, Tatarov.

TATAROV. If you've only come to give back the gown, then you haven't come to the right place. I live here. Miss Tregubova lives somewhere else. But since you found out my address, you must want to see me. Now you don't say anything. I don't understand. Have I offended you?

Lyolya is silent.

But I think you should be grateful to me. By stealing your diary I rendered you a great service.

Lyolya is silent.

The Soviet regime won't last long. It'll be destroyed by the war which will break out before too long. A government will be formed from the scientific, technical and humanitarian intelligentsia. It's no secret to anyone that there will be repression—persecution of Communists and those who serve them most zealously. Well, that'll be it. Vengeance. Of course the new authorities will show mercy. But during the early days—a military dictatorship. The marshal who will take control in Moscow will really be grim—like a Russian patriot, like a soldier. There's nothing to be done about that. The humanists in white vests will drop their eyes for a bit. And just imagine . . .if what has happened had not happened, if your diary had remained in your own possession—let's say, if you returned to Moscow and continued to pretend to be a Bolshevik—and then there was a revolution. Then one fine day at dawn you would be brought to headquarters with a number of others. . . . It would be too late to prove things and go rummaging through diaries. You would be shot like any other Chekist. Isn't that right?

Lyolya is silent.

Now you're in the clear. Your diary has been published. It's read by Milyukov, General Lukomsky, Russian financiers, landowners and—what matters most—by the young people who dream of returning to Russia and taking revenge for their fathers and brothers who were shot, for a youth passed without setting eyes on their fatherland. . . . They read your confession and they think: she was a prisoner, they tortured her, they forced her to serve a power she hated. But in her heart she was with us. And so I've helped you to justify yourself in the eyes of those who will establish order in Russia.

Lyolya is silent.

It's quite clear that somewhere in your subconscious lived an eternal fear, the thought of responsibility . . .for the blood that the Bolsheviks shed while you were silent. Now you have nothing to be afraid of. I was doctor to your fear.

Lyolya is silent.

Now you can be at ease. The fatherland will forgive you. And it will reward you. There isn't long to wait. You'll have your own house, cars, a yacht. You'll shine at balls in a silver gown. We'll meet. I'll be the head of a big newspaper. I'll come to see you at the theater carrying roses wrapped in tissue paper. We'll look into each other's eyes, and you'll shake my hand very firmly.

LYOLYA. Stand up against the wall, you pig!

She gets up suddenly. She has a Browning in her hand; Tatarov flings himself at her and there is a struggle. Lyolya drops the Browning. From behind the curtain emerges Kizevetter, who has been asleep up to this point. He picks up the Browning. Lyolya, her clothing disarranged, lies on the couch onto which she has been thrown. A hush. Kizevetter with the Browning.

113

TATAROV. Give me the revolver.

Kizevetter is silent.

I said: hand over the revolver.
KIZEVETTER. Go away. (*Goes over to Lyolya*). Don't be afraid of me. I'll be your pet dog.

Lyolya is silent.

I don't know you. I've seen you only once in my life. Are you listening? We met in the entryway—remember? You went right through to my heart.
TATAROV. You can conduct this scene without a revolver.
KIZEVETTER. I'm a poor man. But if you're to be bought for money, I'll become a thief and a murderer.
LYOLYA (*making for the exit with a shout*). Let me out! Let me out!
KIZEVETTER (*throws himself at her feet, embraces her knees*). Don't go, don't go. The world is terrible. A black night stands over the world . . . nothing is needed . . . just two people, a man and a woman must put their arms around each other.
TATAROV. Let her go.
KIZEVETTER. Don't come any closer! (*Fires at him*).

Misses. A hush.

TATAROV. An epileptic.

Kizevetter weeps, his head on the table. A noise outside the door. Knocks.

(*Goes over to the door*). What's the matter?
VOICE OUTSIDE THE DOOR. Open up, Russian!
TATAROV. An accidental shot.

Sound of running from the door. Silence outside.

They've gone for the police.

Kizevetter is motionless. Silence.

Where did you get hold of the revolver?

Lyolya is silent.

114

It has an inscription: "Property of Alexander Fedotov, Brigade Commander." Did you get it at the Soviet Embassy? What carelessness! If you were given the job of killing me, you should have been provided with a different weapon.

LYOLYA. Nobody sent me. I decided to kill you myself.

TATAROV. With a revolver belonging to the Soviet Embasssy.

LYOLYA. I stole it.

TATAROV. Ah . . .Well, that's more natural. But the police will find it easier not to believe you. On the basis of this evidence, there'll be created a version that the Soviet Embassy is inducing agents to commit terrorist acts against the émigrés.

Lyolya is silent.

That'll be an excuse for retaliatory acts on our part. Let's say for an attempt on the life of the Soviet ambassador.

LYOLYA. Yes, I understand.

TATAROV. You wanted to settle personal accounts with me, and as a result the Soviet ambassador will meet his death. Do you understand? And after that war could break out. The gunpowder is ready. And in Russia they'll say that you put the spark to it.

Lyolya is silent.

You've gotten yourself in a mess. All right, I'll be of service to you once more.

A knock at the door.

(*At the door*). Who is it?

VOICE OUTSIDE THE DOOR. Open up in the name of the law.

TATAROV (*to Lyolya*). Hide.

Lyolya goes behind the curtain. Tatarov opens the door. Enter two moustached policemen in black capes. Silence.

FIRST. Please be kind enough to tell us what has happened here.

TATAROV. An accidental shot.

FIRST. Into the air?

TATAROV. Yes.

SECOND. At the ceiling?

TATAROV. I think it was the doorpost.

FIRST. Who fired the shot?

TATAROV. He did.

FIRST. May I ask who you are?

KIZEVETTER. My name is Dmitri Kizevetter.

SECOND. Why were you shooting into the air? Is it your birthday today?

Silence.

FIRST. What do you do for a living?

TATAROV. He's unemployed.

FIRST. Aha . . . Where did you get the gun?

KIZEVETTER. I don't know.

SECOND. Let him have one in the kisser, Jean.

FIRST. Wait a moment. Is this your revolver?

KIZEVETTER. No.

FIRST. It's a Russian revolver. Interesting. The Russians supply the unemployed with weapons.

LYOLYA (*coming out*). That's not true.

SECOND. Madam, beautiful women shouldn't get mixed up in politics.

KIZEVETTER. I shot at him because of a woman.

FIRST. Because of you?

Lyolya is silent.

KIZEVETTER. Yes, because of her.

FIRST (*to Tatarov*). Is that the truth?

TATAROV. Yes.

FIRST. You confirm that you made an attempt on his life?

KIZEVETTER. Yes.

FIRST. You can get hard labor for that.

Kizevetter is silent.

SECOND. Give him one in the kisser, Jean.

FIRST. Wait a minute. If you don't want hard labor, then you'd better not insist on attempted murder.

KIZEVETTER. All right.

FIRST. But with a Russian revolver. If an unemployed man fires a Russian revolver into the French air, it means that his arm is held by the Bolsheviks. So this unemployed man wants to make a revolution with the aid of foreigners. In other words, he's a traitor. We've got the guillotine for that. Do you want to go to the guillotine?

Pause.

116

KIZEVETTER. No.
FIRST. So what are we to do?

Pause.

LYOLYA. This man has nothing to do with it . . .do you hear! I'm to blame for everything . . .
FIRST. In what way?
LYOLYA. I brought this revolver.
FIRST (*to Tatarov*). Who is this?
TATAROV.. An actress.
FIRST. Where did you get this Russian revolver?
LYOLYA. I stole it.
FIRST. Where?

Lyolya is silent.

Obviously from the Soviet Embassy. The Soviet Embassy is guarded by the French police. You know that. It's international law. Stealing is bad in general, but stealing from the embassy of a foreign power is impolite into the bargain. If you committed a robbery in the Embassy, I must arrest you as a thief. For that you get put in jail. Do you want to go to jail for plundering the Soviet Embassy?

Lyolya is silent.

TATAROV. The shooting's frightened her and she doesn't know herself what she's saying.
SECOND. Your mistress?
TATAROV. Yes.
SECOND. I like blonds too.

Pause.

FIRST. And so the incident has been investigated. What do we have, forgetting the shot? An unemployed coward and a revolver from the Soviet Embassy. And apart from that we know that a demonstration of the unemployed is going to take place soon. (*Pause*). If you like shooting, why not try it again?
KIZEVETTER. At who?
FIRST. At a lot of people at once.
SECOND. I think the commissar will approve of this suggestion.
FIRST. We'll ask you to shoot at the unemployed.
SECOND. From a Bolshevik revolver.

117

FIRST. They'll respond, and then the militia will have the legal right to smash them. And you'll avoid hard labor. Let's go.

LYOLYA. Bastard! Bastard! You're a bastard!

FIRST. Hide her behind the curtain, Gaston.

SECOND. I'm afraid, she probably scratches.

FIRST. All right then. She'll calm down in the arms of her beloved. Let's go, young man.

Kizevetter is motionless.

Well?...

SECOND. Let him have one in the kisser, Jean.

Kizevetter moves.

FIRST. No. You'll go in front and we'll go a bit behind.

They go out. Silence.

TATAROV. And so instead of marching in the rain to an uncomfortable commissariat, you're staying in a warm room.

Lyolya makes for the door.

Where are you going?

LYOLYA. I'm going home.

TATAROV. Where? To the boardinghouse? You don't have any money.

LYOLYA. To Moscow.

TATAROV. How?

LYOLYA. On foot.

TATAROV. You've gone crazy! I won't let you go...There's a storm outside. You're crazy. Stay here. I'll sleep on the couch.

A knock at the door.

Tss...They've come for you. (*Seizes her and throws her on the bed, pulls the curtain. Opens the door*).

Enter Tregubova. Silence.

TREGUBOVA. On a night like this I can't bear to be alone, Nikolai Ivanovich.

Tatarov is silent.

I've brought a bottle of Lafitte to drink as we used to before. And I've brought you some asters that will remind you of the gardens of our homeland.

Tatarov is silent.

What's upset you? What's happened, Nikolai Ivanovich? (*Catches sight of the gown*). Oh, that's what it is!...My heart didn't deceive me...She's here. (*Pause*). She came to you in a ballgown. Her shoulders are like a young girl's. (*Draws the curtain*).

Lyolya sits like a stone idol.

Good afternoon, ugly duckling. (*Pause*). Why don't you say something? Raise your eyes. I'll scratch them out. Whore! Whore! Streetwalker! Take that! And that! (*Hits her in the face with the bouquet*).

CURTAIN

SCENE EIGHT

PLEA FOR GLORY

Night. A street. Workers.

AGENT. Comrades, I suggest we disperse.
FIRST VOICE. Coward!
AGENT. A hot temper isn't the same thing as bravery. Rashness is a caricature of courage.
SECOND VOICE. You're a caricature yourself.
THIRD VOICE. Speak plainly so that we can understand you.
AGENT. At night it's impossible to speak plainly; at night people either whisper or shout.
ADOLESCENT. Get out of here, lousy police spy!
AGENT. What's that you're yelling, kid? Ginger-headed coot!
ADOLESCENT. Long live Moscow!
AGENT. Numbskull! Do you read the papers?
ADOLESCENT. I can't read.
AGENT. You're a fine one to reorganize the world when you're illiterate! Moscow! Moscow! You dumb fish, you're being deceived. Have you ever been to Moscow?

The adolescent is silent.

You haven't? Well then shut up. Have any of you been?
LYOLYA (*from somewhere in the crowd*). I've been there.
A CHEERFUL VOICE (*singing*).

> In the middle of the market
> You stand behind your basket,
> Blondie,
> Blondie,
> My own little beauty.

AGENT. Well, that's lovely. Then you can tell these ignoramuses about the Soviet paradise.
LYOLYA. Take off your hat when you talk to the workers. (*Pulls off his hat. The crowd roars with approval, some laugh and clap*).
AGENT. Oh you trash! I'll pull your hair for you.

The adolescent kicks the agent in the behind. He collapses.

THE CHEERFUL VOICE (*singing*).

> Today when market's over
> Come and see me, lover
> Blondie,
> Blondie,
> My own little beauty.

Confusion. An elderly gentleman appears with an entourage. They catch sight of the prostrate agent and Lyolya, who is in a state of great agitation.

ELDERLY GENTLEMAN. The revolution hasn't begun yet, gentlemen.
LYOLYA. He's lost his hat, but when the revolution comes his head will follow it.
ELDERLY GENTLEMAN. Who is this fury?
AGENT. A drunken slut.

Silence.

ELDERLY GENTLEMAN. I came here to talk to you. Let's talk calmly.
LYOLYA. You'd better calm down yourself first.

ELDERLY GENTLEMAN. You little fool, if I were afraid of you I wouldn't have come here. Or do you imagine that we're living in the eighteenth century?

LYOLYA. Yes, in my dreams I see princes and dukes strung up on the street lamps.

ELDERLY GENTLEMAN. I'm afraid you're politically immature. The world isn't ruled by princes and dukes in our century and not by kings, but by the machine invented by democracy with the name "Capital."

LYOLYA. Very well. And street lamps are different these days too: they're electrical.

ELDERLY GENTLEMAN. I am a lever of the machine you yourself have invented.

LYOLYA. We haven't been introduced. I'd like to know who you are.

ELDERLY GENTLEMAN (*to his entourage*). You'd think she was an actress hired for a night to play the part of a witch in the French Revolution. What's maddening you? She imagines I'm an aristocrat. My child, I am the son of a street-sweeper, I was poor, in my youth I was apprentice to a blacksmith, then I became a locksmith . . .

ONE OF THE ENTOURAGE. It's too damp this evening for protracted conversation.

ELDERLY GENTLEMAN. I'm working-class by birth and speak your language. What do you want?

A WEAVER. Bread.

LYOLYA. What, just bread? No, no! Why are you afraid of him?

ELDERLY GENTLEMAN. You're in my way. (*Raises his walking stick and pushes it into Lyolya's chest*).

LYOLYA. That hurts.

ELDERLY GENTLEMAN. Don't provoke your comrades. You don't look like a factory worker. I think you're employed by the police.

Lyolya snatches the stick. The elderly gentleman is motionless. Men from his entourage take the stick from Lyolya.

THE CHEERFUL VOICE (*singing*).

I'll take off blondie's frillies,
Her petticoats and stockings—
Blondie,
Blondie,
My own little beauty.

ELDERLY GENTLEMAN. Things will get easier. We only have to wait.

WEAVER. And starve while we're waiting?

121

ELDERLY GENTLEMAN. You get your daily plateful of soup.

WEAVER'S WIFE. And what about our children?

ELDERLY GENTLEMAN. This is no time to breed children. Tell your husband to control himself. I can't be responsible for your husband's pleasures.

LYOLYA. Attack him!

She throws herself at the middle-aged man. His entourage pushes her off. She falls unconscious from a blow on the head. A panic-stricken silence. Then a group of workers appears headed by the unknown man Lyolya had seen beaten up in her boardinghouse. He is Henri Santillant.

THE CHEERFUL VOICE (*singing*).

At first I only tried my luck
By kissing blondie on the back.
Blondie,
Blondie,
My own little beauty.

ELDERLY GENTLEMAN. This is Henri Santillant. May I convey my greeting to a member of the Communist Party and a former Deputy. Have they let you out of prison?

Santillant is silent.

They respect you. You must warn them. They're filling the streets. Morning is approaching. You're preventing the city from awakening. The government would be justified in calling out the militia.

SANTILLANT. We'll disperse if the government listens to our demands.

ELDERLY GENTLEMAN. Say what you have to say. I'll pass it on.

SANTILLANT. It's a long list.

Lyolya regains consciousness and listens.

ELDERLY GENTLEMAN. Dictate then.

SANTILLANT. We demand . . .

VOICE. Nurseries for our children, playgrounds.

ELDERLY GENTLEMAN. Who will dictate?

VOICE. Santillant! We live in slums. Demand that houses be built for the workers.

VOICE. Palaces of culture!

WEAVER. Let sick workers be given treatment in health resorts!

122

VOICES.
> Health resorts for the workers!
> Security of employment!
> Leave for pregnant women!
> No more exploitation of youth!
> Communal kitchens for working housewives!
> Self-determination of nations!
> A six-hour working day!
> Let the workers control the factories!
> Heavy engineering plants!
> Take the land from the landlords!
> Science in the service of the proletariat!
> All power to the workers!

LYOLYA. Bravo! Bravo! Do you hear? Read the list of Soviet blessings, read it.

ELDERLY GENTLEMAN. In order to put this list into effect . . .

SANTILLANT. A social revolution is essential.

ELDERLY GENTLEMAN. My former fellow-deputy—you're a utopian. They've let you out of jail a bit too soon.

VOICES (*shouting*).
> Down with him!
> Down with him!
> Long live the Soviets!

ELDERLY GENTLEMAN. It's getting damper as the dawn approaches. Let's go gentlemen.

The elderly gentleman leaves with his entourage.

LYOLYA. I remember . . . I remember . . . I've remembered everything now! The parks, the theaters, the art for the workers!

VOICES (*shouting*). Long live Moscow!

LYOLYA. I've seen the globe in the hands of a shepherd. I've seen the Red Army.

VOICES (*shouting*). Long live Moscow!

LYOLYA. I have seen the spark of knowledge in the eyes of the proletariat. I have heard the slogan "No more war!" I have remembered it all now.

SANTILLANT. How did you get here?

THE CHEERFUL VOICE (*singing*).

> And so the story's ended,
> Blondie's husband's landed.
> Blondie,
> Blondie,

123

My own little beauty.

The police chief appears with a detachment. A hush.

POLICE CHIEF (*to Santillant*). Who are you talking to?

Santillant is silent.

You must leave Paris by the following route . . .
SANTILLANT. I won't leave Paris.
LYOLYA (*catching sight of Kizevetter, who has just appeared*). That
man . . .be careful . . .I beg of you. The police have ordered him . . .to fire
on you . . .
SANTILLANT. How do you know? You're not employed by the
police, are you?
POLICE CHIEF. We're waiting then.
SANTILLANT. What are you waiting for, hangman?
POLICE CHIEF. Arrest him!

A policeman comes forward.

Give me your hands.

The policeman takes out handcuffs.

Your hands . . .

Santillant is motionless.

Take him by force . . .

*The policeman with the handcuffs moves toward Santillant, who hits
his hand. Kizevetter fires at Santillant. Lyolya manages to shield him with
her body. Panic. Anger.*

VOICES (*shouting*).
They've shot the Russian woman!
Kill them! Kill them!
LYOLYA. No, no, Don't. Don't let them provoke you . . . . This man
has settled a personal account with me . . .Out of jealousy. (*Falls*).

*The police run away. The revolver is thrown to the ground. Santillant
picks it up.*

124

It was I...who stole it...from Comrade...
THE CHEERFUL VOICE (*singing*).

> Two bloody birthmarks now bedeck
> My lovely blondie's pretty neck.
> Blondie,
> Blondie,
> My own little beauty.

LYOLYA (*stretched out at Santillant's feet*). I recognized you...in my boardinghouse...the police...I had come there for that gown...forgive me...(*falls silent*).
VOICES.
> She's a thief.
> He killed her out of jealousy.
> He was her lover.
> They were both with the police!
> She's a traitor!
> The whore!

LYOLYA. Forgive me...I know...I can see: they're coming...they're coming...the Soviet armies are coming...with tattered red banners, their feet bruised by long stony marches...to knock down the walls of Europe.... Comrades...tell them...I've understood everything in the end...I've repented...(*Stands up*). Paris. Paris. This, then, is your glory, Paris! (*Collapses*).

The weaver's wife bends over her.

WEAVER'S WIFE. I can't hear. I can't make out a word.

Lyolya pulls her head closer and whispers.

She wants me to cover her body with a Red flag.
SANTILLANT. Raise your flags. The mounted police are coming. Let's march to meet them.

The unemployed exit in formation. Lyolya's body remains uncovered. The strains of a march are heard.

CURTAIN

THE END

THE THREE FAT MEN

A Play in Four Acts

CHARACTERS

Tibullus—a tightrope walker
Suok—a dancer
Augustus—a trainer and clown   actors in the circus show
Alina—a sharpshooter
Onetwothrees—a dancing teacher
Calliope-Venetia—a distinguished lady
A soldier of the town guard
Captain of the town guard
Doctor Gaspar Arneri
A seller of balloons
Pythagoras—a tailor
Prospero—a gunsmith
An officer of the guards
Aunt Ganymede
Tutti—heir to the Three Fat Men
A cook
First kitchen-boy
Second kitchen-boy
Third kitchen-boy
Fourth kitchen-boy
Fifth kitchen-boy
General Bonaventura
Narcissus the Miller   the Three Fat Men
Cardinal Lapitu
Master of ceremonies
Tutor of Tutti
Tub—a prisoner
Sentry guard
Artisans, wealthy citizens, soldiers of the watch, guardsmen

In the "Jolly Box" show-booth.

TIBULLUS. Bravo, bravo! You're performing like a real actress. How old are you?

AUGUSTUS. Get him! He's asking, and he should know the answer. It's ten years now since Suok joined our troupe.

TIBULLUS. It was ten years ago. Remember, Augustus? Caligula, our pink-cheeked strongman Caligula, was still alive then. He was our show's most famous actor, of course.

Remember, Augustus? That man used to lift a horse on his shoulders. Ten years ago our show was travelling about in the west, in the far west, farther than the city of Till. You must remember that day, Augustus! You were young then . . . . You could manage a double *salto mortale* . .

Two bars of music.

Remember, it was a clear, windy day, the beeches rustled, a man was walking along a green bank, and a girl was running behind him. It was you, Suok. You were really weeping and wailing. A hired killer was taking you to the bay in order to drown you there like a kitten. "It's on orders from the Three Fat Men," he said. The Three Fat Men who rule our country were settling some kind of accounts with you! Do you hear, Suok? How were you guilty in their eyes? You were such a skinny little thing then that even rabbits weren't afraid of you. But the Three Fat Men wanted to drown her. We had a parrot with a red beard. He was called Henry. We offered an unknown man the parrot in exchange for you. He agreed, but asked that it all remain a secret. And so you stayed with us. And now you're thirteen. You've grown and become a pretty girl and a well-known actress. You wouldn't let someone drown you like a kitten now.

SUOK. I love you a lot, Tibullus. Your green cape has got frayed, but I've thought of something: I can sew white squares along the edges. I'll work on it tomorrow. (*Hums a song*).

TIBULLUS. You don't remember, Suok, how clear that day was, how the orioles whistled . . .But you remember the other thing that happened later. We stopped in a place called "The Long Shadow." You climbed over the fence and took a pear from someone's garden. It was an unripe pear, remember? A pear as hard as a fist . . .

SUOK. Then a giant in white trousers appeared in the garden. He was the owner. He grabbed me by the ear with one hand, and started to pull down pears from the branches with the other. He forced me to eat one, then a second, then a third ... When I was eating the sixth, the gardener's son, a red-headed boy, swung his arm and hit the giant in white trousers with a shovel. After that I don't remember too well ... Dogs were jumping about, the giant was sitting on his haunches, the gardener's son clambered up the wall, with the barbed wire scratching him and the servants grabbing at his legs ... then you carried me in your arms.

TIBULLUS. The gardener's son who stepped in on your side was called Prospero. He's a gunsmith now, and they call him the leader of the poor.

SUOK. I know that.

TIBULLUS. Don't fret, Suok. We'll wait a bit. Soon we'll have beautiful capes and gardens filled with pears.

AUGUSTUS. Tibullus is beginning to fantasize. He's dreaming of some wonderful time to come, but in the meantime we're becoming beggars. The coins our audiences throw us get fewer every day.

ALINA. I've got to buy some new pistols. Mine aren't good for anything any more. It's hard to hit a pillow with them, let alone an ace. After all, I am capable of hitting a bee flying around a rose.

AUGUSTUS. There, you see Tibullus ... I'm not able to buy a fox. Soon I'll have to go on stage with a trained chicken ... Our situation is very bad ... As you know, Suok juggles with seven wooden balls. Yesterday we burnt three of them to cook dinner ... We'll burn the rest today ... What will you juggle with, Suok?

SUOK. Nothing. I'll juggle old slippers, or the eggs your trained chicken lays.

TIBULLUS (joyfully). In that case no one will want to watch our performances and we'll have to eat the chicken and the eggs.

Everyone, except Augustus, laughs.

AUGUSTUS. You're really laughing at yourselves. You're a great artist, Tibullus, but you're a hotheaded and thoughtless man. A fantasizer. You believe that the people will be victorious and that a paradise of the poor will come to pass among gardens filled with pears and peaches ... He believes that the power of the Three Fat Men will be toppled. What a crackpot! His thoughts are light, as light as his steps along the tightrope. You're insane, Tibullus.

TIBULLUS (holding a gaudy Chinese umbrella). You see this umbrella? Beautiful, isn't it?

SUOK. It shines and rustles and rings! It is as marvelous as your dreams, Tibullus ...

AUGUSTUS. These are all fantasies! You think that Prospero the gunsmith will take the palace of the Three Fat Men by storm at the head of the poor! You're giving yourself up to dreams, Tibullus, and all the while we're growing poorer, and soon we'll have to sell your marvelous umbrella and make one out of blue apron cloth...And yet you have faith!

SUOK. I have faith too!

AUGUSTUS. Do you know what the shopkeepers call Prospero the gunsmith? They call him "the leader who lost his pants." He doesn't alarm them...Just think of it! The palace of the Three Fat Men is surrounded by moats and defended by guardsmen. What can a band of poor do with stones as their ammunition? It's all so stupid.

A pause. All become sad. They take off their clothes.

SUOK. In the palace of the Three Fat Men there lives a boy called Tutti...

ALINA (*taking up Suok's story*). The Three Fat Men kidnapped a boy...They need an heir...They don't have children of their own...and the people say other things too...

AUGUSTUS. Baloney! You're just a little girl, Alina...You like scary stories! You want to tell us the story of the iron heart!

ALINA. Everyone knows it. On the order of the Three Fat Men a great scientist ripped the heart out of the kidnapped boy and put in an iron heart...

AUGUSTUS (*angry*). No kidding? Was it a complicated operation? And what for?

SUOK. So that little Tutti would grow up cruel.

ALINA. The Three Fat Men will die, and the terrible man with the iron heart will rule our country...

TIBULLUS. Do you hear, Augustus? The Three Fat Men stole a child from the people and want to give them back a monster!

SUOK. Prospero the gunsmith will free the boy!

AUGUSTUS. No one is afraid of your Prospero...Last night I was wandering about town. Lights were burning and happy voices and the sound of flutes could be heard through the open windows, young men and their ladies were strolling the boulevards and pretty flower girls were selling flowers on street corners...Roses were floating in basins like swans...

ALINA (*interrupts him*). Lord save us, you'd think we were living in a country where everyone was as happy as children.

AUGUSTUS (*continuing*). I stopped at a street corner...Two dandies walked past and one said to the other: look, the rogue has made himself a jacket out of beet soup...

TIBULLUS. And you didn't say anything?

SUOK. You should have shouted at the top of your voice, "Down with the Three Fat Men!"

AUGUSTUS. quiet...Shh...Idiot! Have you taken leave of your senses! Don't shout so loudly! Do you want us to be arrested?

131

Enter Onetwothrees.

ONETWOTHREES (*looks around at the door, bows*). This way please . . .It's here . . .Please . . .

Alina, frightened by Onetwothrees, goes unnoticed behind the partition. The Distinguished Lady enters.

DISTINGUISHED LADY. Ah, here it is . . .Ah, here they are . . .the street actors, I believe. Greetings, ladies and gentlemen . . .

ONETWOTHREES. Hello there. If I'm not mistaken, this is old man Brizak's showplace.

AUGUSTUS. Yes, that's us . . .

ONETWOTHREES. Pleased to meet you. May I present a distinguished lady known as Calliope-Venetia. You have the honor to see her beneath your roof . . .I'm called Onetwothrees. I'm a famous dancing teacher. You've probably heard of me.

AUGUSTUS. Sit down, please . . .

DISTINGUISHED LADY. Onetwothrees, you've brought me to a place that doesn't even have chairs . . .

TIBULLUS. You can sit here. (*Indicates a drum*).

DISTINGUISHED LADY. What? On a drum? It's impossible for me to sit on a drum. I'm not a general. One has to sit properly!

TIBULLUS. Madame, it is the best seat in this house. Your servant can sit on that barrel.

ONETWOTHREES. I'm not a servant. I'm a dancing teacher.

AUGUSTUS. Tibullus, control yourself. What can we do for you, madame? What can we do for you, Mr. Onetwothrees?

ONETWOTHREES. Here's what it's all about, ladies and gents. The distinguished lady who has graced you with her visit, Madame Calliope-Venetia, wishes to have a children's party at her dacha the coming Sunday . . .She has invited me to take charge of the artistic section. Unfortunately, the dacha is situated in a place which, while quite attractive, is lacking in elevation, hills and knolls, so essential to echo the joyful exclamations and singing of the guests . . .Yes indeed . . .I'll continue. The esteemed lady's granddaughter happened to be riding in her carriage across Tenth Market Square and was the fortuitous witness of one of your shows. She saw the dancing of your little actress Suok, and she liked it very much . . .

TIBULLUS. Of course she did! Our Suok is a marvelous performer.

ONETWOTHREES. Exactly. And we would like to invite little Suok to take part in our gathering . . .

AUGUSTUS. Well, that would be delightful . . .

TIBULLUS. Quiet, clown. Let him speak his fill.

132

DISTINGUISHED LADY. We are inviting little Suok to play the role of "echo" at the party. Don't you think that's terribly interesting? Let's say the guests take their places at table and your Suok hides in the jasmine bushes. And let's say that one of our little girls suddenly exclaims: "Oh, what a sweet pear!" Suok will have to repeat: "Oh, what a sweet pear!" And let's say another girl will remark: "Look what a wonderful dress I have. No one else has a dress like mine . . ."

ONETWOTHREES. Or suddenly one of the invited boys, filled with military ardor, shouts: "Down with Prospero—the leader who lost his pants!"

TIBULLUS. "Servant," was that what you said?

SUOK. Be quiet, tightrope walker, let him speak his fill.

ONETWOTHREES. Don't you think it's interesting? But there's one thing . . .

DISTINGUISHED LADY. That's right, Onetwothrees, tell them about the most important thing . . .

ONETWOTHREES. It's like this . . . We're inviting little Suok simply as an actress . . . not as a guest. You do understand, don't you? Our party is being given for the children of very rich and distinguished people. It is possible that the party will be attended by one of the Three Fat Men . . . You can understand yourselves that such well-born children would feel awkward if a street actress were to join in their games, sit at the same table with them and so on . . . Suok will have to be kept out of the way.

DISTINGUISHED LADY. You must understand that the children of distinguished parents are used to one kind of food and the children of street actors to another . . . I'm sure that your Suok has never eaten cake, isn't that so? So how can we offer her pineapple then? It would upset her stomach. Let her learn to eat honey-cakes first.

AUGUSTUS. How much do you propose to pay?

DISTINGUISHED LADY. Twelve gold rubles.

AUGUSTUS. All right then, we agree. Suok, you have to agree. It's a good price.

SUOK. Have you said everything you wanted to, Augustus?

AUGUSTUS. Yes, everything, I think.

SUOK. And you, Mr. Onetwothrees, have you said everything?

ONETWOTHREES. Seems like everything.

SUOK. And you madame?

DISTINGUISHED LADY. Oh yes, my child.

SUOK. Well now, Tibullus, do what you wanted to do.

Tibullus snatches a paper disk from the wall, swings it about and slaps it down on Onetwothree's head.

AUGUSTUS. Oh, Tibullus! Oh, madame! Forgive us! He's lost his

133

mind!

SUOK. How's that, madame? Give her curls a pull, Tibullus! I think she's wearing a wig.

DISTINGUISHED LADY (*whining*). How dare you! Rebels!

Tibullus pulls off the Lady's hat together with her wig. The headpiece flies across the stage.

(*Squealing*). Oh! Oh! Oh! Arrest them! Police! Police! They're conspirators!

A detachment of the municipal guard rushes in.

CAPTAIN. Quiet! I'm asking you not to shout! We'll clear it up right away. (*Gives everyone a lookover*). So...Hm...Hm...The notorious stageshow...What's that? Shut up! How? I understand. Shut up, you bums. Conrad, stand at the door. Oliver, over here. Right. Oh, madame...We've known them a long time...They put on shows directed against the power of the Three Fat Men. They sing songs slandering the merchants and shopkeepers. They call the people to insurrection...They are friends of Prospero the gunsmith. Shut up...

AUGUSTUS. Oh, Mr. Captain...Forgive us...

TIBULLUS (*to Augustus*). Quiet, you trained chicken...

DISTINGUISHED LADY. I order you...I'm the wife of General Venetia...I order you to annihilate them...knock down their theater...

AUGUSTUS. Do you hear that! Tibullus! They're knocking down our showplace!

CAPTAIN. Conrad, knock down the wall! Oliver, tear out the door. Madame, excuse the draft. Move over to the side or else you'll feel the wind. One! Two! Three!

AUGUSTUS. Ooh! (*Collapses on the drum weeping*).

ONETWOTHREES. Take that, you miserable buffoons! Here's one for you, tightrope walker!...You called me a servant, did you? Here's one for you! Here's one for you!

The guards pull apart the walls of the showplace. Through the new opening Star Square can be seen with a gigantic lantern, the town wall, the town gates and a tower.

DISTINGUISHED LADY. Oh, I feel a migraine coming on...And I seem to have lost my jaw. Captain, don't step on my jaw...

SUOK. Will we come through it, Tibullus?

TIBULLUS. We will. It's not so terrible. Let them break up all this rubbish! Soon there will be a great holiday...Prospero the gunsmith will take the palace of the Three Fat Men by storm, and then we'll put on a full dress performance in the town's largest circus on Jewellers Street . . .

The sound of battle grows behind the town wall. All listen.

CAPTAIN. Sorry. At ease. (*Listens to the noise. Shouts*). Conrad, to the square!

TIBULLUS. Can you hear it, Suok?

CURTAIN

EPISODE TWO

The square. Everyone is rushing to the square on which appear Doctor Gaspar Arneri and the seller of balloons, drawn by the noise beyond the wall. People from the circus show run past Doctor Arneri, almost knocking him off his feet as they rush toward the open gates.

DOCTOR. Quiet down! Quiet! For God's sake, quiet! What's happened? . . . My God . . . I came out for a walk. Careful . . . My stick . . . Don't step on my feet . . . This is disgraceful. I am Doctor Gaspar Arneri, learned master of amazing devices, surgeon, pyrotechnician, I know a hundred sciences, and they're stepping on my feet as if I were a schoolboy. Quiet! And what's this!! My glasses! They'll break my glasses . . . I'm nearsighted . . . Without my glasses I'll see my surroundings about as well as a normal-sighted man sees with glasses . . . Quiet . . .

SELLER OF BALLOONS (*howling*). Prospero the gunsmith!

DOCTOR. Wait a moment, my dear fellow. One little second. Stop. You are conversing with a great scientist. Wait. Where are you rushing?

SELLER. Can't you hear? (*Extends his arms in the direction of the town wall, beyond which the noise of battle is growing.*)

DOCTOR. I hear noise. What is going on there?

SELLER. Prospero the gunsmith!

DOCTOR. You repeat the name of the people's leader senselessly, and I can't understand a thing. I'm a scientist. I'm accustomed to operating with exact data. For example, I see that you are without doubt selling balloons. They're like varicolored grapes. And I can assume that a good gust of wind could carry you away with your balloons. Then I see that everyone is running to the square illuminated by the biggest lantern in the world, called "Star" for its exceptional light. I also see that your head is like a teapot painted all over with daisies. But in relation to the noise over the town wall, I don't have any data.

Beyond the gates are heard the shouts of the characters who had run there in the previous scene.

CAPTAIN (*commander of the watch*). I beg you not to shout! Please remain in your places.

The whole group returns to the square and stays by the gates.

DISTINGUISHED LADY (*fidgeting*). Where's my hair? Where's my jaw? They've robbed me, captain . . .

DOCTOR. I beg you to explain to me what is going on, captain.

CAPTAIN. Prospero the gunsmith led the poor to storm the palace.

DOCTOR. Oh really? Why won't you let us beyond the gate? I'd like to take a look. I'm a historian. I'm obliged to see everything.

CAPTAIN. Back! (*Stands before the group. Glances at the open gates*). Yes-s. Everything can be seen excellently from here. The road is lit by lanterns. There are about two hundred poor. No more . . . Yes . . . Quiet! The drawbridge is lowering. I see. Of course . . . Guardsmen galloping over the bridge.

ONETWOTHREES. Bravo! Bravo!

CAPTAIN (*to the Distinguished Lady*). This way please, madame. Out of respect I'm offering you a place next to myself. Now you will see the flight of Prospero the gunsmith . . .

DISTINGUISHED LADY. Unfortunately I don't see well without my wig . . .

CAPTAIN. Look, look, madame! The guardsmen have gone into the attack . . . .

DISTINGUISHED LADY. Oh, I'm so glad!

The tailor Pythagoras appears.

PYTHAGORAS (*elbows his way through*). Let me through . . . I'm the well-known tailor Pythagoras. I sew exclusively for the well-to-do . . . I make dresses the color of grapes and goldfish . . .

DISTINGUISHED LADY. You can let him through.

PYTHAGORAS (*looking through binoculars*). Oh how interesting! They're running . . . Excuse me, madame, but when I am filled with happiness, I begin to hiccup . . . The guardsmen are cutting them up with sabers. Stupid loafers, they thought they could take the fortress with their bare hands . . .

DOCTOR. Excuse me . . . I don't understand what's happening. Is Prospero really running away? Are the guardsmen really winning? Let me go forward then . . . I'm a historian. I must be a witness to this great historical event.

CAPTAIN. Why you rat! Did you hear? He calls this sortie of disgusting brigands a historical event.

ONETWOTHREES. Just look, he has excellent glasses! Madame, do you have bad vision? We'll take the glasses off that nose of his that looks like a fig. There you are!

DOCTOR. I don't see anything. Please help me!

CAPTAIN. You've lost your jaw, madam? I can knock out his jaw and make you an offer of it, madam. Ha ha ha!

DISTINGUISHED LADY. Oh you're awfully clever, captain!

DOCTOR. Oh I can't see a thing...Give me my glasses...What an insult...

CAPTAIN. Get the hell out, you old fart!

A shot.

PYTHAGORAS. They're running...Bravo! Bravo!

CAPTAIN. You see. There he is, running...he's enormous...See how his shadow flies after him like a cape.

DISTINGUISHED LADY. Who is that terrible man?

CAPTAIN. It's Prospero the gunsmith. The gardener's ginger-haired son.

PYTHAGORAS. They'll take him prisoner today, and tomorrow they'll cut a nice pattern out of him.

DOCTOR. Has he really been defeated? Did Prospero really lose the battle? I can't see a thing...

CAPTAIN. Yes-s. Move back. Enough. The show is over. The rebels are running for the gates. They want to hide in the town. Some hopes! I'll close the gates.

ONETWOTHREES. And quite right.

PYTHAGORAS. Aha...Ha ha ha! Bravo, commander! Bravo! Excuse me, madame, when I get agitated I begin to sweat. Yes. Just perfect. Close the gates.

DISTINGUISHED LADY. Right under their noses...They've caught them over there...they shouldn't let any survive...Bravo, captain...I'm inviting you to the children's party.

SUOK. There he is. I can see Prospero.

ALINA. He has blood on his forehead.

TIBULLUS. We must save him.

CAPTAIN. And so I'll close the gates. Conrad! Fleming! Over here!

SUOK. Don't you dare close them.

DOCTOR. Oh I can't see anything! Who's that shouting? It's a little girl...What a clear little voice...She has a silvery throat.

SUOK. Don't you dare...Do you hear? Do you hear, nose-face? Get back! I won't allow the gates to be closed.

137

PYTHAGORAS. Ugh, don't confuse us, you flatiron. Don't confuse us. When I'm confused, I begin to get mad.

The gates close.

ONETWOTHREES. Perfect!
SUOK. Open up!
DISTINGUISHED LADY. No don't. It's just right.
ALINA. Let's help! We'll force them open!

Knocking at the gates. Noise and shouting behind them. The powerful voice of Prospero: "Open! Open up! It's me . . . Prospero the gunsmith!" Silence. Prospero's voice: "Hurry! They're catching us. Open! Open up!" Bangs the gates. They shake.

TIBULLUS. I'll open them for you now, Prospero. (*With a blow of his fist he lays out the captain*).
SUOK. One!

Tibullus flattens a soldier with a second blow.

SUOK. Two!
SECOND SOLDIER. Take my pistol, tightrope walker. I don't want to serve the Three Fat Men.
SUOK. Hurray!
PYTHAGORAS. When I'm afraid, I begin to shout. Help! We're done for!

Prospero's voice: "Hurry. They're close . . ." The Distinguished Lady, Onetwothrees and Pythagoras throw themselves on Tibullus.

TIBULLUS (*waving the pistol*). Away!

They do not retreat.

I'm hurrying, Prospero. Suok, help me!

Propspero's voice: "Too late!" Tibullus and Suok open the gates. Prospero tears out, guardsmen behind him. General shouting. The guardsmen have caught Prospero.

TIBULLUS. Forgive us, Prospero. We were too late.
SUOK. Hello, Prospero . . . Don't be angry, we were late. You're not in pain, Prospero? No? Of course you're not! What an idiot I am, asking silly

questions! You don't remember me, Prospero? You've grown . . .Oh, what a big fellow you are. Tell me, is it true that the kidnapped boy has an iron heart?

OFFICER. Plug up his mouth.

Prospero is gagged.

CAPTAIN (*getting up from the ground, indicates Tibullus to the guards officer*). Arrest him. He raised his hand against me, an officer of the town guard.

DISTINGUISHED LADY. He insulted me, the wife of a general.

OFFICER (*to Tibullus*). Stay where you are!

Tibullus runs to a column from which a wire runs to the lantern.

DISTINGUISHED LADY. Hold him!

SUOK. Run, Tibullus! Allez! I know what you want to do.

DOCTOR. I can't see anything. Historical events are unfolding around me.

SELLER. Madame, don't take off the glasses! Watch! The great tightrope walker Tibullus will now demonstrate his artistry.

Tibullus clambers up the column.

DOCTOR. I want to see Tibullus's artistry . . .

ALINA. Bravo, Tibullus!

PYTHAGORAS. Shoot him!

SUOK. Bravo, Tibullus!

Tibullus steps onto the wire. He walks along it, keeping his balance with the help of his green cape.

CAPTAIN. Just a minute. Step aside. I'm the best shot in the regiment. Watch . . .you . . .gunsmith . . .I'll now potshot your little buddy. (*Takes aim*).

The Doctor has approached from behind with the awkward gait of the near-sighted; he gropes about with his hands, one of which holds a stick. He swings it and strikes the officer's hand. The officer drops the pistol.

Damn!

DOCTOR. Oh, excuse me, please . . .I'm near-sighted . . .I can't see anything without my glasses . . .I thought . . .that this . . .was a clothes hanger . . .What a good thing, I thought, they've put clothes hangers up in the square.

ONETWOTHREES. Now just wait. We'll take him alive. No use wasting bullets...I'm a famous dancing teacher. I know how to slither up columns too. Give me some scissors. I'll cut the wire.

PYTHAGORAS. Here are some scissors.

Tibullus is walking along the wire toward the lantern. Onetwothrees clambers up the column and stretches out to the wire with the scissors.

DISTINGUISHED LADY. Cut it! Cut it! I'll pay a hundred gold rubles!

Tibullus has climbed from the wire onto the ring which circles the lantern.

SUOK. Well done, Tibullus! I know what you want to do...

ONETWOTHREES (*opens the scissors*). one...two...

TIBULLUS (*on the ring*). Three. (*He puts out the lantern. General uproar*).

DOCTOR. Oh, I can't see anything. It's awfully quiet and dark, like the inside of a suitcase. I used to be near-sighted, but now I've gone completely blind.

A square of light opens in the cupola; stars are visible. Tibullus has opened a hatchway and escaped through it, emerging on the other side of the cupola.

ONETWOTHREES. He's escaped through the hatch...

DISTINGUISHED LADY. Close it quick! Close it! There's a draft! Blows right through me...I don't have my wig, and I'm without my lower jaw...

SELLER. Oh...something terrible is happening...Close the hatch! Close the hatch! Close the hatch or the gates! A draft! The wind is carrying me away...Oh...Oh...Oh...My balloons...The scissors! Cut off the balloons! My balloons...Hold me...I'm flying away...I don't want to fly! I don't know how to fly . . .

The Seller goes flying, suspended from the string of balloons, right up to the hatch. The stage revolves. The Balloon Seller's flight over the town. As he draws near, the palace of the Three Fat Men rises. The balloons descend and the seller flies into the palace kitchen through a window. He splashes down in the middle of a gigantic pie.

CURTAIN

EPISODE THREE

The palace kitchen. Balloons are bouncing. Squealing of cooks.

COOK. Well hello there!

FIRST KITCHEN-BOY. He flew in the window like a speck of dust heralding the arrival of a letter.

SECOND KITCHEN-BOY. Balloons! What marvelous balloons!

KITCHEN-BOYS:

FIRST. Green!

SECOND. Pink!

THIRD. And yellow!

FOURTH. They're bouncing about!

FIFTH. Hurray!

COOK. The pie's demolished. A beautiful work of the pastry-cook's art has perished. Do you know what it should be called? A tragedy, that's what. In Greek it's katastropha, but God knows what to call it. We worked on this pie, we strove, we wanted to receive an award for it, everything was ready almost, and suddenly some unknown and suspicious man sits down in the middle of our pie without any permission whatsoever. How do you like the flying scoundrel?

FIRST KITCHEN-BOY. When a bird flies, that's as it should be. If an angel flies, that's already suspicious. But if a man flies, it's simply impudence.

COOK. There's to be a gala dinner at the palace today. (*To a kitchen-boy*). Watch the chocolate, it's boiling. Make sure a fly doesn't fall into it. Anyway you're such a gawker that you wouldn't pay any attention even if a turkey fell in. And so there's to be a gala dinner at the palace today. I'm not saying this for you, gawker, but for that turkey there who fell in the pie. Good God, what an ugly puss on him! I'm a mean thing, but I can't help wanting to laugh. And so you've ruined our pie for us, you flying devil. In the meantime there's a triumphal celebration at the palace today to celebrate the repression of the rebel Prospero the gunsmith. The gunsmith is sitting in a cage at the palace in Tutti the heir's menagerie. Hear that, you flying swindler? You understand, of course, that they'll stick you in a cage too, although you're not an eagle, but rather a turkey who should wind up in the chicken coop.

SELLER. I'm afraid to open my eyes. Tell me please, where am I?

COOK. You're in the palace of the Three Fat Men.

SELLER. You're joking. You shouldn't joke about such things. I'm very nervous.

COOK. You're sitting right in the middle of a pie. Surely you can feel that?

SELLER. I can. It's wet. I feel a cold coming on. I'm quite sickly.

141

(*Gropes about with his fingers*). What are these things here?

COOK. Those are candied fruits, you scoundrel.

SELLER. It all happened so fast and unexpectedly, you know, that I thought I must be dreaming. But my eyes are closed—how can a man see with closed eyes?

COOK. He turns out to be a philosopher. So what's your opinion, does it hurt to get it in the neck?

SELLER. Don't hit me. I'm very sensitive.

MASTER OF CEREMONIES (*runs in*). The pie! Where's the pie? Why haven't you brought it? The pie is awaited in the banqueting hall!

COOK. Turn around and get out of here. The pie will be ready in five minutes.

SELLER. May I stand up?

COOK. No, please remain seated.

SELLER. I'm so uncomfortable. It's like sitting on a throne, and I'm very modest.

COOK (*bawling at the kitchen-boys*). Let's have some cream! Cream, the devil take it!

The kitchen-boys bring in cream by the shovel-full. They plaster the Seller with cream.

More! More! Still more cream! Slap on the pistachio!

SELLER. Oh God, what are you doing?

KITCHEN-BOYS. Strawberry topping!
Lemon filling!

COOK. Do you understand me? We'll have a wonderful pie. These balloons . . .This ugly puss that looks like a teapot decorated with daisies.

SELLER. What pie? You mean they're going to eat me? It's really unnecessary. I'm not edible.

COOK (*sculpting the cream*). Good! Just right! This will teach you a lesson! Don't fly! Don't fly! Decorate him with candied fruit! Little stars!

KITCHEN-BOYS:

FIRST AND SECOND. Little rings!

THIRD AND FOURTH. Little roses!

FIFTH. And diamonds!

COOK. More! More! More!

Seller is completely covered in cream and candied fruit. He holds tightly to the string of balloons. Bustle. The kitchen-boys fuss about.

SELLER. I'll open my eyes anyway. I'm very curious. (*Opens his eyes*). Oh no! What have you done? I'd better close my eyes. It has to be a dream. I'll open my eyes when I wake up.

COOK. Let's have some syrup! Syrup, quick, syrup . . .

The head cook is given the syrup. He pours it all over the Seller.

SELLER. Brr . . .Br . . .I love to bathe. I'm very keen on cleanliness.

COOK. Right. Enough syrup, don't you think?

SELLER. I think so.

COOK. Tutti the heir likes a lot of syrup. You, Turkey, do you know who Tutti the heir is? But how would you know?

FIRST KITCHEN-BOY. Tutti the heir is a thin boy who looks like a mean little girl.

SECOND KITCHEN-BOY. When the Three Fat Men die, Tutti their heir will rule the land.

THIRD KITCHEN-BOY. He never leaves the palace. He's never seen living children.

FOURTH KITCHEN-BOY. They built him a menagerie.

COOK. He watches tigers and polecats. He's learning cruelty from the animals.

FIFTH KITCHEN-BOY. He has a doll.

FIRST KITCHEN-BOY. An artificial little girl . . .made of wax.

COOK. It's not wax, you fool. A lot you know! The doll was made from a special paste. It was made by a great craftsman. I had the chance to get a quick look at her. She looks like a pretty girl of about twelve.

SECOND KITCHEN-BOY. Tutti the heir doesn't know that there exist real live boys and girls. He thinks he is artificial himself . . .made of wax.

THIRD KITCHEN-BOY. He's got an iron heart. They ripped out his human heart and stuck in an iron one. He tic-tocks like a clock.

FOURTH KITCHEN-BOY. They say he was kidnapped from his parents when he was a very little boy . . .

FIFTH KITCHEN-BOY. And they say that the people would like to take the boy away from the Fat Men, who stole him.

COOK. You shouldn't speak loudly about it. (*Walks to the side and admires the pie*). Anyway we've wasted enough time chattering. What a miraculous pie. If I were a young scapegrace, I'd compare it to a snow man.

FIRST KITCHEN-BOY. If I were a poet, I'd compare it to a swan.

SECOND KITCHEN-BOY. And me . . .if I were a washerwoman, I'd compare it to a mountain of soap-suds.

COOK. Well since I'm not a washerwoman, nor a poet, nor a young scapegrace, but the head cook, I feel without making unnecessary comparisons that we should stick this swan in the oven so as to put a blush on its cheeks.

SELLER (*crying*). No need to put me in the oven . . .I have a very rosy complexion.

MASTER OF CEREMONIES (*running in*). The pie! The pie! Hurry up with the pie!

Three servants come running in.

COOK. It's ready. Carry it out.
SELLER. Goodbye, ladies and gentlemen, goodbye. I'm very polite...

The servants pick up the platter and carry out the Seller.

FIRST KITCHEN-BOY. Wait! Wait! (*Shouts to the Seller*). Tell Tutti the heir, please, when he's eating you, that he shouldn't eat the wooden balls.

They carry the pie up the stairs. The Cook walks behind with a knife. A procession. A chorus of kitchen-boys.

EPISODE FOUR

Feast of the Three Fat Men. Only the three of them are eating. Everyone else present in the hall is serving them. Each one eats in his own way. The General chomps away as if he were cracking walnuts. When the eating of the Miller is heard, it sounds as if he were belching rather than gulping his food. The Cardinal sighs and moans like a voluptuary. This was the way people ate in the time of Falstaff.

GENERAL. Delicious...Um...Delicious...
CARDINAL. How tasty it all is, how delightful.
MILLER (*to the General*). Don't chomp so loudly. Exercise self-restraint.
GENERAL. Don't disturb me when I'm eating. I'm not chomping—it's you puffing away.
CARDINAL (*masticating a table napkin*). Incomparably tasty.
GENERAL (*to the Cardinal*). You're munching your napkin.
CARDINAL. Really...
MILLER. Spread some butter on it, napkins are tastier that way.
CARDINAL. I got carried away...it's so enchanting.
MILLER (*to the General*). Hey! You've bitten my ear.
GENERAL. Let's not argue. I took it for a fruit dumpling.

Music.

CARDINAL. Shh...You hear...music...

144

GENERAL (*hearing the chorus*). If I'm not mistaken they're bringing the pie. Hurrah!

The kitchen-boys bring in the pie. The pie is set down. The Seller sits with closed eyes, holding tightly to the balloon strings; the balloons float in the air and sparkle.

CARDINAL. Now we'll eat the pie. If I didn't have this damned wart on my chin, I would feel just splendid.

MILLER. You have a marvelous wart. It's so big that a flower grew out of it instead of hair!

GENERAL. Tell me, what kind of flower is it? A petunia or a sweet-pea?

CARDINAL. You'd better look for yourself. The lump that flops around under your chin can be called a "kadyk" or an Adam's apple. But yours, my friend, is not an Adam's apple, but a regular Adam's melon.

GENERAL. Let's not fight. One fool told me that my moustaches look like boots. Well, I stopped waxing them after that. Let's not fight. Let's eat the pie.

SELLER (*softly*). May you choke on it!

MILLER. According to our tradition, he who ate the most at dinner receives the biggest piece of pie. I ate the most!

CARDINAL. No, I did!

GENERAL. Let's not fight. Reckon it up.

MILLER. I ate the following: fifty snails in rice sauce, two dozen potatoes stuffed with magpie fillet, three young pheasants—one with nuts, the second with peas, the third with plums, and I beg you to note also that one of the pheasants had three legs.

GENERAL. That's impossible.

MILLER. I remember distinctly, I ate a three-legged pheasant.

CARDINAL. Remarkable...My pheasant had only one leg.

GENERAL. Let's not fight. He ate your pheasant's second leg. Let's find a way out of this situation.

SELLER (*to the Cook*). I fear it will be a mess when they start eating me...I beg you not to forget that I have not three, and not one, but exactly two legs...Ugh...

CARDINAL. In view of the fact that Mr. Narcissus the Miller cheated, we consider the competition to be void. The best piece of pie will be left for Tutti our heir.

Argument, swearing.

GENERAL. Do you think these balloons are edible?

MILLER. I think they're edible.

CARDINAL. To you everything is edible.

Argument. Swearing.

GENERAL. Let's not fight. Just look at this magnificent pie! Look at the ugly mug that's sticking out of the custard cream . . . An amazing mug. Looks just like a man's head! Charming! I believe it's made of marzipan!

CARDINAL. No, I think it's made of almonds!

MILLER. You don't understand a damned thing! It's made of halva!

Argument, swearing.

GENERAL. Let's not fight. We can find out right now. I'll eat off the nose.

SELLER (*loudly*). Hey!

CARDINAL. Oho! The pie said, "Hey!"

GENERAL. The pie turns out to be mechanical . . . Look! It's shaking, the balloons are jumping . . .

MILLER. Listen, we can't get by without mechanical things. What a joy it is that the pie can talk. A pie shouldn't be able to talk. Today the pie is talking, tomorrow the soup will begin to sing, and the day after tomorrow the cutlets will begin dancing. Cut it up! I want some pie!

Cook raises her knife.

CARDINAL. Wait a minute. I've thought of something. Cook, put down your knife. Prospero the gunsmith is sitting in a cage in the menagerie. I'll order him brought here. We'll offer him a piece of pie . . . Ha ha ha!

GENERAL. Right. I'll order Prospero brought here. I'd like to see that warrior.

CARDINAL. We'll tease him a bit.

MILLER. We'll cut him a piece of pie and give it to him to sniff . . . and then—off with him!! Back to the cage!!

Laughter.

GENERAL (*to the Master of Ceremonies*). Bring the prisoner here. Tutti the heir has the key. Tutti is asleep. The key's under his pillow.

MILLER. They say he's very horrible. He has a terrible head.

CARDINAL. Hate burns through his eyes. You can't make yourself look into them.

GENERAL. They say he's stronger than anyone, stronger than a lion.

CARDINAL. Oh this wart . . . The flower is tickling my nostrils.

146

Exit the Master of Ceremonies.

Tomorrow there's to be an execution in Court Square. Yes. Right now carpenters are erecting ten scaffolds. Prospero will be executed last, after the executioners have beheaded all his friends, all the conspirators.

MILLER. Quite right . . .I don't think anyone would dare to raise a revolt now.

GENERAL. Fools! Dreamers! The filthy sluggards want to do battle with our guardsmen. Those are men of leather and iron! The poor want to do battle with me! Just look at me, I've got fists the size of milk pitchers!

MILLER. The poor must live under lock and key. One look at those freaks makes me want to throw-up. They're disgusting . . .Once, it was long ago, a girl climbed into my garden to steal pears. I wanted to punish her, but just imagine, my gardener's son, a ginger-haired blockhead, stood up for her. He hit me with a shovel . . .He chopped off my ear . . .

Prospero the gunsmith is led in by a convoy.

That's him! The ginger-haired gardener's son!

Silence.

You don't recognize me, Prospero? Greetings, Prospero!

PROSPERO. Greetings, scoundrel!

MILLER. Ugh, how impolite you are. It won't do you any good to swagger. Those stupid ragamuffins took you for an eagle yesterday, but today you're no more frightening than a pheasant. I'm not angry at you. You chopped off my ear with a shovel, and it hurt like hell . . .We're good people, gunsmith, we'll cut off your head without any pain at all.

PROSPERO. I'm not frightened. I have only one head, but the people have hundreds of thousands of heads. You won't cut them off.

MILLER. We won't talk about politics. What are politics compared to a good pie. We would like to treat you to some.

PROSPERO. I won't eat from your trough! Fat pigs!

CARDINAL. How impolite he is, this leader. We invited you to partake of a piece of pie and you utter vulgarities.

GENERAL. I think if he eats the pie on an empty stomach he'll feel sick.

MILLER. You're right, general. That's why we'll give him some pheasant first. (*Grabs a pheasant leg and approaches the gunsmith*). Here, gunsmith. Very tasty meat. Oh, your hands are tied! What a shame! Well try it without the help of your hands. (*Sticks the pheasant leg in his mouth*).

GENERAL. Don't you find it tasty? Chew it up better.

CARDINAL. For some reason he's not eating. Remarkable thing.

147

Perhaps pheasant meat is not to your taste? Perhaps it's too stringy? In that case, give it back! (*Grabs the pheasant leg out of the gunsmith's mouth*).

The gunsmith spits in his face. Silence.

Out! Out! Back to the cage! Take him back to his cage!

The gunsmith is led away.

GENERAL. We must console Mr. Lapitu.

MILLER. It's nothing. Merely a bit of irrigation for the flower in your wart.

GENERAL. Let's not fight. Don't get hot under the collar. Now we'll give you the best piece of pie. I think the best piece is the—nose. We'll cut it off right now.

SELLER. Hey!

GENERAL. Hear that? The pie shouted again . . .I'm almost sure it know how to sing . . .

CARDINAL. What an excellent cook we have. She was the one who thought this up. You're a good girl, cook. Does your pie know how to sing?

COOK. It does.

GENERAL. Well bring it on then. Let it sing.

The Cook pulls the Seller by the nose.

SELLER. I don't know how to sing, I'm very unmusical.

Loud and mournful cries from Tutti the heir resound from the gallery: "Doll! My doll! My poor doll!"

Silence.

GENERAL. Quiet! It's Tutti our heir who's shouting.

Silence. Tutti comes running in in tears. His distraught tutor runs behind him.

CARDINAL. What's this? Why is the heir crying?

Panic at the table.

SELLER. The hell with it . . .They say when children cry it's good to give them something sweet . . .I've had it.

GENERAL. What's wrong, Tutti?

MILLER. I know, you had a bad dream.

GENERAL. Perhaps you dreamt of Prospero the gunsmith.

CARDINAL. Why are you crying? Tell us what you dreamt.

Tutti wants to speak, but, choking with tears, is unable to.

MILLER. He can't speak. His mouth is full of tears.

GENERAL (*to the tutor*). And what's your mouth full of? Explain why our heir is crying.

CARDINAL. Quiet! Why are you crying, Tutti?

TUTTI. My doll! My poor doll!

TUTOR. I'll tell you everything, just as it happened. A terrible thing occurred...Tutti the heir was already asleep...I was nodding in the armchair...I was looking at the stars, testing my knowledge of astronomy...Then in the corridor there resounded heavy steps, the clanging of spurs...It was the changing of the guard...And suddenly a guardsman rushed into the bedroom...

GENERAL. What's that? A guardsman ran into the bedroom of our heir?

TUTTI. Yes! Yes! Yes! He broke in! Are you listening? The guard broke into my room...

TUTOR. It was terrible.

TUTTI. He noticed my doll...It was sitting in the armchair....Are you listening? Oh, if only you knew...The guardsman waved his saber...

CARDINAL. Do you hear that? There's your guards for you!

TUTTI. Don't interrupt.

GENERAL. Inconceivable...

TUTTI. Don't interrupt my story.

MILLER. There's your guards for you.

TUTTI. Quiet! Who's interrupting me? Shut up, do you hear? The guardsman sliced my doll with his saber...

CARDINAL. What's that?

MILLER. The guardsman?

CARDINAL. Ran it through?

MILLER. Our heir's doll?

GENERAL. That's impossible.

TUTOR. He shouted: "Enough of serving the Three Fat Men! Down with the gluttons!! Down with the three fat pigs!!" Alas, I understood the meaning of those words.

MILLER. Did you hear that? Treason, treason in the palace!

TUTTI (*sobbing, stuttering*). He stabbed my poor little girl with his saber and shouted: "So I've settled things with that puppet!" That is, with my doll—understand?—with my doll.

They all want to comfort him.

What? I ask you to be quiet! He called my doll a puppet...And then...and then the guardsman threw himself at me...

CARDINAL. The guardsman wanted to kill our heir?

GENERAL. Tutti! My dear Tutti.

MILLER. And you? What were you doing at the time, you old houseslipper?

TUTOR. I started shouting. I shouted terribly. I shouted so loudly that the geese in far-off villages called back...

TUTTI. Are you listening? He came at me with the saber and said: "Ah...the little wolf...ah...the wolf cub with the iron heart!"

TUTOR. He called the heir a wolf cub.

TUTTI. Shut up! I'm not a wolf cub! You're a giraffe! I'm not a wolf cub! Do your hear?! The guardsman called me a wolf cub...He said: "When the Three Fat Men kick the bucket, this wolf here will take their place..." Could I really be a wicked wolf? You hear—the guardsman wanted to run me through with his saber!

TUTOR. At that point the patrol arrived...But the criminal was able to escape. He jumped out the window. Look, he ripped open my nose with his spur.

TUTTI. What's your nose got to do with it? He's talking about his nose. I don't give a damn about your nose...My doll! My doll...She's got a dark hole in her chest. She's lying about like a rag...and you talk about your nose. My lovely doll! Do your hear? (*Furiously*). Do you hear? They killed my doll...What am I do do? I can't bear it! (*Cries*).

GENERAL. Treason! There's treason among the guards!

MILLER. Don't cry, heir, just look what a pie we've got here!

SELLER. That's it. Now they'll cut off my head.

TUTTI. Oh how dreadful! What's going to happen? She was so good...happy...she shone—you understand? She shone like a jasmine bush...She sang, she danced! Save her! Do you hear? Doctors! Doctors! Her heart is wounded.

CARDINAL. Don't carry on so, Tutti! You have an iron heart. You shouldn't cry.

TUTTI. Not true! Not true! I don't have an iron heart. My heart couldn't have been made of iron. Could an iron heart really feel pain? Oh how my heart aches...aches, like a tooth!

MILLER. The heir's sorrow is without bounds. The doll must be repaired.

GENERAL. We could buy a new one.

TUTTI. What? I don't want another one...I don't need another one...I want my own doll to be resurrected! Do you hear?

TUTOR. The great scientist Doctor Gaspar Arneri...if we entrust

150

him with it, he'll repair the doll...

TUTTI. Doctor! Doctor! Call the doctor!

TUTOR. Doctor Gaspar Arneri is the most learned man in the country. Many take him to be a sorcerer. He's learned a hundred sciences, invented a multitude of contraptions, he's a master of masks, puppets, fireworks and kites shaped like snakes. They say he can turn anyone into a chicken, or a bouquet, or a negro. Of course it's a rumor spread by students who didn't finish their studies, but in any case the people have composed a song about Doctor Gaspar that goes like this:

"How to fly from here to stars,
How to catch a fox by 's arse,
How rock with steam to pair—
Knows our good ol' doc Gaspar!"

TUTTI (*smiles through his tears*). It's a good song. Please ask Doctor Gaspar to cure my doll.

MILLER. You've got an iron heart. You shouldn't ask for anything. You should order. Very good. Take the doll to Doctor Gaspar Arneri immediately. He has to repair the doll. Give him twenty-four hours.

CARDINAL. Postpone the execution. Let Prospero be put to the torture. Give him a day and a night. We must find out how treason has penetrated into the palace.

TUTTI. We must find out how treason has penetrated into the palace.

MILLER. And now, at long last, the pie.

GENERAL. Cook, give the knife to our heir. He has an iron heart. It must be pleasant for him to hold a knife in his hand. Tutti, cut yourself a piece.

Tutti approaches the pie.

SELLER (*shouts*). Oh! Oh! Oh! Help! (*Jumps out of the pie, cream and candied fruit fly in all directions*).

Panic.

Oh! Oh! Oh! Save me! I want to live! I'm very life-loving! (*Runs, knocking over the heir*).

Panic. The assembled guests howl. The Three Fat Men howl. The General pulls out his saber.

SHOUTS. Treason!
Treason!
Treason!

Plates and fruit are flung at the Seller. He scatters balloons as he runs.

GENERAL. Stop the celebration! Put off everything! Call a council meeting! All civil servants, all judges, all ministers, all executioners! Postpone today's execution! Treason in the palace! Treason has penetrated into our food!
    SHOUTS. Hold him!
          Hold him!
          Hold him!

The Seller is chased around the palace. Finally he runs into the kitchen.

CURTAIN

EPISODE FIVE

The kitchen. The Seller has run into the kitchen.

SELLER (*agitated*). Save me! Save me! Why should I have to fly? I'm not a bird . . . Why do I have to sit in a pie? I'm not a pineapple! Why do I have to run? I'm not a horse. Why does fate torment me? I'm very unlucky.
    FIRST KITCHEN-BOY. What lovely balloons you have!
    SELLER (*agitated*). You think so, you little scoundrel! Maybe you'd like to eat them up?
    SECOND KITCHEN-BOY. Remarkable balloons.
    THIRD KITCHEN-BOY. Make me a present of one.
    FOURTH KITCHEN-BOY. Yes, this one.
    FIFTH KITCHEN-BOY. The pale blue one.
    SELLER. Have you gone mad? Oh how unhappy I am. They're pulling me to pieces . . .I want to sleep . . .They want to eat me. What do you want, snub nose? Cut me up! You want an ear? Or a hip? Or a heel? Eat up! Eat up! Only don't step on my corns.

Noise of approaching pursuit.

SELLER. Oh! They're running! Miller! Miller! He'll eat me! Oh save me . . .
    FIRST KITCHEN-BOY. In the first place, don't jump around on one leg.
    SECOND KITCHEN-BOY. You're not a ballerina, not even a heron.
    THIRD KITCHEN-BOY. In the second place, we can save you . . .
    FIFTH KITCHEN-BOY. If you give us your balloons.

FOURTH KITCHEN-BOY. You'll have to crawl into a saucepan.

SELLER. What's that? Where? First into a pie, and then into a saucepan? First in the cream and then in the soup? Oh what do they want from me...Have I been nominated for the plat du jour or something?

The noise comes closer.

Oh! The Miller is getting closer! Oh! How many feet does a pheasant have? Two? Three? How many feet has a miller? Oh, I'll lose my mind! Balloons! My dear balloons! Carry me away from here! I want to fly away. (*Jumps up and down*).

FIFTH KITCHEN-BOY. We're speaking quite seriously—crawl into the saucepan. This way. (*Takes the lid off a large saucepan*).

SELLER (*peers in*). Empty! It's empty! There's no bottom to it! It's dark like a well...

FIRST KITCHEN-BOY. Crawl in.

SECOND KITCHEN-BOY. It's an underground passage.

SELLER. Very well. I'll crawl in. It's all the same anyway. Well what a day I've had of it—first I fly under the clouds, and now I'm going to travel under the ground. I'm very undemanding. Well so long, youngster...

THIRD KITCHEN-BOY. Hey...no! Where are you going?

FOURTH KITCHEN-BOY. And the balloons? The balloons...Give us the balloons...

FIFTH KITCHEN-BOY. Otherwise we won't let you through...

KITCHEN-BOYS. Balloons!

Balloons!

Balloons!

SELLER. You'll get them! What kind for you? A blue one? Here. And you? A yellow one? Here you go! Here you go! They should only burst! (*Crawls into the saucepan. Out of the saucepan*). You should only blow up too! (*Disappears*).

The first kitchen-boy puts the lid on the pot.

KITCHEN-BOYS (*with balloons*). Balloons! Balloons! Balloons!

The pursuit tears into the kitchen. In their fear the kitchen-boys go running into the audience and let go of the balloons, which fly about the auditorium.

SHOUTS. Where is he?

Where is he?

Where is he?

They run into the audience after the kitchen-boys. They search.

Where is he?
Where is he?
Where is he?
Light! Give us some light!

A light is given.

ACT TWO

EPISODE SIX

The tower of Doctor Gaspar. Doctor Gaspar walks through the auditorium to the stage.

DOCTOR. I don't understand a thing...I don't see anything. This damned dancing teacher Onetwothrees, this person like a cross between a grasshopper and a squealing violin, this horrible personage with a head no bigger than an unripe pear, took away my wonderful glasses...Help me...I wandered about all night. I can't get home. I looked for a cab but couldn't find one. I mistook a respectable lady for a horse, although she looked more like a cow than a horse...Terrible...terrible...a dreadful night...it's awful to be near-sighted when historical events are taking place...Where's my tower? Where's my tower? Ah...Excuse me, if you please...I think I can smell a ham omelette...Yes, that's it, yes...I think I've found my house. Only an omelette cooked by my dear aunt Ganymede could smell like that. In that odor, valerian drops may be clearly sensed. Ah...Hurrah! Here's my tower. (*Mounts the stage. Searches for his glasses on the table and finds them.*). Whew...Well, I'll put my glasses on at last...That's it (*puts them on*), good. True, they're old glasses. But that's all right. Glasses don't have to be new, they're not slippers...Yes-s. I'll have a bit of omelette and then lie down for a rest, I didn't sleep the whole night. It's very difficult to sleep without glasses—you have to see your dreams, and I see very poorly without them.

A noise behind the Doctor. He looks around. Tibullus crawls out of the fireplace. Silence.

TIBULLUS. Your glasses are on now, Doctor Gaspar.
DOCTOR. My glasses are on, but I don't believe my eyes all the same. Only devils come crawling out of fireplaces. I'm a scientist and know there's no such thing as devils. Who are you?

154

TIBULLUS. Doctor, you are called a friend of the people.

DOCTOR. I'm a scientist, and a scientist cannot be a friend of the people.

TIBULLUS. If I were to shout: Long live Prospero the gunsmith, what would you do?

DOCTOR. I'd say that I was very happy. If you want to hail him, that means he is still alive. (*Pause*). It's still strange that you crawled out of a fireplace. Since there are no devils, you are apparently a chimney sweep.

TIBULLUS. Did you have occasion to see Uncle Brizak's travelling theater?

DOCTOR. I'm a scientist, a scholar. I don't have time for the theater.

TIBULLUS. Have you ever seen the tightrope walker Tibullus?

DOCTOR. Once. Yesterday evening. On Star Square. But without my glasses. I don't even know what color he is. And probably I'll never find out. The tightrope walker Tibullus was taken prisoner, most likely, and will be executed along with Prospero the gunsmith.

TIBULLUS. I am Tibullus the tightrope walker.

The Doctor adjusts his glasses. Silence.

DOCTOR. Long live Prospero the gunsmith!
TIBULLUS. Down with the Three Fat Men!

A handshake. Silence.

DOCTOR. Are they looking for you?

TIBULLUS. I clambered over the roofs like a cat. I managed it at night, when all cats are gray.

DOCTOR. I understand: you need to change your appearance.

TIBULLUS. If the gunsmith is executed, the poor will lose heart. The people will take fright, and the power of the Three Fat Men will seem to be unconquerable. I've got to free Prospero—but they're after me.

DOCTOR. When you slid down here you became half black. I'll help you to become completely black. Take off your clothes. There are rumors going round that I can turn a man into a pig, a bouquet or a negro. Those rumors are somewhat exaggerated.

A knock.

If I could turn people into pigs, then that's what I'd do to the Three Fat Men. If I could change a man into a bouquet, then I would have transformed that girl who cried out in such a clear voice in Star Square last night, though to judge by her voice the girl is such a charmer that there'd be no sense in turning her into a bouquet, since a bouquet of the most gorgeous flowers couldn't be better than a pretty, brave, noble girl . . . I'm not a sorcerer, fortunately. Long live negroes. I'll turn you into a negro.

TIBULLUS. That means you are a sorcerer.

DOCTOR. That isn't sorcery, tightrope walker, but exact science. A combination of acids, salts and alkali. Crawl into this barrel.

TIBULLUS. That's easy enough. Only don't do it wrong, doctor, don't turn me into a pig. (*Crawls into the barrel. From the barrel*). Because if you turn me into a pig, I won't be able to walk on a high wire.

A sound like a shot is heard behind the door.

DOCTOR. What's that? The guards are shooting. They're in our way. You won't have time to turn black and you'll be transformed into a zebra.

Auntie Ganymede runs in with a mousetrap.

What is this? Who's shooting? The guards?

AUNTIE. It's a mouse. A mouse. A mouse.

DOCTOR. Auntie Ganymede, you're talking nonsense. A pig can't walk on a tightrope and a mouse can't shoot.

AUNTIE. A mouse. A mouse. A mouse.

DOCTOR. If you keep going on like that, I'll turn you into a bouquet.

AUNTIE. Hurrah! Hurrah! Hurrah!

DOCTOR. If you keep on shouting, I'll turn you into a zebra.

AUNTIE. She got caught, my mouse. Here she is. I've been hunting for her for three days. She was the one who ate my cinnamon. And she spilled my valerian drops too . . .

DOCTOR. A mouse likes something sour, that's why it eats cinnamon. Let's have an omelette.

AUNTIE. All night I waited for you. You haven't caught cold? They didn't kill you?

DOCTOR. I'm hungry. Let's have an omelette.

AUNTIE. Coming up. Coming up. It's ready . . .

DOCTOR. Cook another one. Only don't add valerian drops instead of salt . . .

AUNTIE. What? Two omelettes?

DOCTOR. Yes. For two people.

AUNTIE. And who's the second?

Tibullus appears from the barrel, having been transformed into a negro.

Oh! Oh! Oh! (*Drops the mousetrap*). A negro!! An omelette! Oh! Oh! Oh! A mouse.

156

TIBULLUS. Don't be frightened, Auntie Ganymede. I'm not a zebra, a bouquet, or a pig. I'm the most harmless of negroes. And I want to eat an omelette.

AUNTIE. Oh! Oh! Oh! A mouse likes something sour, a negro likes an omelette. Give me some valerian drops. (*Rushes to the door*).

The Captain of the town guard and the Master of Ceremonies appear carrying a doll. Auntie Ganymede runs to the door, almost knocking them off their feet.

CAPTAIN. Where does Doctor Gaspar Arneri live? (*Raises his nose in the air*). Aha...judging by the smell (*sniffs*) of valerian drops, Doctor Gaspar Arneri lives here. Aha...Pleased to meet you...Are you Doctor Gaspar Arneri?

DOCTOR. I am Doctor Gaspar Arneri.

MASTER OF CEREMONIES. Stand up and pay attention.

CAPTAIN. Just a moment. Are there any outsiders here? (*Notices Tibullus*). Ah...a negro? What are you doing here, negro?

TIBULLUS. I'm not a negro. I'm a negro puppet.

DOCTOR. Yes, that's quite right. This is a negro puppet. And quite smart too. He knows himself that he's a puppet.

CAPTAIN. Hmm...So you're a puppet?

TIBULLUS. A puppet.

CAPTAIN. So you can't see anything?

TIBULLUS. Nothing.

CAPTAIN. And you can't hear anything?

TIBULLUS. Nothing.

CAPTAIN. Well then, everything is in order. Read.

MASTER OF CEREMONIES. Stand up and pay attention.

During the reading, Tibullus steals out of the room.

(*Reads*). "In the name of the government of the Three Fat Men, Doctor Gaspar Arneri is assigned to cure the doll of Tutti the heir by noon tomorrow. In the case of the successful fulfilling of the order, Doctor Gaspar Arneri has the right to any reward he desires; if the order is not fulfilled by Doctor Gaspar Arneri, he will be put in a cage which will be opened on the day of Prospero the gunsmith's execution."

DOCTOR. I have a question.

CAPTAIN. A question? Well, make it quick.

DOCTOR. I am a scientist and therefore express myself precisely and succinctly. Will Prospero the gunsmith be executed today?

CAPTAIN. The execution has been postponed until tomorrow. Unfortunately.

157

DOCTOR. You are not a scientist and therefore express youself carelessly. Not unfortunately, but fortunately.

CAPTAIN. Let's not fight. For such precise expressions I should arrest you. But then who would cure the heir's doll?

The Master of Ceremonies pulls back a cover. The doll is revealed.

DOCTOR. Ah...This girl really does look like a doll. Only her little face has grown pale and taken on a sad expression...You say she's unwell?

MASTER OF CEREMONIES. She has a hole in her chest.

DOCTOR. Oh, the poor little girl!

MASTER OF CEREMONIES. Not a little girl, a doll.

CAPTAIN. Let's not fight. The order is delivered. The doll must be well.

Noise, stamping, shouts.

What? Who? Why?

DOCTOR. It's Auntie Ganymede; she's been hunting a mouse.

AUNTIE (*runs in*). She darted in here. Hold her! (*Trips over a spur*). Oh, what long spurs. They're longer than a comet. Oh where's my mouse...my mouse.

CAPTAIN. Don't upset yourself. She's been captured.

AUNTIE. Where? Where?

CAPTAIN (*tapping his toe*). Right here...under my boot.

The mouse is under the Captain's boot.

Where's your mousetrap?

AUNTIE. See that, doctor...You're a great scientist, and you weren't able to capture the mouse. And here the captain caught her right away. Here's the mousetrap. (*Hands it over*).

CAPTAIN. Well now. Let's not fight. I'll open the cage and shut the prisoner up in it. (*Takes the mouse by the tail and shoves it into the mousetrap*). Done. Ha-ha. We've got experience in this business. Yesterday we caught Prospero the gunsmith and put him in a cage.

DOCTOR. To keep a mouse in a cage isn't difficult. But I, as a scientist, must inform you that it is much more difficult to keep a lion in a cage.

CAPTAIN. Ha-ha. Let's not fight. Goodbye. Madame, chop off your prisoner's head. (*Exit*).

Auntie Ganymede notices the doll for the first time.

AUNTIE (*greatly surprised*). What's this, doctor?

Enter the Captain.

CAPTAIN. One moment. Excuse me. Couldn't you sell me the negro puppet?

DOCTOR (*looking about, notices the absence of Tibullus*). Oh . . .it's already sold . . .

CAPTAIN. Excuse me . . .I'm sorry. (*Exit*).

AUNTIE. What's this, doctor?

DOCTOR. I don't know myself.

AUNTIE. A doll?

DOCTOR (*shouts*). It's a girl, a doll, a devil, a chimney sweep, a pig, a bouquet, a negro, a zebra, a puppet and an omelette.

Auntie Ganymede runs out, deafened, leaving the Doctor with the doll. The doll is the double of Suok.

DOCTOR (*looks at the doll*). I've seen you somewhere before, doll. No . . .Funny . . .Where could I have seen you, Tutti the heir's doll? (*Comes closer*). Her eyes are closed . . .Her hair is the color of little gray birds' feathers . . .Her dress . . .is it pink? No . . .if we say pink, we're not saying anything. Pink can be the color of soap or the tongue some little imp sticks out at you . . .Such an idiotic comparison. Oh, I know. If the doll came to life, got up and twirled round the room, then her dress would crackle and shine and give off a delicate perfume, like golden summer rain . . .(*Calls*). Doll! Doll! (*Pause*). Oh, how familiar her face is to me. Where have I seen you? It's as if I saw you not long ago through a mist, through a veil . . .My charming child . . .Oh, how I regret that I am not a sorcerer and cannot turn this delightful but dead bouquet into a living girl.

Auntie Ganymede looks in at the door. The stage slowly darkens. Lights gleam above the stove and lights of various colors appear in the Doctor's retorts above the crucibles.

Well, I'll begin the treatment. It's a dark wound. Who ran the doll through? Ah . . .it's the mark of a saber wound . . .I see. A guardsman stabbed the doll of Tutti the heir. (*Takes up his instruments*). Most likely she could sing and dance, possibly smiled, and without doubt she grew, developed in size, became prettier, like a live girl. A great master created this thing . . .All right . . .first we'll take out this spring . . .

The doll gets up.

159

AUNTIE. Oh! (*Slams the door shut*).

The doll sits down again.

DOCTOR (*in the direction of the door*). Auntie Ganymede, if you're going to get in my way, I'll turn you into an omelette and feed you to the negro.

The doll gets up. Her dress begins to shine. She moves rhythmically around the room. Delicate music comes from her.

Bravo! Bravo! Bravo! Auntie Ganymede, come here.

Auntie Ganymede sidles over timorously. She has noticed the doll. She sits down in the entryway, throwing up her hands.

Just look. Look. She's alive. In a moment we'll give her back the gift of speech...Give me that measuring-glass. Quick.
AUNTIE. I'm afraid...There's a negro sitting there.

The Doctor grabs the measuring-glass and performs some manipulations. The light becomes even brighter and the musical accompaniment still louder.

DOCTOR (*in a whisper*). Do you hear? Auntie...Do you? A great master created her...This is Tutti the heir's doll...Auntie...I'm terribly afraid...I don't understand a thing...I have the feeling that she was a living girl...and she was turned into a doll...(*Shouts*). Doll! Doll! Doll! Who are you?
DOLL (*sings*). Turn the arrow at my back,
        Twist the lever round,
        Tighten up the azure screw
        Until the silver ring is sound.
        Light I'll be, and supple too,
        Like a little fish, a vine,
        On my lips a smile will curve,
        And with joy my eyes will shine.
DOCTOR (*grasps Auntie Ganymede's hand and squeezes it*). Oh... did you hear that?
AUNTIE. She's asking you to turn the little screw...
DOCTOR. No...Not that...Her voice? Her voice?
AUNTIE. Well yes. She has a charming little voice.
DOCTOR. Auntie Ganymede...I heard that voice once before... Perhaps yesterday...Oh, how strangely disturbed I am...

160

AUNTIE. Twist the screw . . .She's asking . . .

DOCTOR. The screw . . .(*Looks for it*). What kind of screw? . . .Yes...
I'm so upset that I'm afraid I'll turn it the wrong way . . .Yes . . .I'm
turning it . . .

The doll turns around abruptly and hits the Doctor on his bald spot.

AUNTIE. What's the matter, doctor?

DOCTOR. That's what happened. I twisted it the wrong way . . .

AUNTIE. Twist it back quickly.

DOCTOR. I can't.

AUNTIE. Why not?

DOCTOR. That pig broke my glasses. I can't see anything. I'll wash
my eyes right away with a compound that strengthens vision.

The doll walks toward Auntie Ganymede.

AUNTIE. Oh! Oh! Oh! . . .She's walking.

The Doctor has lowered his head into a pot.

Oh! Oh! Oh! She's coming straight at me. Doctor, save me . . .

DOCTOR. Oh! I can't pull my head out... (*Lifts head along with pot*).

AUNTIE. Oh! (*Runs from the doll and hides in a barrel*).

*The doll suddenly staggers, crumples and falls. Onetwothrees has
crawled in through the window.*

DOCTOR. The devil take it, I don't like this. (*He has a clay pot on his
head*). Doll, where are you?

ONETWOTHREES (*squeakily*). I'm here.

DOCTOR. Don't move . . .

ONETWOTHREES (*in the same manner*). I don't care to remain in
the same place . . .

DOCTOR. How dare you disobey me?

ONETWOTHREES. Goodbye, old buffoon. I'm taking off.

DOCTOR. Don't you dare. Don't you dare. Hold her. Auntie
Ganymede, hold her. She has betrayed me.

Onetwothrees runs off with the doll. Silence.

Auntie Ganymede, what's happened? Where are you? Help me squeeze out
of this pot . . .

AUNTIE (*crawls out of the barrel, having turned into a negress*). Oh,
poor doctor . . .Just wait a moment! (*Pulls at the pot, but can't get it off*).

161

DOCTOR (*shouts*). Ouch...What are you doing? You'll pull my head off.

AUNTIE (*pulls*). O-o-one...I can't...Maybe with a poker...(*Takes a poker and smashes the pot with it*). O-o-one!

DOCTOR. Be more careful. If you break my head, I'll turn into a pig.

AUNTIE. Two!

The pot disintegrates. The Doctor sees that Auntie has turned into a negress.

Why are you looking at me that way? Did I turn into a bouquet or something?

DOCTOR (*roars*). Ah-ah-ah! Help! Help! Dolls, devils, negroes! (*Runs for the door*). I'll find you! I'll catch you! You can't run for long without a spring. Where is she? Where is she? Where are you, you damned doll? Oh, turn me into a pig, I've lost the doll. (*Runs out*).

AUNTIE. Incredible things are happening...(*Becomes thoughtful*). Why was it that the doctor looked at me so intently? Though I long ago noticed that the doctor was a little in love with me...(*Takes a mirror*). Of course, he's in love with me, that's it...(*Looks in the mirror*). Oh! (*Falls in a faint*).

The stage revolves. The town at night. Doctor Gaspar runs about in search of the doll. Onetwothrees is carrying the doll along the roofs. The Doctor bumps into the stage of the travelling circus from Act One.

CURTAIN

EPISODE SEVEN

The travelling circus.

DOCTOR (*looks in at the door*). May I come in? (*Goes in. Catches sight of Augustus, who is asleep, wrapped in a panther's skin. Becomes frightened*). Ah! A panther! I seem to have landed in a menagerie. (*Hides behind a drum*).

AUGUSTUS (*wakes up*). Who? Who's there? Guards? What a fearful night. How hard it's become to keep alert and to sleep. And it's all the fault of that tightrope walker Tibullus...The soldiers of the watch just about ruined our stage on Star Square...Now, because of that very same Tibullus, the guardsmen won't let us perform either day or night. It wasn't enough for him to walk the tightrope...now he wants to walk the sharp edge of an axe. (*Turns to the wall*).

162

The Doctor crawls out of the drum.

(*Jumps up*). Who's that? Spies?

The Doctor is frightened and sits down on the drum with a bang.

DOCTOR (*gets up, stands on the drum*). I will no longer . . .

Silence.

AUGUSTUS. A tiny little man who looked like a moon dweller is standing on a drum in a scarf, a cape and huge glasses. It seems I'm asleep and having a funny dream.
DOCTOR (*from the drum*). I'm not a spy . . .I'm a doll . . .That is, I'm Auntie . . .that is, Doctor Gaspar Arneri.
AUGUSTUS. Ah pleased to meet you. We know that you have good relations with the poor.
DOCTOR. Tell me, have I landed in a menagerie?
AUGUSTUS. No. You've landed in uncle Brizak's travelling theater. I'm uncle Brizak.
DOCTOR. Then why is there a panther here?
AUGUSTUS. Where?
DOCTOR (*points to the panther skin*). There . . .a spotted one . . .
AUGUSTUS. That spotted thing was once a panther, but now it's a blanket . . .Oh doctor . . .Once we had a panther who was called Lenore. I presented a trained panther to the public. She could juggle bottles and colored balls with her nose . . .Apart from that, she could put on spurred boots and do tricks with swords like a guardsman. Ah doctor . . .One time she almost bit off my hand . . .And now? Do you think a blanket could put on spurred boots? She died, our Lenore who had a skin like an astrologer's coat. You should feed a panther with raw meat . . .but we were poor, doctor . . . . We fed her potatoes . . .(*Cries from grief. Heaves the panther skin in the Doctor's direction and walks out*).

The Doctor is frightened. Sits down on the drum with a bang. Alina jumps out from behind the curtain.

ALINA. Who's here? What's that noise? Spies? (*Notices the Doctor sitting on the drum*). Oh . . .A spy? . . .Stop . . .Caught you, my friend. (*Pulls down a pistol from the wall*). Let's see. I'm one of the best shots in the country. You've never seen how I shoot? I can hit a bee buzzing round a rose. It's true my pistol is the worse for wear . . .But I can easily hit you in that barrel. Don't move. (*Raises the pistol*). I'll shoot.

163

Sound of a misfire. The Doctor jumps.

Misfire. Again. I'm taking aim.

Sound of a misfire. The Doctor jumps.

Misfire. Again. I'm taking aim.

Sound of a misfire. The Doctor jumps.

DOCTOR. Am I dead or did you have another misfire?

Augustus enters.

ALINA. A misfire. I've told you, Augustus, that you can't fire a pistol like that one.

DOCTOR. You have to feed pistols raw meat, and you feed it potatoes.

ALINA (*to Augustus*). Who's this?

DOCTOR. I'm a scientist, but I would like to become an actor in your theater.

ALINA. Is it so bad to be a scientist?

DOCTOR. Accept me into your troupe . . .I'll be a conjurer . . .I know chemistry and physics . . .I have to quit being a scientist . . .I've got to hide . . .

AUGUSTUS. Oh, doctor, that means the guards are after you too.

DOCTOR. I was assigned the task of curing Tutti the heir's doll. I began to treat her, but before I could finish she fled from me. I pulled out one of her springs and she most likely collapsed and is lying like a rag in some side street by now.

Suok comes out from behind the small curtain. The Doctor sits down on the drum, stands up, sits down again.

SUOK. Why is that little man jumping on the drum? Am I dreaming all this, Augustus? Or is it really happening?

Silence.

DOCTOR. The doll! The doll! Tutti the heir's doll!

AUGUSTUS. I don't understand anything.

DOCTOR. But I understand it all. Where is your enchanting dress? Do you want to make a blanket of it?

164

Silence.

SUOK. A very strange little man. First he jumps on the drum and now he's calling me Tutti the heir's doll.

DOCTOR. Don't play the innocent with me....

SUOK. I'm not a doll, I'm a girl.

DOCTOR. Don't put me on. You're a doll. I recognized you right away even though you managed to change your clothes. I recognized your voice—you couldn't forget that, having once heard it. Well, pull yourself together...I'm very happy that you're well. Oh you naughty little mouse...So you pretended to be ill on purpose...I'm very happy. Quick! Get ready! It's a long way to the palace. If we go now we can get there on time. At noon we'll present ourselves before the Three Fat Men.

SUOK. I'm not a doll. I'm a girl. I'm an actress and I'm called Suok.

Tibullus the negro enters.

(*Screeches*). A negro!

TIBULLUS. You're frightened? Suok, people who work in the circus must not know fear. Don't you recognize me? Augustus, open your eyes. It's me—Tibullus.

SUOK. How handsome you are. I didn't think that negroes were so beautiful. You're probably the most handsome negro in the world...

ALINA. Only he smells of burnt cork.

SUOK. That's just negro eau de cologne...

DOCTOR. It's not cork and not perfume, but a combination of acids.

SUOK. Hello, my dear tightrope walker. I dreamt that you and Prospero the gunsmith were taken to execution...I cried, I howled, I threw myself on the executioners, I scratched them...

TIBULLUS. The execution is postponed. They're going to execute him tomorrow.

AUGUSTUS. We've got to escape, Tibullus. Or else they'll capture you too.

TIBULLUS. We've got to rescue Prospero. But how to do it?

DOCTOR. I know how to do it.

SUOK. I do too...I think I can guess...

DOCTOR. Do you have a fancy dress?

SUOK. Hooray! Hooray! Hooray! I guessed...Listen to me, black-skin...They ordered Doctor Gaspar to cure Tutti the heir's doll.

DOCTOR. I wasn't successful. I only half cured her...

ALINA. And then she ran away.

SUOK. It came out afterwards that Tutti the heir's doll looks like me...

DOCTOR. ...and so, seeing little Suok...

AUGUSTUS. . . .Doctor Gaspar took her for a doll . . .

DOCTOR. Really, the likeness is so striking . . .

AUGUSTUS. . . .that you could call it a miracle.

DOCTOR. There are no miracles. Science calls miracles by the magnificent name of phenomena . . .But this likeness was rather spoilt, my charming phenomenon. The doll was pale and sad and had a wound in her chest . . .But you . . .are cheerful and coquettish, you shake your hair and your eyes sparkle . . .And then . . .the doll was so fancily dressed that she looked like a princess or, at the very least, like a toy on a Christmas tree.

TIBULLUS. Let's not waste time. I've got it now. You'll go to the palace of the Three Fat Men and play the role of Tutti the heir's doll.

SUOK. And as far as the dress goes, like a Christmas tree toy, I can assure you that the dress, you know, Tibullus, the one I sewed from the Spanish flag . . .

DOCTOR. Bravo! Bravo! To hell with princesses and Christmas tree toys. Put your Spanish flag dress on quickly . . .and we'll make a blanket from the Christmas tree toys. And we'll feed the princess raw meat . . .

SUOK. Well now I'm content! We'll save you, Prospero.

DOCTOR. Ah!

TIBULLUS. What's the matter?

DOCTOR. I just remembered . . .I know . . .I recognized it . . .It was your voice I heard on Star Square when the gunsmith was taken prisoner . . .Why was the doll singing in your voice?

SUOK. A phenomenon, doctor. I'll put on my dress now. I'll put my dress on now. It looks so good on me, you know, that it shines and crackles . . .I feel like eating myself, like a caramel.

ALINA. Hurry, Suok.

DOCTOR. You aren't frightened, my child?

TIBULLUS. Suok, remember how we walked the tightrope. We stood on a tower. I got down on one knee and you stood on it. I said, "Allez!"— were you awfully frightened?

SUOK. No I wasn't. When you said, "Allez!" it meant I should be ready, calm.

TIBULLUS. Suok, I'm saying, "Allez!" to you now. You will save Prospero the gunsmith!

SUOK. I want to kiss you, doctor. I've got to do it now because when I put on my new dress that looks like a pound of caramel I won't want to wrinkle it. (*Runs up to the Doctor, who is sitting on the drum, and embraces him*).

Suddenly the drum rises up and overturns. The head of the Balloon Seller sticks out of the ground. Silence.

ALINA. What's this? A spy? Where's my pistol? I'll smash this teapot

166

decorated with daisies right now.

SELLER. I'm not a teapot. I'm a phenomenon.

Silence.

Pull me out, please don't be shy. Grab me by the cheeks and pull. I'm very malleable.

TIBULLUS (*pulls him out of the ground*). Now, tell us quickly where you've come from.

SELLER. And you won't eat me?

TIBULLUS. I don't eat raw meat.

SELLER. I began by selling balloons. Then I flew. Then I sat in a pie. Then they wanted to cut off my heel. Then I crawled into a saucepan. There was an underground passage from the pot. Then I crawled along underground. Then it turned out that the underground passage ended here. That's the whole story.

TIBULLUS. The underground passage ends here, but where does it begin?

SELLER. It begins in the palace of the Three Fat Men, in the kitchen, in that big saucepan with a picture of a red lobster on it. Perhaps you would be interested to know where the key to Prospero the gunsmith's cage is to be found? Tutti the heir has it. And that's all. I'm very precise.

SUOK. And very simpatico. (*Kisses the Seller on the lips*).

SELLER. And very tasty.

SUOK. Where's my Spanish flag dress? Alina, close the curtain. I'm going to change clothes.

CURTAIN

ACT THREE

EPISODE EIGHT

The Palace of the Three Fat Men. Sunset. A group looks at the road from the tower.

TUTTI. Are they coming? Please concentrate—are they coming or not?

TUTOR (*looks through binoculars*). I'm a teacher of geography and therefore I have a better understanding than others of such concepts as horizon, mirage and so forth. In my opinion, they're coming.

TUTTI (*jumping up and down*). They're coming! They're coming!

TUTOR. Don't jump like that or you'll go over the top. Although a teacher of gymnastics has been stationed below to catch you in flight, he may have fallen asleep under a bush as he's lazy . . .

TUTTI. They're coming. I can see now. (*Grabs the binoculars from the geography teacher*). Hurrah! (*Throws down the binoculars*). That's so the teacher of gymnastics will wake up. Wake up, they're coming. Why haven't bouquets been prepared? I'll order the whole garden to be cut and brought to Doctor Gaspar. He can spend the rest of his life sniffing it.

TUTOR. We may conclude that the doll is completely recovered. She's walking unaided, and she seems to be laughing.

TUTTI. Do you hear that? My doll is coming back!

Music. Suok steps into the palace, behind her Doctor Gaspar walks with mincing steps.

TUTTI. Hello.

Suok is playing the doll. Astonishment. Applause.

She is completely cured. I don't believe my eyes, doctor.

DOCTOR. I've dressed her in a new dress.

TUTTI. It's green. It's pink. It's white. It's scarlet. It looks like a rainbow that's won the prize in a rainbow competition.

DOCTOR. I've improved her voice.

TUTTI. Let her sing something.

SUOK (*sings*). By some mysterious science
        Fanning in crucibles its flare,
        To life I was brought back again
        By worthy Doctor Gaspar here.
        Just look at me, my lips have smiled,
        And did you hear, I sighed.
        And once again I stand up straight,
        Most wondrously revivified.
        I've rushed to you through all my life,
        Down many mingled roads I came—
        So don't forget your sister Suok,
        Your sister Suok's sweet name.
        Without you I have sorely pined,
        And, slipping into silent sleep,
        Have seen you in a tender dream,
        Have seen you sigh for me and weep.
        Just look at me, my lashes tremble,
        A wisp of hair curls on my brow.
        Don't forget your little sister,
        The name of Suok keep with you now.

TUTTI (*repeats*). Suok...Suok...What a fine name...When I repeat it I feel like laughing and crying at once, as if I had a cold in the head and was eating cake...

The Three Fat Men approach. A procession.

GENERAL. Very good. I see that Tutti the heir is satisfied.

CARDINAL. You are truly a great scientist. I would like to ask you a question, doctor. As you can see, I've got a wart here. A flower has grown out of it, doctor.

DOCTOR. It's a petunia.

MILLER. Judging by the size of your wart, you can expect a sunflower to grow there next year.

CARDINAL. I want to ask you, doctor, how can I go about getting rid of this wart?

SUOK. It's best to get rid of the entire head at the same time...

Silence.

GENERAL. Who said that?

MILLER. The doll did.

GENERAL. Let's not fight. Dolls can't talk.

CARDINAL. And so it was an illusion.

DOCTOR. Yes, an illusion. Let's not fight. We'll postpone the execution of the wart by two days.

TUTTI. The doctor should get a reward. He cured my doll.

DOCTOR. I beg you to revoke the death sentence on Prospero and all the rebels.

Panic. Indignation.

GENERAL. Prospero the gunsmith will be executed tomorrow.

Suok begins to tremble, droops—she has gone wrong.

TUTTI. Oh doctor! Doctor! She's broken again. (*Rushes to pick up the doll, which collapses*).

DOCTOR. If my request is not granted, the doll will be completely ruined. The fact is, that when I was working on the repair of her mechanism, my thoughts were preoccupied with the forthcoming execution...I was very upset...And my nervous tension was communicated to the sensitive substance from which the mainspring is made...Do you understand me?

TUTTI. Explanations are unnecessary. I demand that the doctor's

169

request be granted.

MILLER (*leading the Cardinal aside*). We'll pretend to agree. Say, "Very well, the rebels will be pardoned." What does it matter? Let the boy calm down. And then we'll see.

CARDINAL. Very well. We will grant Doctor Gaspar's request. Prospero the gunsmith and the other rebels will not be executed. Execution will be replaced by life imprisonment in the menagerie.

GENERAL. Let's not fight.

TUTTI. Bravo! Bravo!

The doll comes to life.

MILLER. The ceremony may be considered at a close.

DOCTOR. Goodbye, dear doll.

TUTTI. Farewell, farewell.

All leave except Suok and Tutti.

I'm terribly hungry. I'll have some cake now. I'll eat this here...with grapes. (*Eats*). And now this here...with cream.

SUOK. I want some cake too.

Tutti drops the cake in fright.

The last time I had cake was a year and a half ago. But Augustus said it wasn't really cake but pastry.

Tutti is silent, amazed by Suok's ability to speak.

SUOK (*eats one cake, a second and a third*). Why are you looking at me like that?

TUTTI. I don't understand a thing...

SUOK. I'll have one more. This one...with grapes.

TUTTI. You didn't talk before.

SUOK. You can thank Doctor Gaspar; he taught me how to talk. And to eat cake.

TUTTI. That's remarkable.

SUOK. He also taught me to see dreams.

TUTTI. Oh how interesting.

SUOK. He repaired my heart and made me lie down motionless for half an hour. And I fell asleep. I had a dream; I dreamt that I became a living girl.

TUTTI. What does that mean?

SUOK. Listen further. I was a real live girl, a circus actress...I worked in Uncle Brizak's travelling theater. I could do acrobatic tricks, I played in pantomines . . .it was so interesting. The theater travelled from place to place. We would stop in green meadowlands, slap together a wooden stage . . .The wind would stir the colored rags we used instead of flags . . .The peasants would come from near and far in their striped leggings, fishermen, hunters. We performed only for the poor. When the landowner on whose land we had stopped would drive up in his carriage, we would get our horns and blow them for all we were worth. The horns would blare, the horses would rear, the landowner would stop his ears with his fists . . .and take off. We didn't care for the rich at all.

TUTTI. And what does that mean?

SUOK. Once a rich miller forced me to eat unripe pears because I had got into his garden. "It's not your garden, it's my garden," he said.

TUTTI. And what does that mean?

SUOK. Last week we were in the town of Till. We performed in the harbor. I saw war vessels going out to sea. The sailors had revolted against the rich and the gluttons.

TUTTI. What does that mean?

SUOK. We put on a big show for the sailors there in the port. I played a waltz on apricot pits.

TUTTI. What does that mean?

SUOK. You can make whistles out of apricot pits. I made twelve whistles and whistled a waltz.

TUTTI. Oh how interesting. Too bad you don't have any on hand. You could show me.

SUOK. I can whistle with the help of a key.

TUTTI. I have a key. Here it is. See? (*Unbuttons his coat and takes a key from a chest pocket*).

SUOK. Ah good, give it here. Now listen. (*Whistles a waltz*).

TUTTI. I could listen forever. It's so beautiful. But I feel very tired, I want to sleep. You didn't talk before, didn't eat cake, didn't whistle waltzes.

SUOK. You shouldn't get tired—after all, you have an iron heart.

TUTTI (*nodding off in the armchair*). And what . . .does that . . . mean?

SUOK (*alone*). And now I've got to find the way to the menagerie. (*Goes out*).

The Miller, the General and the Cardinal enter.

MILLER. He should sleep all night and all day tomorrow.

CARDINAL (*shows a phial*). We have to give him three drops in the ear from this phial. It's very simple. He'll sleep without waking for a whole day.

Approaches Tutti and bends over his ear.

One, Two. Three.

GENERAL. That's it.

MILLER. The gunsmith will be executed tomorrow. And when the boy wakes up . . .let him bleat like a lamb if he wants to.

Suok walks through the palace. At the entrance a guardsman on duty is asleep. At his feet is a lantern. Suok creeps up on tiptoe.

GUARD. What the devil? Isn't that just wonderful? It's incredible that a soldier should have such a magical dream . . .a doll goes strolling round the palace . . .Amazing. How d'you like that! A live girl . . .nothing less. But it was a dream . . .a dream . . .I've lived in this world a long time, and this is the first time I've had an interesting dream. Usually I dream of ordinary things: a boot, a cookie, a shovel, a cow . . .And then all at once such beauty. If only I hadn't woken up.

SUOK. You don't have to wake up. (*Takes the lantern. Plucks a rose from her dress and plants it in the strap of the guardsman's helmet*). You won't wake up? I'll come back right away and check.

GUARD. All right. The devil!—of course I'll sleep. If I wake up this beautiful rose will disappear . . .It's the first time I've dreamt of a rose. And I always dreamt of ordinary things: a roof beam, hair in a nostril, plaster . . .

SUOK (*takes the lantern and goes into the menagerie. It is dark. The lantern swings in her hand. Shadows swirl*). Where is he? Am I frightened? Nonsense. I'm not afraid. People who work in the circus shouldn't know what fear is.

A voice from the cage: "Suok!" Silence. In the cage, Tub.

SUOK. Who's calling me? Is that you, Prospero?

TUB. I'm not Prospero.

SUOK. Who are you?

TUB. I'm dying, Suok . . .I'm cold, so cold . . .Everything is written here . . .Take this board . . .Farewell, Suok . . .Farewell . . .

Suok takes the board. Silence.

SUOK (*screams*). He's dead! (*Drops the lantern*).

Darkness.

VOICE OF PROSPERO. Suok! Suok! I'm here. I knew you would save me.

172

Noise. Lanterns at the entrance to the menagerie. The Three Fat Men and Onetwothrees with the real doll. The guardsman is asleep.

ONETWOTHREES. It's treason. A cunning plot. Here's the doll, here's the real doll, poor thing. I found her lying in the street like a pink rag . . . Doctor Gaspar smuggled the actress Suok into the palace.

CARDINAL. It's the girl who ordered me to be drowned ten years ago.

MILLER. Treason! Treason! Search her out! Where is she? Execute her!

ONETWOTHREES. I believe I've acted in a way deserving of reward. I think you should appoint me court dancing instructor.

CARDINAL. We must immediately search the palace, we've got to ransack the place.

ONETWOTHREES. I think you should reward me. I would like . . .

CARDINAL. Devil take it, I've had enough of you. What is it you'd like? A present? A trophy? Music? Flowers? Here you are then—a flower from me, devil take it. (*Pulls the flower out of his wart*). Here, smell it.

Onetwothrees sits down on a small column and smells the flower.

GENERAL. Let's not fight. You got your reward.

GUARD (*wakes up and jumps to attention*). Concerning flowers . . .

GENERAL. Why do you have a rose in your helmet? What is it? A new uniform? (*Pulls off the rose*).

GUARD. What? A rose? Didn't she disappear? She tricked me. I'm naturally stupid. The doll tricked me. Damn. She's in the menagerie, look for her there. (*Sits down*). Oh you fool, you fool . . . Why did I betray such a nice girl . . . Can't be helped, I'm naturally stupid.

ALL. To the menagerie!
    To the menagerie!

A general rush.

CARDINAL. General, why are you running with a rose, like a girl?

GENERAL. Let's not fight. I present the rose to you. Stick it in your wart.

Prospero emerges from the menagerie, carrying Suok on his shoulders. A panther bounds along beside them. Everyone falls back.

SHOUTS. A panther!
    A panther!
    Back!

PROSPERO. Make way!

SUOK (*to the guardsman*). What, you woke up before you were supposed to? I did ask you to wait.

CARDINAL. The doll! The doll! The devil is carrying the doll.

SUOK. Where are your scissors, Onetwothrees? Cut off his wart.

Everyone runs.

GENERAL. Guard! Guard! Guard!

SUOK. Into the kitchen! Quickly! There's a saucepan there . . . An underground passage.

They run.

CURTAIN

EPISODE NINE

The kitchen. Prospero and Suok are running. Frightened cooks and kitchen-boys hide in a corner.

SHOUTS. The doll!
    Damn!
    The doll's come to life!

SUOK. Here she is! Here she is!

PROSPERO (*takes the lid off the saucepan*). Climb in. I'll be after you.

Suok climbs into the saucepan.

Well?

SUOK. It's the wrong saucepan. It's got a bottom. I made a mistake.

The pursuit rushes in. Onetwothrees, the General, guardsmen. Prospero is seized by the guardsmen.

ONETWOTHREES (*slams the lid over Suok*). Stop! Caught you, little bird—you won't get out of this net.

GENERAL. Yes-s. Excellent. We've got them.

Prospero struggles.

Hold him tight. Is he breaking loose? All right then, stick him in the saucepan until reinforcements arrive. In this one here.

The guards lower Prospero into a saucepan and close the lid.

That's it. (*Bangs on the lid*). Sit still, pheasant. We'll make you into a soup.

The Miller and the Cardinal run in.

MILLER (*puffing*). Whew . . .ooh . . .The panther has been chasing us around the entire palace . . .
CARDINAL. It'll come running in here any minute.
GENERAL. Guards, get your pistols ready. The doll has been captured. The gunsmith has been captured. Now we'll capture the panther.
MILLER. Everything's clear. The girl stole the key from our heir and opened the cage. The gunsmith let the panther loose to scare us and to clear an escape route for himself.
CARDINAL. We shouldn't shoot the panther. It's a rare specimen. We should capture it alive.
GENERAL. We'll leave that to the gunsmith. He knew how to let it loose, so let him catch it.
ONETWOTHREES. And let the girls applaud him.

They both lift off saucepan lids. Suok sits in a saucepan.

GENERAL. Crawl out then, animal trainer. Let's not fight. (*Looks into the saucepan*). He's not there. The saucepan has no bottom. Prospero has escaped.
SUOK. Bravo, Prospero! Bravo, Prospero!

The panther appears. Squeals, shouts. The panther runs to the saucepan.

CARDINAL. Capture it alive.
GENERAL (*grabs the panther by the tail, a piece of hide is left in his hand*). Let's not fight. Goodbye. (*Disappears*).

Silence.

ONETWOTHREES (*pulls Suok out of the saucepan by the hair*). You'll answer for all this.
CARDINAL. We'll instigate an investigation and trial.
MILLER. Ten years ago I was ordered to drown you. You remained alive. This time it will be different. Put her under guard. I'll be your executioner myself.

175

The Executioner appears, wearing black and in a mask. Suok closes her eyes in fear.

EXECUTIONER. Who summoned the executioner?

ONETWOTHREES. I think you're shaking, little kitten. Here's the exeuctioner. Just look what a well-built and elegant fellow he is—he seems to be in better shape than your Tibullus. You've been sitting in a saucepan, chickadee—well, here's your cook.

EXECUTIONER. Who summoned the executioner?

GENERAL. Yes...We summoned him.

EXECUTIONER. I'm Horatio the executioner. I was called from the city of Bourbona for the execution of Prospero the gunsmith and the rebels. I was informed that the execution will take place tomorrow. Why was I summoned ahead of time?

CARDINAL. There's the girl. Take her. We assign you to guard her.

GENERAL. Mr. Executioner, keep a close eye on her. She was drowned, but she didn't drown...She was a doll and became a girl...It seems that she's the devil himself.

EXECUTIONER. Come over here, little girl. She won't run away, that I guarantee. Come here, little one...Oh you little mousey...You've been naughty, and now you're crying. Come here then, under my black wing. Don't be afraid, don't be afraid.

SUOK. I'm not afraid. I'm not afraid. I set free the gunsmith Prospero and now I can die...(*Weeps*).

The Executioner takes hold of her; she struggles and scratches.

Tibullus! Darling Tibullus! Where are you, Tibullus? Save me!

The Executioner carries Suok.

GUARD. Take this too, or before you can blink this puppet will turn into a girl.

The Executioner carries off the doll and Suok.

MILLER. Call the heralds. Announce the trial!

CURTAIN

ACT FOUR

EPISODE TEN

Suok's trial.

GENERAL. I've just received the report. There was a rumor going around the capital that war-ships from the city of Till were coming to aid the gunsmith and the rebels. What an idiotic rumor. Even if the ships came, our coastal batteries would open fire and the ships from the city of Till would sink like a bunch of kittens.

CARDINAL. But don't you think that...Listen to me...Doesn't it seem to you that the town is buzzing...as if thousands of voices were singing a song...buzzing.

GENERAL. Quite right. You get an impression that we're sitting inside a guitar and someone is plucking the bass string.

MILLER. Rubbish. It's because we all slept badly. Enough. It seems you're beginning to be afraid of the man known as the leader who lost his pants. Enough. It's time to begin the trial. There's the cage in front of us. It's the cage where Prospero the gunsmith was imprisoned. Now Suok is there. As you can see, the cage hasn't gone empty. Mr. Executioner, open the cage and bring out Suok.

The Executioner opens the cage and carries out Suok, whom he seats before the court. He stands beside her.

GENERAL. Call the witnesses.

Enter the Distinguished Lady, the Tailor and Onetwothrees.

DISTINGUISHED LADY. Ah, here she is, the famous actress... Where's that pertness of yours? She's silent. Ha-ha-ha! She's pale.

GENERAL. Let's not fight. She's afraid.

CARDINAL. Well give us an answer then; how did you deceive Tutti the heir and obtain the key?

Suok is silent.

MILLER. Doesn't she hear? Mr. Executioner, give her ear a tug.

The Executioner pulls Suok's ear.

GENERAL. Pull the other one.

177

The Executioner pulls the other one.

DISTINGUISHED LADY. Pull the third one.
GENERAL. Madame, you are talking nonsense. A pheasant has two legs, a man two ears.
MILLER. Your silence irritates me.
CARDINAL. Perhaps she is talking, but so softly that we can't hear?
GENERAL. Let's not fight. She doesn't wish to speak.
MILLER. Mr. Executioner! Give her a slap on the forehead.

The Executioner smacks Suok.

CARDINAL. Once more.
ONETWOTHREES. Will you allow me?
DISTINGUISHED LADY. Bravo! Bravo! Smack her, Onetwo-threes.

Onetwothrees strikes a pose, does a pirouette and delivers a slap—the doll trembles. Onetwothrees bows.

TAILOR. Excellent. That sent the sparks flying.
CARDINAL. Now we'll ask her about something else. Let's try. Ten years ago an order was given—to drown you. How did you manage to avoid your fate?
Suok is silent.

TAILOR. Why does she keep silence? Once I heard her sing a song in the square. A song about a dumpling that agreed to be cooked, but only on condition that it wouldn't wind up in the stomach of someone rich. She sang very clearly. Where is that voice of yours? Perhaps we should entreat you? Caress you? I'll caress you if you like . . .with a hot iron.
CARDINAL. Just one moment. Do you hear that buzzing? I have a feeling that we're sitting inside a bomb.
MILLER. It only seems that way to you. You slept badly.
CARDINAL. I'll ask the executioner. He, no doubt, slept well last night. Mr. Executioner, don't you hear a certain buzzing around here . . .a buzzing that's getting louder?
EXECUTIONER. That's my iron heart buzzing.

Silence.

MILLER. I don't see any reason to continue this interrogation. I'll write the sentence right now. (*Writes. He is dictated to in exclamations; he helps himself to write with exclamations of his own*).

178

GENERAL. The main thing is—she set Prospero the gunsmith free!

MILLER. She deceived the heir!

DISTINGUISHED LADY. She insulted distinguished ladies and gentlemen!

TAILOR. She sang insulting ditties!

ONETWOTHREES. She entertained the poor!

MILLER. I'll read out the sentence. (*Reads*). "The sham doll by means of deceit penetrated into the palace and, taking advantage of the credulity of Tutti the heir, released from his cage the chief rebel and enemy of the Three Fat Men, Prospero the gunsmith. The impostor is sentenced to death. Let her be quartered, and, having been quartered, let her be thrown into the pool where the sharks live! Let her quartered body be devoured by sharks."

TAILOR. Bravo! Excuse me, madame. When I'm overjoyed I begin to hiccup.

ONETWOTHREES. Do you hear, Suok? They're going to quarter you. That means that first they'll pull off one arm . . .

TAILOR. And then the other . . .

DISTINGUISHED LADY. And then the third.

GENERAL. Madame, don't talk nonsense.

MILLER. Mr. Executioner, begin your work.

EXECUTIONER. Very well. (*Stands over the pool*). One! (*Tears off one of Suok's arms*).

VOICES. Bravo!
Bravo!

ONETWOTHREES. Why don't you scream, Suok? Scream! Call out! Call for help! Call for the help of Tibullus!

EXECUTIONER. Two! (*Pulls off the other arm*).

VOICES. Bravo!
Bravo!

CARDINAL. She doesn't scream. A stubborn girl!

MILLER. Mr. Executioner, throw her into the pool. Maybe she'll scream when a shark bites off her head.

VOICES. Excellent idea!
Bravo!

The Executioner throws the doll into the pool. Everyone rushes over to look.

TAILOR. Look, look! A large shark has seen her . . . Good . . . Good . . . Very interesting . . . The large shark is opening its mouth . . .

ONETWOTHREES. Snap! The shark bit off her head.

CARDINAL. She didn't scream . . .

DISTINGUISHED LADY. Why don't you scream, Suok! Scream!

Call the ships from the city of Till! Maybe they'll save you!

A cannon blast.

MILLER. What could that be?
CARDINAL. Mr. Horatio, what was that?
EXECUTIONER. That was the ships from Till.
MILLER. That's not possible! It's a lie!
ONETWOTHREES. I'll go look right now. Let me through. (*Runs to the tower*).
MILLER. Quiet! Quiet! Listen, he'll tell us. Well, what? What do you see?
GENERAL. Rubbish. What could he possibly see? Ships from the city of Till—that's a fairytale.
MILLER. Well, what? What? Do you see ships?
GENERAL. Give him some spectacles.
DISTINGUISHED LADY (*runs to the tower*). Here, I have excellent glasses. These are the glasses which Doctor Gaspar kindly brought me on Star Square. (*Puts on glasses and looks*). I see . . .
VOICES. What?
What?
What?
DISTINGUISHED LADY. I see . . . one, two, three, four . . . I see ten ships.

A cannon shot.

GENERAL. We're done for. (*Falls in a faint*).
CARDINAL. Doctor! Doctor!

Enter Doctor Gaspar with two pistols.

You're right on time, doctor. The General has fainted. He slept badly last night. Give him an injection of something.
DOCTOR. Unfortunately, I don't have any syringes at hand.
CARDINAL. But those things you're holding in your hands—aren't they syringes?
DOCTOR. These are pistols. I request that you all raise your hands. Hands up!

Silence.

ONETWOTHREES. What are you listening to the old man for? We'll quarter the old goat.

180

MILLER. Doctor Gaspar, you are a great scientist, and great men have their eccentricities. You got it into your head to go about with pistols. It's very funny, but we're not disposed to laugh. Get the hell out of here!

DOCTOR. I'm aiming at a rose flying around a bee. Or rather, the reverse. Doesn't matter...Hands up!

GENERAL (*regaining consciousness*). Let's not fight. Let's put them up.

DOCTOR. The guards have gone over to the side of the people. Ships from the city of Till have sailed into port. The capital is in the hands of the rebels. I was authorized to arrest you and guard you until the arrival of Prospero the gunsmith.

Again a cannon blast. Enter Prospero, representatives of the people, among whom are Alina and the Seller of Balloons. The guard stands watch.

MILLER. It's a revolution! Get back!

CARDINAL. Stop that howling. We slept badly last night. It only seems to be happening.

MILLER. It seems to me that you're an old fool.

DOCTOR. I request a word.

PROSPERO. Quiet. Let Doctor Gaspar Arneri speak!

DOCTOR. I think the Three Fat Men should be put in the cage.

SHOUTS. In the cage!
  In the cage!
  In the cage!

CARDINAL. Are we going to fight or aren't we?

GENERAL. Let's not fight.

SHOUTS. In the cage!
  In the cage!
  In the cage!

The Fat Men are chased into the cage.

GENERAL (*from the cage*). As you see, the cage is never empty.

MILLER. I request a word.

DOCTOR. Shall we let him speak, gunsmith?

PROSPERO. Let the miller speak.

MILLER. Perhaps you'd like to see the girl who saved you, Suok?

SHOUTS. Suok!
  Suok!
  Where's Suok?

PROSPERO. Where is Suok?

MILLER. Mr. Executioner, perhaps you could relate to our leader of the populace what became of the little dancer, Suok?

EXECUTIONER. I threw her into the pool as food for the sharks.

Pause.

PROSPERO. You did that? You dared?
VOICES. Death!
  Death!
  Kill him!
  Death to the Executioner!
PROSPERO. You dared? (*Seizes the Executioner by the collar. His cape falls from him. It is Tibullus*).
SHOUTS. Tibullus!
  Tibullus!
  Tibullus!

Tibullus opens the wall clock and takes Suok out of a box.

SHOUTS. Suok!
  Suok!
  Suok!
SUOK. Well here I am. Hello Prospero.
DOCTOR. This has to be investigated. Ever since dolls began turning into girls, tightrope walkers into negroes, executioners into tightrope walkers, the defeated into the victors—it has become necessary to subject each event to careful analysis. Too bad I don't have a certain pair of glasses. Although, allow me, allow me...good day, madame...If I'm not mistaken, these are my glasses. Alina, take the glasses off from her. (*The glasses are taken off the Distinguished Lady*).
DOCTOR (*puts them on*). So. Very good. (*Goes over to Suok*). But it's not enough. I'll get my listening tube. (*Gets his stethoscope*). I'll have a listen. Yes, it's the real Suok. I can hear her heart of gold beating.
SHOUTS. Suok!
  Suok!
  Suok!
PROSPERO. Come to me, Suok!
TIBULLUS. No, to me. Come to me, Suok!
DOCTOR. No, to me.
SELLER. No, to me.
ALINA. No, to me.
AUGUSTUS. No, to me.
THE PEOPLE. To us, Suok! Come to us, Suok!
SUOK. Ah, I've dropped it!
TIBULLUS. You've dropped your little board.
SUOK. It was entrusted to me by a man dying in the cage . . .I'll read

it . . . can't see. The letters are almost rubbed away . . .

DOCTOR. Give it to me. I've got two pairs of glasses. (*Reads*). "I, Tub, a great scientist, am writing this. I believe that the time will come when you, Suok, and you, Tutti, will read these lines. You are brother and sister. You were kidnapped from your parental home on the orders of the Three Fat Men. I was summoned to the palace. They showed me you, Suok, and ordered me to make a doll identical to you. Make a doll, they said, which will grow and change just like a living being. I made such a doll. And you, Suok, a living girl, the Three Fat Men ordered you drowned. Tutti started to live in the palace. The doll took the place of his sister. Then they said to me: tear out the living heart from the boy and put in an iron one. I refused. Then they put me in the cage . . . And they forced the boy to believe that he had an iron heart. I'm going to die soon . . . Forgive me . . . We were all treated badly by the Three Fat Men. Forgive me, Tutti, which means, "the parted one." Forgive me, Suok, which means, "all of life."

PROSPERO. Where's Tutti? (*To the Fat Men*). We've come for the boy you stole from us. Answer us, where is Tutti?

A cannon shot. Tutti appears.

TUTTI. Who's shouting? I was asleep . . . I was sleeping soundly. Suok! Hello, Suok. I was sleeping and had a dream . . . I dreamt that you were a living girl, that you were my sister, Suok . . .

DOCTOR. Go on, Tutti. Go and embrace her. She is your living sister.

TUTTI. Oh what happiness! I still don't quite understand what is happening but it seems that what is happening is happiness. My iron heart will break from happiness. I want to be joyful, but a man who has an iron heart doesn't have the right to be joyful.

DOCTOR. Allow me, I'll listen to your heart. (*Listens*). You have an ordinary living heart, a human heart, which cannot be replaced by iron, or stone, or ice. You may cry to your heart's content.

A cannon shot.

TUTTI. What's that?
SUOK. Those are the ships from the city of Till.

They both run to the tower.

THE PEOPLE. Ships from the city of Till!
Ships from the city of Till!

CURTAIN

A STERN YOUNG MAN

A Play for the Cinema

Dedicated to Zinaida Raikh

A garden.

A verandah.

On the verandah a table.

Four sets of eating implements.

The table is elegantly set.

A warm day. Shifting foliage and shadows.

Dragon-fly reflections of glasses on the walls.

The house is surrounded by a garden.

It is a small building of modern design, white, airy, with many windows.

It is the summer residence of Dr. Stepanov.

In the garden, not far from the verandah, a man sits in a wicker chair.

Beside the chair a small table.

On it is a box of cigars, an ashtray, a cigar-stub in the ashtray.

On the gravel by the armchair is a newspaper.

Here is Fyodor Yakovlevich Tsitronov, a friend of the master of the house.

He has an unpleasant appearance.

Imagine a face on which there is constantly a dozing expression. His lower lip sags.

His cheeks are like jelly.

Nor is he young.

And he has eaten and drunk a great deal in the course of his life, indulging himself to the full.

He has always been inclined to obesity. There was a period when this obesity was particularly apparent. But a catastrophe occurred, possibly physical in nature, perhaps a kidney complaint, and as a result there occurred a sudden loss of weight, which resulted in a certain sagging now to be observed in this man. All the same, an observer would say that he was fat rather than thin.

A garden.

Flowerbeds

The flowers are completely still.

Only the thick leafy clusters move.

Luncheon is being prepared in the kitchen.

The cook. He is wearing a cap.

The kitchen windows look out onto that part of the garden which is less clean and orderly. Backs of dachas. Here there is something in the nature of an aviary.

There are birds.

There is a guinea-fowl.

Having sat down on a step, a girl is churning ice-cream in a mixer.

Inside the house there is cleanliness, polish, tall glass doors.

186

Paths strewn with gravel, arbors, flowerbeds can be seen through the window.

The flowers are completely still.

A river. On the bank a young woman.
This is Masha, the wife of Dr. Stepanov.
She has just been bathing.
She is returning home.
She puts on her watch.
Her hand is still wet.
She looks to see what time it is.
She walks past the dachas.
Bathers walk toward her.
They look back.
She walks on.
A warm day.
The road.

A garden. Tsitronov is seated in the wicker chair.
Masha comes through the dacha gates.
The seated man and the woman who has entered see each other from a distance.

It turns out that the man with the drowsy face has very lively eyes.
The woman is lightly dressed.
She knows that his eyes are fixed on her and feels uncomfortable.
He knows that she feels uncomfortable and this gives him pleasure.
She walks to the verandah.
A car approaches the cottage.
Tsitronov hears the car approaching.
He hurriedly makes his way to the gate.
He stands at the gate.
The car draws nearer.
Tsitronov waves in greeting.
The car is driven in.
It is the latest model, a powerful, comfortable, expensive car.
The new arrival gets out of the car.
Dr. Julian Nikolaevich Stepanov, a well-known surgeon. He is forty-eight years old. Thick-set. Clean-shaven.
Masha runs to meet him.
Tsitronov.
Stepanov.
Masha.
Stepanov draws his wife to him. Kisses her.
All three of them walk along the path.

187

Tsitronov walks behind, carrying the hat and walking stick of the new arrival.

The dacha station.
A train comes in.
Among those alighting is a young man in white pants and a white shirt.

At the dacha.
In the garden.
The train whistle is audible.
Masha. Stepanov.

MASHA. Yes . . . That's Grisha arriving.

Looks at her watch. Continues.

Yes . . . It's him. We agreed on four o'clock.

The table. Four sets of knives and forks.

STEPANOV. But will he find the way?
TSITRONOV (*breaks into the conversation*). How can he miss it? He'll ask. Everyone here knows where Dr. Stepanov's dacha is.
STEPANOV. No, no, Mashenka, you go all the same. To meet him. Awkward. The man has come here for the first time.

Masha goes out.

The young man stands on the platform.
The train has gone.
The young man has been traveling for quite a long time. He brushes off, as it were, the traces of the railway coach's crush. He somehow expresses a certain primitiveness characteristic of himself.
The dacha district lies before him.
Masha comes out onto the road.

At the dacha.
Dr. Stepanov is in the garden by the wicker chair in which Tsitronov is sitting. The little table with cigars on it stands by them.

STEPANOV. Fyodor!
TSITRONOV (*shouts back*). What's the matter?
STEPANOV. Have you been smoking cigars?
TSITRONOV. Yes.

STEPANOV. Smoking is forbidden, if you don't mind.
TSITRONOV. Not allowed?
STEPANOV. Not allowed.
TSITRONOV. Are you speaking as a doctor?
STEPANOV. No, as the master of the house.
TSITRONOV. You must be joking.

The road.
Masha is walking.
At the dacha.

TSITRONOV. I see you're not in a good mood. Why? Don't you like your wife going out to meet this young man?
STEPANOV. Fool!

The young man walking.

At the dacha.
The pantry.
Gleam of tiles.
A housemaid.
A kitchen-boy.
The housemaid is young and not without a certain chic.
She takes a bottle from a basket. It is brandy.
A foreign label.

Young man walking.
He walks past the dachas.
People are playing tennis.
A clumsy shot.
The ball flies beyond the fence.
The young man looks around as the ball whistles past.
A slope.
The ball rolls down the slope.
The young man sees this.
Grass. The ball lies in the grass.
The young man descends the slope.
At this moment Masha passes above.
He throws the ball to the players.
Masha turns a corner.
They have missed each other.

At the dacha.
By the door onto the verandah.

The fresh air of the garden.
The little table.
The varnished surface of the table gleams.
A man can be heard walking with a tray with glass on it.
The glass clinks.
It is Tsitronov.
He puts the tray down on the table.
On the tray is a bottle, large goblets, a crystal basin in which there are pieces of ice, a tumbler with straws, syphons.
Having put down the tray, Tsitronov draws a deep breath.
It was a heavy load, after all.
He sets about uncorking the bottles.
A column of light shines on the bottles.

TSITRONOV. I've gradually turned into your lackey, Julian. To hell with you. But I'm not insulted. You're a great man.

Young man walking.
He approaches the dacha.
He is struck by the splendor which opens before him.
He slows his pace.
He is rather overwhelmed.
The fence.
Clumps of trees.
The young man looks over the fence.
Beyond the fence is a rich, strange house.
The young man sees a gardener attending to a flowerbed.
People washing down the car with a hose.
The young man is ready to give up the idea of entering the garden.
The gate.
The young man watches.
The fierce indifference of the dogs.

TSITRONOV. Who do you want?

The young man has no time to reply.

MASHA (*shouts from the distance*). Grisha! Grisha!

Before she called out, she was walking quickly, almost running.
Having called out, she walks more slowly.
The young man looks around.
She goes toward him.
He stands in embarrassment and confusion.

190

There is a type of male appearance which has developed as a result of the evolvement of technology, aviation, sport. From under the leather peak of a pilot's helmet, a pair of gray eyes, as a rule, look out at you. And you may be sure that when the pilot takes off his helmet then it will be fair hair that will be gleaming before you. A tank is moving along the street. The ground trembles beneath your feet. Suddenly a trap-door opens in the back of this monster, and a head appears through this trap-door. This is the tankman. And, needless to say, he will also be pale-eyed.

Light eyes, light hair, a thin face, a triangular torso, a muscular chest—such is the modern type of male beauty. This is the beauty of the Red Army soldiers, the beauty of the young men who wear on their chest the badge "GTO." It comes about from frequent contact with water, machines and gymnastic equipment.

Such is the appearance of the young man who now stands before Masha, on the grass, in the midst of camomile, in the bright sunshine.

The meeting.

Tsitronov moves away accompanied by the dogs.

He glances round at the young people.

At the dacha.
At the table.
Stepanov, Tsitronov, the young man, Masha.
They are eating lunch.

TSITRONOV. Well, what do you think, is it a good brandy?

YOUNG MAN. Very good.

TSITRONOV. It's Julian Nikolaevich's favorite. The government sends it to him.

YOUNG MAN. Who sends it?

TSITRONOV. The government. Why are you surprised?

YOUNG MAN. I wasn't surprised. I simply didn't hear properly.

Masha emerges from behind the table.
Stepanov is uneasy.
Inside the house.

MASHA. Forbid him to speak to Grisha in that way. It's annoying.

She doesn't want to return to the table.

MASHA. Why do you always have that man with you?

STEPANOV. But Mashenka, he's my friend.

YOUNG MAN. That's not true, you like the way he flatters you.

At the table.

YOUNG MAN. There aren't many such people as Julian Nikolaevich.
TSITRONOV. And people like you? A lot of them?

The young man understands that he is under attack.

YOUNG MAN (*smiling*). Yes, a lot.

Masha and Stepanov return to the table.

TSITRONOV. It seems, Julian, that under socialism too there is a lot
and a little.

In the garden.

MASHA. But won't you come for a stroll with us?
STEPANOV. No, Mashenka, I'm too old. I feel like sitting down after
lunch.

*Two people remain at the table: Stepanov and Tsitronov. Masha and
the young man walk off.*
At the table.

STEPANOV. Well, I suppose it's completely natural.
TSITRONOV. What's natural?
STEPANOV. That she likes this young fellow.
TSITRONOV. Only he's poor.
STEPANOV. Apropos of what do you say that?

The young people come in. The room seems fuller.

TSITRONOV. I'm trying to comfort you.

The garden.
An arbor.
The washed, gleaming car.
The young people come in.

TSITRONOV. She won't leave you. Ever. She's gotten used to luxury.

In the kitchen.
The cook.
He is gnawing at a chicken leg. Washing it down with wine.

192

In the bedroom.
The housemaid is putting Masha's underwear in a cupboard.
Expensive underwear.
The young people walk in close proximity.
At the table.
STEPANOV. You mean that I bought her?
TSITRONOV. Yes.
The young people walk in very close proximity.
At the table.
Stepanov grasps a bottle.
Tsitronov immediately jumps up.
Terrified. Runs to one side.
Cries out in a voice in which fear is mingled with entreaty:

—Julie! Julie!

He runs out into the garden casting frequent panic-stricken glances behind him:

—Julie! Julie!

Stepanov lets go of the neck of the bottle.
He gets up.
Goes out.
Tall glass door.
This is the door to the library.
In the library. A wall of books.
But it isn't stuffy here. Because the garden is outside the windows.
This closeness makes the room airy.
Every object, even if placed in a far corner, reflects sky, twigs, clouds.
Stepanov is walking through the library.
His anger has not yet abated.
He is smoking.
Tsitronov is at the door.
He knocks softly.

TSITRONOV. Julie...Let me in, Julie...Don't be cross...I said a terrible thing...She loves you, Julie...I know...Loves you madly...

The young people are returning to the dacha.
Masha leaves the young man in the garden.
The young man is alone.
Masha in the library.
Masha.
Stepanov.

MASHA. Grisha is leaving. Can we take the car? I'll give him a ride to the station.

Stepanov and Masha go out into the garden.
They walk through the garden.
The young man is alone.
He joins them.
Tsitronov lags behind them.

STEPANOV. Come and see us on the tenth. We're having a farewell party. I'm going to London, you know. To an international congress on cancer.

Masha is bustling about by the car.
The young man feels very awkward at the present moment.
He wants to look at Masha.
But the great doctor stands before him.
He is a student and a member of the Komsomol, and he is full of respect for this remarkable man. He can't allow himself to turn away and look at Masha. He listens to the doctor and looks him in the eye, but this is an unnatural and tormenting effort.

YOUNG MAN. Yes, I know. You'll be making a report. And what's the theme?

He manages, almost out of the corner of his eye, to catch a glimpse of Masha. She seems especially attractive to him next to the elegant car.

TSITRONOV. What's the theme? Current events, young man. How can you ask what the theme is? You're not a specialist, after all. Theme: the resurrection of men and women. Julian Nikolaevich literally resurrected people. And you ask about it as casually as if it were a report to the local committee.

The young man is at a loss.

TSITRONOV. Amazing familiarity . . . Someone finds himself in the house of a great scientist . . .
STEPANOV. Get out!

Tsitronov stands there.

STEPANOV. Did you hear what I said to you?

194

Tsitronov moves away toward the verandah.

STEPANOV. I'm afraid he has adopted this manner of boasting about me . . .
MASHA. You like that.
STEPANOV. You're talking nonsense.

They take their leave.
The car drives off.

A lawn outside the dacha.
Camomile.

On the lawn stand Stepanov and Tsitronov.
From here they can see the road. It's quite a distance. The air is transparent. They see details of the distant landscape which have become very miniature. Little trees. Little bushes. Little houses. A little car appears, moving rapidly.

The road.
A car which has come to a halt.
The woman driver and the passenger are beside it.
Something is wrong with the motor.
The young man sets about putting it to rights.

On the lawn.
Tsitronov comes running with a pair of binoculars.
He adjusts the focus.
The car and the two young people, visible through the binoculars.
Suddenly their outline becomes less precise. Mistiness envelops them.
And only gradually does the picture become clear again.
On the lawn.
Stepanov is looking through the binoculars.
He is a big man. His legs are pillars.
Big steps.
In the midst of camomile.

By the car.
The young man is busy repairing the engine.

YOUNG MAN. I dreamt that a car just like this had arrived at the stadium. And there is a woman at the wheel. I watch from the distance . . . it seems to be you. Her hat's like yours, similar from a distance. Surely it can't be her, I think to myself . . .

MASHA. Well...was it me?

YOUNG MAN. No, I run up...suddenly she gets out of the car...And I see she's a foreigner...a German woman with a big nose and glasses...very plain.

On the lawn.
Stepanov removes the binoculars from his eyes.

—Interesting, what can they be talking about?

Raises the binoculars.
Sees the young people, the car.
The young people are chatting.
He sees moving lips. Masha laughs. Loudly, one would imagine.
But Stepanov doesn't hear anything. For him it is silent cinema.

On the road.
The car drives away.

On the lawn.
Stepanov and Tsitronov leave the lawn.

The car turns on a square near the platform.
The young man walks onto the platform. He looks around.
The car is driving away.
The young man watches.
Masha stops the engine, calls out:

—So don't forget, Grisha. The evening of the tenth.

He waves.
The car drives away.
Grisha stands on the platform.
He is waiting for the train.

Grisha Fokin returns home.
It is evening.
He lives in a big building, in a communal apartment, together with his old mother.
The young man goes up the stairs.
A room.
He enters.
A desk.
Books.

The son calls out:

—Mama!

His mother isn't there.
A door along the corridor swings open. His mother looks out.
She says:

—Grisha! I'm here.

She is at a neighbor's.
The neighbor's room.
A mirror.
The neighbor is seated in front of the mirror.
His mother is in the doorway.
Her son goes up to her.
He sees that the neighbor is seated before the mirror.
The neighbor.
The mirror.
The neighbor says:

—Good morning, Grigory Ivanych.
SON. Why do you look in the mirror so often, Katya?
NEIGHBOR. Because I'm not good-looking.
SON. That doesn't matter, Katya. Beauty is a dialectical concept. It can only arise between two people. It will never be known what a person is like when he is by himself: beautiful or ugly. But when another person approaches and says: "I love you," then the first one immediately becomes beautiful. Do you understand?
NEIGHBOR. Really?
SON. But of course!
NEIGHBOR. But already someone has come up to me and said: "I love you."
SON. That means you're already beautiful.
NEIGHBOR. Really?
SON. But of course.

He picks up the mirror.
Looks into it.
Asks:

—Mama, am I good-looking?
MOTHER. But of course you are.
SON. But nobody has yet said to me: "I love you."

197

NEIGHBOR. But you're good-looking, all the same.

Morning.
At the stadium.
Corridors. Passageways.
A staircase.
Paths.
Squares.
Grass.
Trees.
Notices.
Numbers scrawled with lime on sand.

Training is in progress.
A group of young people. They are resting. Girls and young men.
A bright summer day.
Tall trees.
An enormous sky.
Below on the tarmac stands a group of jumpers with a pole.
Among them is Grisha Fokin.
A young man goes up to the resting group with a discus.
A discus thrower.
The discus thrower. He is stripped. A pair of brief shorts is all he has
on.
Sunburned. In his hand is a heavy stone discus.
The resting group. Conversation.

FIRST YOUNG MAN. He assembled the third physical training
group.
SECOND YOUNG MAN. Who did?
GIRL. Grisha Fokin.
THIRD. What does that mean?
GIRL. Do you mean to say you don't understand?
THIRD. No.
FIRST. A complex of spiritual qualities. The spiritual qualities of a
Komsomol member must develop.

The discus thrower transfers the discus to the other hand. As if he isn't
listening. He sits, leaning lightly on his elbows. His tanned body gleams in
the sun.

FIRST. For example?
GIRL. Surely you understand?
FIRST. Modesty. That's the first thing. So that there's no rudeness or

198

familiarity. Next: sincerity. So as to speak the truth. Then: generosity . . .

SECOND. In what sense?

GIRL. Surely you understand?

FIRST. Not to get pleasure from his comrades' mistakes.

The discus thrower remains seated.

FIRST. Generosity. To overcome the feeling of private ownership.
—And then sentiment.

DISCUS THROWER. Oh, sentiment too?
—Within certain limits. To like not only marches, but waltzes too.

GIRL. Go on, go on—what next?
—A harsh attitude toward egotism.

GIRL. That's right.
—Well, and chastity.

DISCUS THROWER. What do you mean by chastity?

GIRL. But surely you understand?

Grisha Fokin in the circle. Sun. Grass. Camomile. The discus thrower
sits.

SECOND. But surely those are bourgeois qualities.

FIRST. They are human qualities.

SECOND. What does that mean, "human?"

GIRL. But surely you understand?

FIRST. The bourgeoisie have perverted these concepts. Because there
was the power of capital.

GIRL (*quickly*). And since now there's no power of capital, all these
feelings are purified. Surely you understand?

A car drives up to the stadium.
The car stops.
Masha gets out.
From above the young man looks through his binoculars.
He calls the girl.

—Shurka! The foreigners have arrived.

Sensation.
The tennis players watch.
A track man sitting on the parallel bars watching.
He wipes his hands with a handkerchief.
The group of reclining athletes. Heads turn at the shout of the young
man with the binoculars.

199

—What is it?

GIRL. The foreigners have arrived.

Masha is in the stadium grounds.
The car is stopped. A doll hangs in the window.
The discus thrower catches sight of Masha.
General interest in the stranger walking through the stadium grounds.
She was the car's driver.
She is very elegant.
In the car sits Dr. Stepanov.
Masha looks round.
She waves to her husband.
Sunshine. Space. Masha stands with hand uplifted.
Dr.Stepanov does not respond. Masha is shocked by his failure to respond.
She repeats her gesture.
Masha with uplifted hand.
Dr. Stepanov lights a cigarette.
Masha returns to the car.

—What's the matter . . .are you angry?

Silence.

—Surely you're not jealous? You ought to be ashamed of yourself.

Silence.
At the stadium the scene is observed.
The discus thrower and Fokin.
Fokin is wearing a dressing gown.

DISCUS THROWER. What is it? Is it her?

Fokin remembers his dream. His heart beats strongly. He cannot answer.

GIRL *(from above)*. What are you standing there for, Grisha? You should go forward. Surely you understand?

The discus thrower and Fokin stand motionless.

DISCUS THROWER. What particular moral quality are you developing at the present time? Shyness? In my opinion, cowardice.

At the car.

MASHA (*angrily*). Let's go back, please.

DOCTOR (*with irritation*). No, it'll be awkward now. As everyone has seen us.

The discus thrower walks through the field.
The dark, gleaming figure of the athlete moves against a large open space.
He slowly waves an arm which seems to be straight because he is holding a heavy discus,
The girl is beside Fokin.
Fokin is all movement forward.
The discus thrower moves forward.
At the car.
Dr. Stepanov.
Masha looks round at the approaching discus thrower.
He comes up to her. Bows.

—Have you come to see Grisha Fokin?

MASHA. Yes.

DISCUS THROWER. He know you've come. He saw you. But he's hiding.

MASHA. Hiding?

DISCUS THROWER. Yes. He's afraid to look at you because he loves you.

The girl, Fokin.
Fokin pushes the girl away.
Rushes forward.
He is already standing among the group by the car.

FOKIN. What did he say? What did you say? Masha . . .

DISCUS THROWER. I said that you love. . .the comrade. . . here. . .

DOCTOR. Masha, I think this is a silly conversation.

MASHA. And the entire stadium knows about this?

FOKIN. No, no, Masha . . .No one knows. Only him. My friend.

Masha sits down behind the wheel.
A scandal. Dr. Stepanov is outraged.
He says:

—Strange. Very strange. Like a dream. A naked man comes up and says that somebody loves my wife.

The car drives away.
Fokin stands, disheartened.
He gazes after the departing car.
The discus thrower stands further off.
The girl runs up.
The discus thrower says:

—I am right, aren't I? According to this theory, a komsomol member has to tell the truth. And I just told the truth.

Fokin does not move.
The car vanishes in the distance.
The discus thrower calls:

—Grisha!

The latter is motionless.
The discus thrower again:

—Grisha!

The latter is motionless.
The discus thrower once more:

—Grisha!

The latter is motionless.

GIRL. He doesn't hear anything. Surely you understand that?

The discus thrower turns about and flings the discus.
The discus falls at Fokin's feet.
He is motionless.

Before us stands Dr. Stepanov.
Addressing himself to an invisible interlocutor, he speaks in English.
His intonation and gestures are somewhat pompous.
It is as if he is imitating an orator.
This is happening in the library.
Masha is sitting at the desk.
In front of her are sheets of paper and open books.
Tearing herself from her work, she listens to her husband.

MASHA. What was that you said?

STEPANOV. Respected gentlemen! To conclude my report, I wish to enumerate my colleagues, assistants and graduate students, who took part in this work, the results of which have just been brought to your attention, respected gentlemen. At the top of the list I have to put the name of my wife...That's what I'll say at the international conference in London.

In the garden.
Tsitronov is sitting in the wicker chair.

In the library.
Masha is sitting at the desk.
Stepanov picks up a sheet of paper.

STEPANOV. Mark these pages with Roman numerals. And I'm afraid you've mixed things up, my good lady. We refer not to Bruno Weber but to Walter Weber.

In the garden.
Tsitronov gets up.
He looks at the library windows.
Stepanov is at a window.

STEPANOV (*shouts*). Do you want a cigar, Fyodor?
TSITRONOV. Very much.
Goes in the direction of the verandah.
Stepanov stands on the verandah holding out a cigar.

TSITRONOV I see that your mood has improved. What have you done? Made peace?
STEPANOV. Yes. We decided not to receive him any more at our house. Just think...Masha's name is bandied about the entire stadium. A limit must be put to this.
TSITRONOV. And the party? The party's tomorrow. After all, you did invite him.
STEPANOV. Think of something...An invitation can always be withdrawn.

A theater.
The theater dressing room.
A tailor. He is an old man.
He is sewing.
The discus thrower walks through the theater.
It is an opera-house.
Morning in the opera-house.

The aria of the tenor in rehearsal can be heard.

The discus thrower listens.
Corridors. Passageways.
Ballerinas are rehearsing.
In the corridor the discus thrower encounters a ballerina.
She was going to the stage. She is wearing a tuttu.
The ballerina sees a handsome young man in front of her.
The discus thrower sees a beautiful girl in front of him.
Both have come to a halt.
Then she performs the function of his guide.
Where are they going?
This will become clear now.
The theater in the afternoon.
Passageways. Corridors.
A tenor is singing.
A door into the theater's property room.
A keyhole. The ballerina and the discus thrower. He glances in.
Then he thanks the ballerina.
The discus thrower goes into the room.
It is the property room.
The discus thrower stands in the doorway. He says:

—Uncle!

The old man looks around.
It is the tailor. He smiles joyfully. Nods his head. Says:

—Hello, Kolya.

The discus thrower goes in, sits down. He says:

—Uncle, I need a dress coat.

Wardrobes. A row of wardrobes.
Uncle and nephew walk by the wardrobes.
The uncle opens one of them. Dress coats are hanging inside.
The old man says:

—But you'll bring it back, Kolya. I'm responsible, you know. I'm committing a crime, Kolya.

The discus thrower examines the dress coats. He pays no attention to the uncle.

204

OLD MAN. I'm committing a crime, Kolya.

The old man with the dress coat. The coat is on a table. All the accoutrements to the dress coat.
The old man gets hold of a large box.
The discus thrower takes an occasional drag at a cigarette.
As he packs the dress coat, the old man says:

—This is from "Traviata." I'm committing a crime, Kolya.

The discus thrower pays no attention at all to his uncle.
He picks up the package.
He goes to the door.
The old man after him:

—Do you hear, Kolya? It's a dress coat from "Traviata."

The door closes behind the discus thrower.
The theater.
The discus thrower comes out of the theater with the package.
The ballerina appears high up in one of the theater windows.
It is to be assumed that she is watching the young man.
The discus thrower looks back.
The ballerina at the window.
Very distinct sounds can be heard from the orchestra at rehearsal.
A side street.
The discus thrower appears in the side street.
An open window on the first floor.
The discus thrower goes over to the window. He knocks on the glass of the open shutter.
A boy appears at the window.
The discus thrower turns around.
He waves his hand, indicating a building to the boy.
The boy looks.
A house. In this house lives Grisha Fokin. His window.
A white sports jersey hangs down from the windowsill.
The boy nods his head.
The discus thrower puts the box down on the windowsill.
Then he indicates to the boy the gleaming white face of the tower clock in the distance.
The boy nods.

In Grisha's room.
He prepares to shave.

He lays out his shaving things.
His mother brings a glass of water.

SON. All the same, mama, I don't know whether to go or not.
MOTHER. You yourself said that a komsomol member must be resolute.
SON. Yes...But they left the stadium without saying a word to me.

A staircase.
The discus thrower mounts the staircase together with the girl who was at the stadium.
She is excited.
She is saying something to the discus thrower.
He goes ahead up the steps. But she stops him.
Because of this they mount the stairs in some confusion.
The girl says:

—It is necessary that all desires be satisfied, then man will be happy. Surely you understand that. But if desires aren't satisfied, then man becomes unhappy. Desires cannot be suppressed. Suppressed desires give rise to bitterness. This is the theory. If you want to sit down on a step—then sit down.

The girl sits down on a step.

If you want to get up—get up.

The girl gets up.

In Fokin's room.
Behind the wardrobe. The mother is knotting her son's tie.
The door swings open.
Enter the girl and the discus thrower.

GIRL. It's so simple. If you feel like jumping—jump.

She jumps.
The mother peers from behind the wardrobe. She doesn't understand anything. Why is the girl jumping?

GIRL. If you feel like knocking over a glass—knock it over.

With the violence of a fanatic she knocks a glass over.
Overturned glass.

Water on the oil-cloth.
Having knocked over the glass, the girl immediately sits down—she is
as tired as a dancer. Fans herself.

GIRL. Phew, this playing around exhausts me!

The son emerges from behind the wardrobe.
He sees the glass lying on its side, water on the oil-cloth. Asks:

—What's come over you?

GIRL. A person shouldn't suppress desires. I felt like drinking water,
and I drank some.

SON. I see. And then you felt like pouring it out? Perhaps you'll feel
like wiping it up?

GIRL (*stretching*). No, I don't feel like that yet.

FOKIN (*with mild irony*). Oh, you don't feel like it?

GIRL (*jumping up*). I feel like it. I feel like it.

From now on she is wiping the table.
The discus thrower looks at Grisha.

DISCUS THROWER. Are you going like that?

FOKIN. What do you mean "like that?"

DISCUS THROWER. They won't let you in looking like that.
Everyone will be in evening dress there. It's the Soviet aristocracy.

Fokin makes no reply.
Goes out.
Fokin knocks at the door of his neighbor across the hall. She opens it.
Seeing the dandified Fokin, she steps back. Throws up her hands.
Fokin in the neighbor's room.
A mirror.
Fokin looks in the mirror.
He finds it dark.
Picks up the mirror.
Goes out onto the tarmac.
The neighbor after him.
Fokin hands the neighbor the mirror.
The neighbor holds the mirror in front of him.
Here it is light.
Before he has time to be reflected in the mirror, Fokin sees Tsitronov
in it.
In the room.
Tsitronov stands in the doorway.

207

He measures everyone with a glance.
He sees the mother,
   the discus thrower,
   the girl,
   Fokin.
   The discus thrower stands, his arms folded on his chest. His sleeves are rolled up. Beneath the light material of his shirt one can sense the bulging interlaced muscles.
   The girl stands beside him. She snuggles up to his elbow. As if finding a refuge from danger behind his elbow.
   Tsitronov.
   He is wearing a hat. With a walking stick.
   Turning to Fokin, he says:

—Dr. Julian Nikolaevich Stepanov and his lady will not permit you to enter their house. Do you understand that?

   The mother exlaims:

—Why won't they permit him?

   Tsitronov casts a contemptuous glance in the mother's direction, then he says:

—They request you not to come here again.
   FOKIN (*quietly*). Very well.

   The discus thrower stands with folded arms. The girl beside him. Snuggles up to his elbow.

   TSITRONOV. You said yourself that there aren't many like Dr. Stepanov, and that there are a lot of people like you. Is that true?
   FOKIN. Yes.

   In indignation the discus thrower goes into action. The girl withdraws still further behind his elbow.

   TSITRONOV. And so you're the one who believes that socialism means inequality?
   FOKIN. Speak more simply. Of course there shouldn't be levelling downward.
   TSITRONOV. What shouldn't there be?
   FOKIN. Levelling downward.
   TSITRONOV. That isn't a philosophical term.
   FOKIN. Yes it is a philosophical term.

The girl comes out from behind the elbow. She goes over to Fokin and kisses him.

And, having done this, she explains to the discus thrower, glancing up at him:

—I felt like kissing him. Desires have to be satisfied.

And again withdraws behind the elbow.

FOKIN. Who sent you?
TSITRONOV. Dr. Stepanov and Masha.
FOKIN (*hoarsely*). And Masha?
TSITRONOV (*relishing the pause*). Yes, and Masha.

Fokin stands with bowed head.
Tsitronov holds the walking stick. You might well think that he wanted to thrust up the young man's bowed head with his stick.

TSITRONOV. Well? Why are you hanging your head? You want to come to the party? Yes? It's so beautiful at our place—isn't it? Over the fence. Flowers. And today there will be guests, there'll be a holiday, there'll be a concert. Masha will shine in a ballgown. How delightful to sit at dinner opposite the woman you love. She eats pastry, you gaze at her and it seems to you that her every gulp is like a kiss. But you haven't even got a dress coat. Do you have a dress coat? You don't? Well, all right. I've let my tongue run away with me.
Goodbye, young people.
Goodbye, my little gray one . . .
Live your gray little life.
GIRL (*interrupting him*). That's a fascist interpretation of communism. Surely you understand that.

The discus thrower pushes the girl away. Restrains his anger. Says:

—And who do you think you are? . . . How dare you talk like that?
TSITRONOV. I? I am one who emphasizes inequality.

The discus thrower clenches his fists.
He says, turning to the girl:

—How do you put it, Lizochka? One has to satisfy one's desires. And if I have a desire to give this fellow one in the kisser?
GIRL. Don't suppress your desire. Hit him.

209

The discus thrower advances on Tsitronov.

TSITRONOV (*raising the palm of his hand*). But, but . . .

Fokin grasps the discus player's arm.
He has a very strong grip.
The discus thrower's gust of anger is cut short.
The discus thrower cools down.
Tsitronov goes through the door.

DISCUS THROWER. And it isn't your fence. Oh you scoundrel. One who emphasizes inequality—did you hear? That means lack of faith . . . complete lack of faith in us . . . in the young . . . in our strength, intelligence . . . in culture. Did you understand? . . . Grishka, how dare he? We'll be great men too . . . How dare he? Let go of me. He should be done away with . . .

Up the staircase comes a boy with a package.
He comes in the door.
The tarmac. For a while it is deserted.
The boy comes out of the door.
He descends the stairs.
The tarmac. For a while it is deserted.
Suddenly the door is flung open. The discus thrower comes flying out.
Then the girl comes flying.
Then a dress coat and a dicky come flying.
The coat lands on the bannisters.

DISCUS THROWER (*rubbing his shoulder blade*). I purposely sent the dress coat. So that he would understand. So that he would feel ashamed.

Turns to the door. Shouts resentfully:

—Fool, spoiled brat! I'll show you. You have to fight for what is yours . . . Oh, what a . . . If I were in his place . . . I'd win Masha over from the professor. A komsomol man should be brave.

Fokin comes out onto the tarmac.

FOKIN. The root of the matter is that Masha doesn't love me. Doesn't love me, and that's all there is to it. She loves him. And not me. That's all there is to it. A komsomol man should be accurate.
DISCUS THROWER. If you like, I'll put the dress coat on and go to

the ball.

GIRL. Ooo yes. And bring back some pastries. He made the pastries sound so appetizing.

DISCUS THROWER. Do you hear, Grisha? I'll put the dress coat on and I'll be kissing Masha.

Fokin yanks the dress coat from the bannisters and brandishes it.

DISCUS THROWER. Grisha! What are you doing? That dress coat is from "Traviata."

Fokin throws the dress coat at the discus thrower.

The party at Dr. Stepanov's house.

Cars at the entrance. The latest models, powerful, comfortable, expensive cars. Dolls hang at the windows, toy animals, roses.

In the garden.

Lanterns. Little tables.

Bottles in buckets clammy with cold. Snow-white table napkins. Pyramids of fruit. Cut glass.

Flowers which have fallen on the gravel.

Moths circle the lanterns.

Fall on the tablecloth.

Guests.

A group of foreigners.

Among them is a family: a husband, wife and adolescent son. The boy is wearing a jacket, has close-cropped hair and an upturned nose; fair-headed with a cowlick on the crown of his head—lively but obedient. He pushes forward eagerly but looks round at his parents.

Masha appears.

Masha is walking through the garden. Alone.

Everyone looks at Masha.

Masha's appearance, her gait, the movement of the pleats of her dress are so strange, so beautiful, so unusual that the adolescent cannot restrain himself, and running forward clasps his hands.

Masha asks the guest to come into the drawing room.

The drawing room.

Grand piano.

Guests.

Dr. Stepanov and Masha.

The garden.

The sound of the piano is heard.

The discus thrower clambers over the fence.

He is wearing a dress coat. An athlete. Broad-shouldered. His polished

shoes gleam.
    He advances.
    Sound of the piano.
    The discus thrower sits down at a table. Tablecloth. Wineglass. A
moth circles the glass.
    In the drawing room.
    A pianist is playing.
    Guests.
    The discus thrower enters the drawing room.
    Masha sees him.
    He sees Masha.
    Masha is disturbed.
    The pianist plays.
    Masha gets up.
    She goes over to the discus thrower.
    The pianist is irritated by the movement.
    He stops playing.
    Masha notices the silence:

—What?
    STEPANOV. You're disturbing us, Masha. (*To the pianist*). Please
excuse us.

    The pianist continues playing.
    Masha looks at the discus thrower.
    The discus thrower looks at Masha.
    Masha smiles.
    The discus thrower smiles.
    The pianist stops playing.

    MASHA. What?
    STEPANOV. You're disturbing us,Masha. (*To the pianist*). Please
excuse us.

    A moth settles on Masha's shoulder.
    A moth settles on the discus thrower's shoulder.
    The pianist stops playing.

    MASHA. What?
    STEPANOV. You're disturbing us, Masha.

    Fokin appears. He shouts:

—What does that mean, "disturbing?" She is music itself.

The guests freeze.
Fokin goes over to Masha, says:

—She is music itself. Masha . . .

She goes to meet him. Fokin says:

—Look at the way she moves. Listen.

He raises her hand.
The hand sings.
He strokes her head, says:

—You see the way she carries herself. Listen.

Her hair sings.
He puts her head on his chest. Says:

—Here is her heart. Listen.

The heart sings.

—Here is her kiss. Listen.

He kisses her.
The kiss sings.
The pianist collapses head down on the keyboard.
The adolescent raises his top hat in the air.
But the discus thrower is in the garden.
He picks up a tray of pastries.
Tsitronov appears.
He gives chase to the thief.
The thief climbs over the fence with the tray.
The public comes running out.
They all stand around in a semi-circle.
They shrink back.
They are afraid.
The thief is sitting on the fence.
Tsitronov rushes over to him.
The thief throws pastries at him à la Chaplin.
Cream pies.
Tsitronov's face is smeared with cream.
In the drawing room.
Fokin is at Masha's feet.

213

He kisses her, embraces her.
The whole of her is singing. Masha's melody.
Tears run down her cheeks.
The tears fall on Fokin's face.
Music.
Fokin wakes up.
He is sleeping under the birches.
Rain.
His face is wet with tears.
In the distance the dacha.
A car drives out.
The gates close.
A watchman, a gardener.
The watchman says:

—The ball was cancelled. This morning. The boss was called out to operate . . . Someone important has been taken sick.

Grisha Fokin returns home.
Early morning.
His mother is asleep behind the screen.
There is a visitor. The discus thrower.

DISCUS THROWER. Where have you been?

Fokin makes no reply.

DISCUS THROWER. Well, it's clear.

Voice of the mother behind the screen:

—Grisha!
SON. Go to sleep.

Silence.

DISCUS THROWER. I came this evening, Grisha, to see Olga. I wanted to talk to her. But she turned out to be ill. I wasn't allowed to see her. Then I came here You weren't in. I decided to wait and I've been sitting here all night.
FOKIN. What did you want to talk to Olga about?
DISCUS THROWER. About Dr. Stepanov . . . Listen to me, Grisha . . . I wanted to ask Olga whether Dr. Stepanov wasn't committing a terrible crime against our society . . . Against a society which will soon be

214

classless . . .

FOKIN. All right then. Say what you have to say. I know what it is you want to say . . .

DISCUS THROWER. You know? I want to talk about the basic law that lies at the foundation of a classless society . . .

FOKIN. What law is that?

DISCUS THROWER. Man cannot have power over man . . .Right?

FOKIN. Right.

DISCUS THROWER. But he . . .this great man . . .has misused his greatness . . .He sent a man to make a mockery of you . . .Just think of it. Yes, that's the way it was . . .And you don't know . . .But perhaps she . . .Masha . . .loves you . . .

FOKIN. No.

DISCUS THROWER. No? You're convinced that she doesn't?

FOKIN. Convinced.

DISCUS THROWER. That's not true. Simply out of great respect for him . . .you persuade yourself . . .that she doesn't love you . . .In order to remove yourself and not disturb his life . . .You're a good komsomol member . . .that's what's at the bottom of it. If the party takes care of him, you don't consider yourself entitled to spoil his happiness. It's like that, Grisha, like that . . .

FOKIN. Shut up. Do you hear? Shut up.

DISCUS THROWER. What a pity Olga has fallen ill . . .She knows everything. She would explain everything . . .Is this man exerting power over man or not . . .

FOKIN. It's power in a pure form . . .He's not a banker . . .He's a great scientist, a genius . . .Do you hear?

DISCUS THROWER. And geniuses are allowed to retain their power?

FOKIN. The power of genius? The worship of genius? That is, of science? Yes. That remains. For me—yes. For a komsomol member. Yes. I'm ready to agree to anything . . .I'll go away . . .Do you hear? Yes . . . That's what I'm telling you . . .Yes . . .The influence of a great mind . . . That's a fine power.

DISCUS THROWER. Oh what a pity Olga's ill . . .She would have explained to me . . .

Voice of the mother from behind the screen:

—Grisha!

SON. What do you want?

MOTHER. You say that there are a lot like you and that he is unique.

SON. Yes.

MOTHER. But aren't you also unique?

215

SON. For you.

MOTHER. Yes.

SON. You're a mother. You have to think that your son is better than the rest.

MOTHER. Yes, you're better than the rest.

SON. For you, for a mother. But for the country?

MOTHER. Grisha! You mustn't forget that half the country is made up of mothers.

SON (*to the discus thrower*). Do you know something? I think the old woman's right...

A knock at the door.
A nervous knock at the door.
The girl comes running in.

—Comrades! Olga is dying...Some fellows came. They took her away to the hospital.

DISCUS THROWER. What's that you're saying?

MOTHER. Who is this Olga, Grisha?

DISCUS THROWER. Well, Olga. A member of the central committee of the komsomol. Remember...she visited us. Such a beauty...

In the hospital ward.
The sick woman.
Her face.
She may possibly be a Korean.
Or a Tatar.
Or a Cossack.
Or a half-breed—the result of an intermixture of Asian and Russian blood.

Her eyes slant toward her temples. High cheekbones. Her face is beautiful with the amazing delicate, doll-like, ancient beauty peculiar to people of the yellow race. At the moment this face is distorted with suffering. Death is gazing into it. Death bends low over her.

The hospital ward.
The sick woman.
The staff.
In the waiting room.
Young people crowd about.
Remarks:

—An immediate operation.

—Poor Olga!

—But who will perform the operation?

The operating room.

216

It has the very latest equipment.
Preparations are in progress.
The surgeon Stepanov washes his hands.

STEPANOV. What shall I bring you from London, Ivan Germanovich? A hat?
ASSISTANT. A hat. A hat would be possible. Good. A hat.

The ward.
The sick woman.

In the waiting room.
An elderly man, a worker by the look of him, is drinking water. His hand trembles. Beside him sits a young sailor. The elderly man hides his face on the young man's chest.
A group: the discus thrower, the girl.

GIRL. That's her husband. Surely you understand that.

The operating room.
Final preparations.
Stepanov stands with his hands lifted in the air.
Gloves are put on them.
He is wearing a mask.
A table. An injection needle.
The sick woman's face.

In the waiting room.
All are seated.
Immobility.
The clock.
A small room.
Tsitronov is wearing a dressing gown.
A table. A bottle of brandy. A glass.
Two peaches on a plate.

In the waiting room.
People.
The clock.
A woman dressed in white runs down a staircase in the distance.
The elderly man hides his face against the sailor's chest.
Discus thrower. Girl.
The girl takes the discus thrower by the elbow. She wants to say something to him. She hasn't said anything, but he pushes her away and

says:

—Sshhh!

The clock.
The operating room from the outside.
A bird flies past. The bird's shadow on the window.
A circular flowergarden outside. Flowers.
The sick woman's face in a mask.
The elderly man gets up.
He is seized by the arms. He throws off those who seize him. A glass is knocked over. The sailor sees the woman in white standing in the distance.
The discus thrower rushes forward.

—Is she dead?

The operating room.
A man in a doctor's smock carries the sick woman in his arms.
She is small. He is enormous.

In a room where Tsitronov is sitting.
Stepanov runs in. Shouts:

—But what size is the hat? Ask what the size of the hat is . . .Ask quickly.
TSITRONOV. Calm down, Julian.

Gives him a peach. He eats the peach greedily (like a monkey). He eats the peach using the entire palm of his hand. Juice drips down. He takes the pit out of his mouth.
Tsitronov gives him a second peach.
He eats it in the same way. Says:

—I'll have to call in at Copenhagen. Copen-hagen. Copen-hagen. Who ate the other peach? Fyodor. You rascal! Rascal! Rascal! Did you eat the other peach?
TSITRONOV. Calm down, Julian.

Gives him a glass of brandy.

The flowergarden.
Flowers.
The flowers sway in the breeze.
Weeping face of the sailor.
The sailor goes over to the staircase.

A woman in white stands there.
He stops in front of her.
She brushes the tears from his face with the palm of her hand.

The clock.
Ray of sunlight on the clock.
Ray of sunlight on the sick woman's hair.

GIRL. If you want to jump—jump.

Stepanov says to his assistant:

—I'll really bring you back a hat. I'll really look around the shops. I'm a member of the British Academy.
ASSISTANT. But I don't need a hat. I'm bald.

In the waiting room.
The sailor to the woman in white:

—But her temperature? . . .What's her temperature?
WOMAN IN WHITE (*wiping the tears from his face*). She's alive.
SAILOR. And can I wait here?
WOMAN IN WHITE. She's alive.
SAILOR. And can I give the professor a present?
WOMAN IN WHITE. She's alive.

The staircase leading up to Grisha Fokin's room.
Fokin is at the desk.
In front of him are sheets of paper, an inkwell.
He is writing.
The door swings open.
The discus thrower and the girl run into the room.

DISCUS THROWER. Grisha. He has resurrected her. She is alive, Grisha. I saw she was dying . . .Grisha . . .She's alive.

The ward.
The sick woman is asleep.
The peaceful face of the sick woman.

Fokin's room.
Fokin.
The discus thrower. The girl.

DISCUS THROWER. In your physical training group...among the qualities which a komsomol member must develop in himself, the first rule should be—do you know what?

FOKIN. What I wrote was...

Reads:

"The komsomol member should raise himself to the level of the best among us. The best are those who create science, technology, music, thought ... These are lofty minds...Those who struggle with nature, the conquerors of death..."

DISCUS THROWER. That's right.

GIRL. If you want to live—live!

A street.
The clinic building.
A car is waiting.
At the wheel, Masha.
The ward.
The sick woman.
It is light.
A multitude of flowers.
Among the flowers the small head of the sick woman. Above her a fan of flowers. The head of the sick woman is like the stub of a fan.
Dr. Stepanov at the bed.
Members of the staff.
Young people—youths and girls—who have come to visit.
A glittering seaman.
He is wearing epaulettes, buttons. A round, blond, close-cropped head.
The doctor says:

—By the type of profession I follow, I am a humanist. I see a great deal of suffering around me. Old men who are afraid of death, mothers weeping over their children.

He turns to the sailor.
The latter immediately rises.

—I was told how you wept. There you see...you, a sailor...what is your rank according to the old system?

SAILOR (*rises*). Admiral.

STEPANOV. There you are, an admiral, but you wept like a chamois. And so...why am I saying all this?...The point I want to make is that the

220

elimination of capital does not mean the elimination of unhappiness. That's how it is. Man's life consists of the alternation of joy and sadness. Isn't that true?

PATIENT. True.

STEPANOV (*to the sailor*). True?

SAILOR. True.

STEPANOV. And a man is only a man when he rejoices and suffers. Do you find a man who never becomes lost in thought attractive?

PATIENT. No.

STEPANOV. But if a man becomes thoughtful, it means that he is either doubtful of something or hopes for something...In a classless society will there be people who become lost in thought?

PATIENT. Yes there will.

STEPANOV. When the mists of mammon have lifted, when there is no longer the division between rich and poor, then suffering becomes a lawful part of human life. That's what I think. And it seems to me that I am not mistaken. And I think that to be able to bear unhappiness is the highest humanity. (*To the sailor*). True?

SAILOR (*gets up*). True.

STEPANOV. Don't get up. What are you getting up for? Where did you get such politeness from? Such good manners? Eh? What are you by birth?

SAILOR. A peasant.

STEPANOV. A fantastic thing.

Dr. Stepanov gets up. Everyone gets up.
The smiling invalid.

STEPANOV. All right then. Soon you'll be getting up. You can read. Something light, pleasant, idealistic...I'll send you...Would you like some Hamsun?

The invalid gets some sheets of paper from beneath her pillow. She says:

—I've got some already. Thank you. Light, pleasant and idealistic reading...I'll read you how it begins. The epigraph, shall I?

Reads:

"If you love without awakening a response, that is, if your love fails to arouse a mutual feeling, and you cannot by behaving as a loving person become a beloved person—then your love is both powerless and unhappy."

STEPANOV. Yes, that's good. Remarkable. About love. About

unrequited love . . .That is to say, about the most magical combination of happiness and unhappiness. Will there be unrequited love in a classless society?

SAILOR. There will.

STEPANOV. Where did you read that from? From Hamsun? Yes? There you are. I guessed that you like Hamsun.

INVALID. No, that's not Hamsun.

The same quotation appears on the screen.
And the signature:

K. MARX.

STEPANOV. A fantastic thing.

The invalid. In her hand she has sheets of paper.
She gets the sheets out from beneath her pillow. Many sheets.
The whiteness of the flowers, the whiteness of the sheets of paper, the whiteness of the pillows and the dark little face of the invalid—and on the dark face the whiteness of a smile. She says:

—Do you know what this is? This was sent to me by a friend of mine, a komsomol member . . .Physical training group number three. The spiritual qualities a komsomol member must develop.

Voices:

—Read the first paragraph.
—The first paragraph.

The invalid reads:

"Equality does not and cannot exist. The very concept of competition destroys the concept of equality. Equality is immobility, competition is movement . . .Raise yourself to the level of the best. That's the first rule."

The invalid interrupts her reading.
She throws a smile in the direction of Stepanov and says:

—The first rule has to do with you, Dr. Stepanov.

Stepanov listens.
Everyone smiles.
The invalid reads:

"Raise yourself to the level of the best. But who are the best? The best are those who invent machines, struggle with nature, create music and thought. Admire lofty minds and science as they deserve . . ."

STEPANOV. Who wrote that? A poet?

INVALID. A friend of mine. A future engineer. A student. Grisha Fokin.

Dr. Stepanov comes out of the clinic.
Stairs.
The car.
Masha isn't in the car.
Stepanov is surprised.
Where can she be? A strange surprise.
The empty car.
Strange.
Dr. Stepanov sees:
A group of passers-by has gathered.
They are watching.
There has been an accident in the neighboring street.
A tram wire has broken.
A crowd.
Trams are waiting.
A mass of trams.
Traffic has stopped.
It is a kind of theater.
Enormous scale.
Houses, street entrances, sidestreets.
Spectators. They watch from the rooftops. From windows. From balconies.
They throng the streets.
A boy sits high on a ledge. He has a fragment of mirror in his hand. He is catching the sun. Rays burst from the boy's hands. He turns round. A star flares up in the boy's hands.
A car waits by the steps. Empty.
Dr. Stepanov approaches the place of the occurrence.
He sees: a repair turret has been erected. There are several men on it.
But where is Masha?
Somewhere in the crowd.
The boy with the mirror catches sight of Stepanov.
It is this comrade alone who attracts the boy's attention: a thickset heavily built comrade.
He directs an arrow of sunlight at him.
Dr. Stepanov is dazzled.
Masha stands amid the crowd.

She watches the repair turret.

There, in the square, people are working. They are wearing rough tarpaulin jackets which make them seem enormous, as a diver's suit makes a man enormous.

They are wearing gloves.

Working at the wire, they hold their faces raised.

Masha watches.

One of the men on the turret turns his head.

He is hot.

He takes off his hat. A fair curl falls onto the sweaty forehead. His gray eyes gleam in a face dark with heat.

It is Grisha Fokin.

Masha looks.

Fokin looks.

They have caught sight of each other.

Boy on the ledge.

Stepanov catches sight of Masha. Why is her face shining?

She is looking at the turret.

Stepanov wishes to understand what is making Masha's face shine.

He looks in the direction Masha is looking.

The boy directs the ray at Stepanov's face.

And dazzles him.

On the turret, Fokin.

On the turret, the discus thrower.

Fokin turns his head away. Don't let her think he has seen her.

Stepanov stands, covering his eyes with his hands, in the pose of a man who has been hit by a wave.

Laughing boy on the ledge.

Masha catches sight of Stepanov.

Goes over to him.

They walk together.

On the turret. Fokin turns round.

Stepanov turns round.

The boy sends out a ray.

Dazzles Stepanov.

Again Stepanov can't see anything.

Masha leads him by the arm.

Laughing boy.

At the car.

From the turret Fokin sees the little car and two figures.

STEPANOV. I can't see anything. There are blue flowers in my eyes...pansies...

Masha kisses him on one eye, says:

—One pansy—*kisses him on the other, says:*
—Two pansies.

Fokin looks.
The boy is dazzling him. Fokin doesn't see anything.
The car drives away.
A pigeon hops along the cornice. An arm's length from the boy. The boy stretches out his hand.
Drops the mirror.
The pigeon flies away.
Keeping clear of the accident, Fokin and the discus thrower walk along the street.

DISCUS THROWER. Why are you so cheerful?
FOKIN. Cheerful? So it seems to you.

Fragments of mirror on the sidewalk.
Fokin picks up a fragment. Looks at it. Says:

—Cheerful, but all the same with a touch of sadness.

At the entrance to the house where Grisha Fokin lives stands Dr. Stepanov.
The discus thrower approaches, having caught sight of Stepanov in the distance.
They exchange greetings.
Go into the hallway.
The stairs leading to Grisha Fokin's room.
The girl watches from the landing.
She leans over.
A surprising visitor mounts the stairs.
Dr. Stepanov.
Advancing steps. The girl lies with her stomach to the bannisters. She is all ears. All attention.
Then, as if uttering a silent scream, she rushes to the door.
In Grisha Fokin's room.
Grisha Fokin, girl.

GIRL (*in a fearful whisper*). He's coming.

They are both excited.

FOKIN. I'll hide. Do you hear? I'm not here . . .It will be hard for me to resist . . .I don't want to make peace with him.

Stepanov and the discus thrower mount the stairs. A wardrobe. The rough sleeve of a fur coat hangs down.
Stepanov enters. Says:

—Good afternoon.

Silence. Dr. Stepanov quickly glances around the room.
He sees: a desk,
    a shelf of books,
    draughtsman's sketches,
    a couch, the wardrobe with the sleeve protruding.

STEPANOV. And the man who lives here? Where's the man who lives here?
DISCUS THROWER. Where is Grisha?
GIRL. He's not here.
STEPANOV. A pity, I came to beg his pardon. Tell him . . .He's a remarkable young man. He said that there were a lot of people like him, but he proved that there aren't many people like him. Yes . . .And I'm ashamed. Tell him that. Dr. Stepanov is ashamed. And it's very unpleasant when a grown man feels ashamed.
DISCUS THROWER. Why do you speak like that? He respects you.

Silence.

STEPANOV. Tell him . . .We're leaving for London. And we are arranging a party. And we would like him to come . . .
GIRL. He won't come.
STEPANOV. Why not?
GIRL. Surely you understand that.

Silence.

STEPANOV. But I am begging his pardon.
DISCUS THROWER. He'll come. What nonsense you're talking. He dreams of it . . .He is fond of . . .(*Stumbles, realizing that he is saying more than he should*).
STEPANOV. Well, never mind . . .He's fond of Masha. I know. You were the one who told me about it all. Remember? You were stripped to the waist.
GIRL. All the same he won't come. You insulted him . . .

226

STEPANOV. Tell him that Masha very much wants him to come.
GIRL. Masha too?
STEPANOV. Masha too.
GIRL. Such a pity he isn't here . . .Oh all right, if you feel like opening a wardrobe, open it.

Opens wardrobe.
In the wardrobe is Fokin.

FOKIN. I won't come. A komsomol member should be proud.
STEPANOV. A man stands in a wardrobe and talks of pride. A komsomol member should have a sense of humor . . .
FOKIN. Tell Masha that I won't come.

Stepanov descends the stairs.

In the room.
The discus thrower locks the wardrobe door.

—Just sit there, you fool . . .Just sit there . . .

Desperate banging at the wardrobe door from the inside.

At the dacha.
Preparations are in progress for the reception of visitors.
Waiters cover the tables in the garden.
Snow-white napkins.
Pyramids of fruit.
Cut glass.
Lively activity in the kitchen.
Mountains of pastries.
The drawing room.
Musicians in the drawing room.
They take their places.
Tall white glass doors.
Straw matting leading up to them.
Footsteps.
Tsitronov comes walking along the mat.
Tsitronov. A cigar in his mouth.
Tall white door.
Glass handle of door.
It is the door of Masha's bedroom.
Bedroom.
Masha is getting dressed.

Footsteps.
Masha listens.
In the corridor.
Tsitronov. A cigar in his hand.
Detail of bedroom.
Dressing table.
Window shutters.
Bottles.
Crystal vessels.
Powder-compact.
But Masha cannot be seen.

Tsitronov in the dining room.
Sees Masha's gloves on the table. Picks them up.
Raises them to his face.

Again the same detail of the bedroom comes into view.
Bottles.
Bottles.
Bottles.
But Masha is not to be seen.
Tsitronov throws down the gloves.
Looks into the garden.
Bunches of leaves.
A statue in front of them.
A stone girl.
Bedroom.
New detail.
Scattered articles of clothing.
But Masha is not to be seen.
Tsitronov at the door.
Masha enters the doorway.
Dressed.

Tsitronov is in the library. Sitting in an armchair. Sunk deep into it.
Head lowered. His chin resting on his chest. His arms hang over both arms
of the chair. The chair seems to be holding him by the armpits.
Music can be heard from the drawing room.
Masha emerges from the gates.
Music can be heard.
Stepanov approaches the gates.
Stepanov in motion.
He sees: Masha coming toward him.
They meet.

Masha.
Stepanov.
They stand still.
Move.
She begins to walk away.
He stands still.
Asks:

—You're coming back?

Pause.
Masha's face. She smiles at her husband:

—But of course.

Stairs leading to Grisha Fokin's room.
Masha ascends the stairs.
Masha in the corridor.
Sensation among the neighbors.
They peer out of their rooms.
Girl in the corridor.
A room.
Grisha is sleeping on the couch.
A meal awaits him on the table.
A little girl comes running out onto the tarmac.
The yard.
Children in the yard.
The little girl calls out from the tarmac:

—Lyalka! Lyalka! Come here. Quick!

Little girl in the yard asks:

—Why?
—There's a smell of perfume here in the corridor.

Above the sleeping Grisha.
Books. Desk.
The mother rouses her son.

—Grisha! Grisha! Wake up!

Son sleeps.

MOTHER (*more loudly*). Grisha! He's been working all night, you know. (*Still more loudly*). Grisha! Get up!

Son sleeps.

MOTHER. You could fire a gun.
MASHA (*softly*). Grisha.

Son wakes up.

At the dacha.
Verandah.
Brandy. Glass. Syphon.
Stepanov stands. He is thinking.
Pours water from syphon.
In several squirts.
Without looking at the syphon.
Presses it again.
No more water.
Goes from the table.
Tall white glass door.
Door to Masha's bedroom.
Straw matting.
Steps on the matting. Stepanov.
On the floor next to the door lies an extinguished cigar.

STEPANOV (*shouts*). Fyodor!

Tsitronov with a table napkin hurriedly walks through the garden.
Among the tables.
Stepanov on the verandah.
Tsitronov in front of him. He sees Stepanov's face terrible with anger.
Shrinks. Sinks into chair. Drops napkin.

—You stood at Masha's door while she was dressing?

Tsitronov is silent.

STEPANOV. Pig! You dare to think about her in that way.

Stepanov grasps a bottle by the neck.
Tinkle of smashed bottle.
Wet spot on the wall.
Tsitronov runs through the garden. Wet. Panic-stricken.
Knocks over tables, pyramids of fruit, mountains of pastries.

He runs out of the dacha grounds.
He runs far into the distance.
He sits on the grass.
Shaking. Wet.

Masha and Grisha.

—Why have you come?
—Shouldn't I have?
—No.
—What a stern one you are.

Masha descends the stairs.

The son sits at his desk over a book. He has sat down with an abrupt movement.
The mother leans over the dressing table.
Masha descends the stairs.
The son rushes headlong past his mother.
To the door.
Son on the tarmac. Door flung open.
Masha has already left the staircase.
She walks along the sidestreet.
Dusk.
The porch.
She is on the porch.
She moves forward.
Looks back.
Catches sight of him.
Both stand still.
They begin to advance toward each other.
She stops beneath the balcony.
The balcony above her.
The door is open.
A light is burning.
A piano is being played in the room there.
She stands beneath the balcony.
He approaches.
The playing stops. A man runs out onto the balcony.
Leans over the bannister.
Shouts:

—Who's there? What's the matter?

Sees them below.
Their faces are lifted.
Shouts:

—What's the matter? What are you standing there for? As soon as you start playing they come along to eavesdrop.

They stand beneath the balcony.
Twilight thickens.
View of them from the balcony.
They move away.
Again the sound of the piano.
Twilight thickens.
The sounds suddenly stop.
The man runs out on the balcony.
Shouts:

—They've gone. Well that's a fine thing! Eh? To play for loving couples? I don't want to. Meetings. Partings. Farewells. The whole area falls in love to the accompaniment of my music. I don't want that.

The two have gone away.
A crossing.
The piano can be heard in the distance.

SHE. I want to make a suggestion. Can I?
HE. Go ahead.
SHE. To walk on a little bit.

They walk.
The piano can be heard.

SHE. I want to make a suggestion. Can I?
HE. Go ahead.
SHE. There's a wonderful bench over there. I noticed it. Let's sit down for a bit.

They move forward.
The piano can be heard.
They approach the bench.
The two of them sitting on the bench.
Balcony. The musician runs out.
Leans over the balcony.
Shouts:

—Nobody there? I can play then!

Sounds of the piano.
The two stop at a bridge.

SHE. I want to make a suggestion. (*Slowly*). Can I?

He looks at her.
Her face in front of him.

HE (*slowly*). Go ahead.

They kiss.

At the dacha.
The party.
Visitors. Masha comes out to greet the guests. Her gait, the movements of the pleats of her skirt, her entire appearance are so amazing, strange and beautiful that the visitors exchange glances, and one of them— a young foreigner—cannot contain himself and softly, as if to himself, begins to clap.

May—June 1934
Odessa.

THE BLACK MAN

A Fragment

I am working on a play in which I want to consider creativity.

The central hero of the play is the writer Zand.

He wants to write a large work about construction, about the proletariat, about the new man, about the life of the young world. He dreams of being the writer of the rising class.

The writer Zand asserts that in order to become a writer in harmony with his epoch it is necessary to turn away from a number of themes. There are themes which, interesting though they might be, are unnecessary to our times. More than simply unnecessary, they are harmful and reactionary if only because they are pessimistic. They discourage the reader occupied with construction. Such themes must be struck from the writer's notebook.

But is this the solution, to cross out a theme? Will it leave our consciousness? Thrown out of the notebook, it still remains in the mind. It will stand astride the mind and stop it creating. Driven within, it will lurk and at last creep out onto paper.

If the writer Zand occupies himself with a new important, vigorous, life-affirming "sunny" theme, it makes no difference one way or the other— the black lizard theme will poke its foul-smelling tail or poisonous head out of his new creative work.

What is to be done? How to destroy such a theme? How to kill the lizard theme . . .you know that the chopped-off parts of lizards grow back again! There are many such themes, a whole nest of poisonous lizards. The theme of murder, for example, has taken control of Zand. He wants to kill a certain man. He dreams that he is killing him (why he wants to kill him is a special question to be treated in the play). How can Zand devote all the power of his mind to creative work in which all our new life would shine brightly when his mind is poisoned with the thought of death, of decay?

And then he encounters the Black Man. This man is some sort of graphologist, a palmist (a cynic, charlatan and poisoner).

This is a man whose ideology is a parody of Freud, Spengler and Bergson. He will be portrayed as a caricature of the European thinker of the period of capitalism in decline, as a parody of those who in our time write of the doom of progress and the destruction of man at the foot of the machine, of sunset.

The play is concerned with Zand's struggle with the Black Man, to the struggle of the idea of death in creative work with the idea of the re-creation of the world through art.

Petty bourgeois room. Six o'clock in the evening. Sorokina and Zand are on stage. Sorokina is young, the mistress of the house.

SOROKINA. Sit down for a bit. He'll be coming soon.
ZAND (*politely*). Thank you.

Silence.

Is your husband at work?
SOROKINA. Yes.
ZAND. And where does he work?
SOROKINA. In the thirty-first postal section. He's assistant to the director of the dispatch office. But haven't you come on business?
ZAND. No.
SOROKINA. What are you here for then?
ZAND. I've come about a personal matter. I can see you're worried. Please don't get the wrong idea. I'm a writer.
SOROKINA. A writer?
ZAND. Yes. My name is Zand. Modest Zand the writer.

Steps in the corridor.

SOROKINA. There's Kolya now. (*Opens the door*).

Enter her husband Sorokin. He is about thirty-five. Silence.

Kolya, someone is waiting for you.
ZAND. Hello.
HUSBAND. Hello, comrade. What do you want? (*Takes off his overcoat, puts his briefcase on a book-stand*).
ZAND. I would like to speak with you.
HUSBAND (*guardedly*). What have you got to say?
ZAND. You're probably going to have dinner?
HUSBAND. Yes.
ZAND. Well go right ahead please. I'll wait.
HUSBAND. But what's it about?
ZAND. Well, you see . . .it's difficult to explain just like that. If you're tired and not disposed to talk, then say so, I can come later . . .
HUSBAND. Sorry, do you need a signature or something?
ZAND. No. I've already told your wife about it. I'm a writer. Modest Zand. Perhaps you've read something of mine.
HUSBAND. No.
SOROKINA. Did you have something to eat at work today? Nothing to eat? How can you . . .Really.

236

ZAND. You work in the postal section?

HUSBAND. Yes.

SOROKINA. They have a terrible buffet there. He doesn't have a thing to eat all day.

HUSBAND. All right, all right.

ZAND. That's not good, you know. One must eat four times a day. Englishmen eat four times a day in all circumstances. At war, traveling and in a foreign country—on some wild island where there are only turtles and fruit . . .

SOROKINA. Do they really eat turtles?

ZAND. They make turtle soup.

HUSBAND. Sorry, excuse me . . .

ZAND. Yes, yes . . . I'll explain it to you right away.

HUSBAND. Have you come from the editorial office? About our way of life?

ZAND. Yes, yes. Something like that. I want to see how ordinary people, workers, live . . . I'm writing a play . . . My hero is an ordinary man, a city dweller . . . He comes home from work . . . Understand? So his wife welcomes him . . . they talk . . .

HUSBAND. But why come to me?

ZAND. It was chance. I didn't choose. I simply came in through the gate and went up the stairs . . . I knocked on the first door.

HUSBAND. Pleased to be of service.

SOROKINA. We'll be eating now.

ZAND. Don't pay any attention to me.

Sorokina goes out.

Have you lived in this apartment for long?

HUSBAND. Not long. My wife lived here with her first husband. I arrived not long ago.

ZAND. A nice room.

HUSBAND. They've promised to refit it.

ZAND. Forgive me for asking so many questions.

HUSBAND. It's all right . . . You keep apologizing.

His wife comes in carrying dinner.

SOROKINA. Perhaps you'll have something to eat with us?

ZAND. Nice of you, but I'm completely full. Thank you.

SOROKINA. You really should try some. It's pea soup.

ZAND. Many thanks, I feel awkward but that's how it is.

SOROKINA. Suit yourself.

HUSBAND. How about a drop of vodka?

ZAND. No, no thanks.
HUSBAND. Get it out of the briefcase.

His wife takes a bottle out of the briefcase.

HUSBAND. So it wasn't smashed in the tram today. (*Opens the bottle*). Don't you want any?
ZAND. Pour yourself some, please.
HUSBAND. A glass of vodka—can't do without it. I always have one. You can write that down.
ZAND. Before dinner?
HUSBAND. Absolutely.

The married couple eat.

ZAND. I've just had dinner in a restaurant. You know we writers are wealthy people. How much do you make?
HUSBAND. Two hundred twenty.
SOROKINA. And deductions?
HUSBAND. Oh sure. Two hundred of it's gone straight away. You can write that down. And provisons aren't included, I'm afraid.
ZAND. Yes. That's not much.
SOROKINA. We won the other day.
ZAND. What did you say?
SOROKINA. We won two hundred rubles in the third lottery.
ZAND (*with gentle animation*). Are you really serious?
SOROKINA. Word of honor. We got the cost of the ticket back too. Altogether it came to two hundred and fifty.
ZAND. And what did you do with the money?
SOROKINA. Kolya deposited it in our savings account.
ZAND. You want to pile it up?
HUSBAND (*to his wife*). That's enough from you . . .
SOROKINA. Come on darling! He's bashful. He has a long cherished dream.
ZAND. What kind?
HUSBAND. Come on Nadya . . . This is too much!
ZAND. No, tell me, what kind of dream?
SOROKINA. To buy a bicycle.
ZAND. Seriously?
HUSBAND. I'll let you buy it. Do you know how much a bicycle costs in the commission shop?
ZAND. No.
HUSBAND. Eight hundred.
ZAND. It's a good thing to have a bicycle. Just think of the rides you

can go on. All those green fields. Do you have a healthy heart?

HUSBAND. I'm healthy all right!

ZAND. And you sleep well?

SOROKINA. We get up early you know. At seven.

HUSBAND. A little glass? Please have one.

ZAND. No, no, you drink. Thanks, but I don't feel like it after dinner.

Silence.

HUSBAND. You can't do much on two hundred, you know . . .And she has relatives too . . .

SOROKINA. My brother and mother live in Borisov. He's a forestry specialist.

HUSBAND. So we sometimes get a bird. Some lard now and then. That's how it is—we're quite poor.

SOROKINA. Want some cranberry juice?

HUSBAND. Let's have some.

His wife goes out.

We've only recently married, you know. (*Pause*). We started living together not long ago. She had a husband.

ZAND. Yes, yes . . .

Silence.

HUSBAND. So you write?

ZAND. Yes.

HUSBAND. Is it difficult to be a writer?

ZAND. It is difficult.

HUSBAND. Why?

Wife brings in cranberry juice.

ZAND. You know there was a great writer, Goethe?

HUSBAND (*busy with the cranberry juice*). Sorry, what were you saying?

ZAND. Goethe, a great writer, he wrote "Faust." There's an opera "Faust." It's something else, a rehash of the subject. But the original is a poem, a drama—"Faust." It depicts a man who has attained the greatest wisdom. And that same Goethe who created that most intelligent of men, do you know what he said? He said that man's greatest misfortune is—to think . . .

HUSBAND. Sorry—what was that?

SOROKINA. What's with you...had too much already?

HUSBAND. Don't interrupt.

ZAND. Man's greatest misfortune—to reflect on things. That is, to think. Understand, he who thinks is automatically unhappy.

HUSBAND. I can tell you—it's necessary to think.

ZAND. No, I'm speaking in a...philosophical sense.

HUSBAND. Care for some cranberry juice?

ZAND. No thanks.

HUSBAND. As you like.

Silence.

ZAND. Tell me...I want to ask...You went to court? True? For an attempt on someone's life...You wanted to kill?

HUSBAND. Afraid so—how do you know? (*Elbows away a phrase his wife doesn't even have a chance to utter*). Don't interrupt.

ZAND. I found out. That's why I came to you. Specially. I didn't want to tell you at first, that I came to see you specially. Maybe it's unpleasant for you?

HUSBAND. W-w-why? It's fine.

ZAND. I've broached such a theme...I've been looking for exactly such a man...I've been to prison offices. They told me...they named various people who had served prison terms. I found out your address. You don't have anything against it?

HUSBAND. Nothing.

ZAND. I am writing a play. I need a person like yourself.

HUSBAND. My name too, if you don't mind me asking?

ZAND. No, no...Just to talk...An ordinary man, a Soviet workman, who has made an attempt on another man's life...

SOROKINA. He was in jail for four years.

HUSBAND. They gave me six years.

SOROKINA. Well yes...Let him out early.

HUSBAND. Six years including pretrial imprisonment and without any loss of rights.

ZAND. Yes, yes. You see, it's all so interesting. So often we hear...murder...I've been to the courts.

SOROKINA. They don't write about murders in the papers these days.

ZAND. Quite right.

SOROKINA. Although they wrote about you in the "Moscow Evening News."

HUSBAND. Yes, but only about the trial.

ZAND. I inquired at the prison administration specially. As a writer.

HUSBAND. Do they let you in there?

ZAND. Yes, they showed me a whole series of cases. But I needed a murder out of jealousy . . . And by an office worker . . . You did it out of jealousy, didn't you?

HUSBAND. Yes.

ZAND. It was because of you, Nadezhda . . . pardon me . . .

SOROKINA. Mikhailovna . . . Yes, because of me.

ZAND. And did he . . . remain alive, your former husband?

HUSBAND. The devil himself doesn't want that sort. I got him in the neck. Right here. The spine wasn't touched. He's healthy now.

ZAND. Perhaps I could do with a little glass of vodka.

HUSBAND. But of course, of course.

SOROKINA. Coming right up . . . (*Gets a glass from the sideboard*).

ZAND. Thank you.

HUSBAND. You should have had some earlier . . . I'll drink with you anyway.

SOROKINA. You've had enough.

HUSBAND. It doesn't concern you, madame. How about a snack?

ZAND. No, this is fine.

HUSBAND. Well, to your health.

Silence.

ZAND. Do you have a nap after dinner? Yes? If I'm keeping you from . . .

HUSBAND. Another one?

ZAND. No, I'm fine . . . just fine. I don't want any more. You say that it's necessary to think. It's not necessary. Take you . . . a strong man . . .

HUSBAND. Let's see who has the stronger arm. Put your elbow on the edge of the table.

ZAND. No, I had in mind . . .

HUSBAND. Go ahead, put it there . . .

ZAND. But you'll beat me, of course.

They arm-wrestle.

HUSBAND. Oho . . . Here we go . . . one, two—bam! Sorry! Too much for you! Didn't I tell you. I have an acquaintance, a jockey. Antsiferov, Fyodor Denisovich. You've undoubtedly heard of him.

SOROKINA. Do you go to the races?

ZAND. Yes . . . but rarely.

SOROKINA. Antsiferov is on tour in Kharkov.

HUSBAND. You really need to know where Antsiferov is on tour, don't you. I arm-wrestled with Antsiferov, you know . . . Came out even. But just think of a horse. Straining its shoulders. Imagine what strong arms you've got to have!

Silence.

(*Suddenly*). But he's an oddball—a writer. Sorry—but weren't you acquainted earlier?

ZAND. With whom?

HUSBAND. With her. (*Nods at his wife*).

ZAND. Why are you asking?

SOROKINA. He's getting jealous.

HUSBAND. She's somehow looking very attentively in your eyes.

SOROKINA. I don't like those kind.

HUSBAND. You like Antsiferov.

Silence.

ZAND. You didn't understand what I wanted to say about strength.

HUSBAND. We understood everything.

SOROKINA. Don't have any more to drink.

HUSBAND. Sorry—we understood everything.

SOROKINA. What did you understand?

HUSBAND (*very roughly*). Get out, you! (*Threatens her*).

Sorokina collects the dishes.

She still remembers her first husband.

ZAND. Who you...

HUSBAND. Missed, I'm afraid.

ZAND. How did you...Walked up to him and pulled the trigger?

HUSBAND. She grabbed my hands.

SOROKINA. I was afraid for you. That you would kill him.

HUSBAND. They've been waiting a long time for that one in the other world.

ZAND. Was he a bad man?

HUSBAND. Ask her.

SOROKINA. He was my husband. (*Goes out*).

ZAND. I know. I read the trial transcript.

HUSBAND. Maybe she's still living with him in her mind.

Silence.

He turned her head when she was still a girl. I was best man at their wedding. He was all painted and dyed, a painted moustache, a wax flower in his button-hole, tall, completely moth-eaten. Rather hump-backed.

ZAND. An old man?

HUSBAND. Ask her. (*Pause*). Such an old man you wouldn't believe it. A Polack. (*Pause*). Name of Brszowski. He could figure a person's character by their handwriting. Sat at a little table in the moviehouse. An educated man.

ZAND. A graphologist?

HUSBAND. Who the hell knows. Sorry—I'll lie down. You don't mind? (*Lies down*). Nadya! Where did she go? Nadya!

Sorokina comes in.

SOROKINA. Lies down in his boots. Take off your boots. Let me help.

ZAND. I only want to ask you one question. You decided beforehand to kill, didn't you?

SOROKINA. He dickered for a whole month for a revolver.

ZAND. Weren't you afraid?

Silence.

Is he asleep?

SOROKINA. He knew there would be a trial. That's what he was after. Served four years. (*Caresses sleeping husband*). My damned little devil. Yes, damned. That's the word. He's asleep.

ZAND. I would have been afraid.

SOROKINA. Of what? Killing?

ZAND. Yes.

SOROKINA. What is there to be afraid of?

ZAND. No, not conscience...No. Once there's no Christianity, there's no conscience...I would be afraid of my mind, my own mind. They say there are apparitions...That the mind breaks down, that thought decays. It means that punishment is already waiting in the mind.

SOROKINA. And you would like to kill, is that it?

ZAND. No, I'm writing a play. And I want to describe a murder out of jealousy in it.

SOROKINA. Something like what happened with us.

ZAND. Yes. I was thinking about strength, you understand.

SOROKINA. About what?

ZAND. About strength. They say that strong unusual people are the chosen ones. Prophets, generals, geniuses...no, no...That's not it. Those are men possessed. It's not strength—it's a mania, a disturbance...That's just the opposite, that's out of weakness, out of fear of death. But strength is in something else. The strong are ordinary people. Take him, for example—in order to live with you, he decided to kill another man...Have you read "Crime and Punishment?"

SOROKINA. No.

243

ZAND. Perhaps I'm talking too loudly?

SOROKINA. Don't worry. He's asleep—when he's had a drop of vodka, you could fire a cannon.

Brszowski comes in unnoticed by Zand. He is painted black. He wears a coat and hat. His appearance is marked by a high starched collar, out of which hangs his stalactite of a neck.

ZAND. In that novel a student decides to kill an old woman, in order to test his strength. He kills her...and then conscience takes over. But these days there's no conscience. The revolution killed thousands...Was that class justification?

BRSZOWSKI. Class justification is as murky a concept as conscience.

ZAND (*turns round in surprise*). Who's this?

BRSZOWSKI (*puts his finger to his lips and makes frightening eyes, indicating the sleeper*). Ssh...

SOROKINA. Get out, get out, do you hear!

BRSZOWSKI. But what's happening?

SOROKINA. I'm telling you to get out. He's against you today.

BRSZOWSKI. Is he drunk?

SOROKINA. A little.

BRSZOWSKI. Doesn't matter.

SOROKINA (*introduces him to Zand*). Here he is...my very first husband. This is a writer. Let me introduce you.

ZAND. Zand.

BRSZOWSKI. Modest Zand?

ZAND. Yes.

BRSZOWSKI. The writer Zand here? In a house that doesn't have a single book? Oh yes, there is one. A savings book.

SOROKINA. You know him?

BRSZOWSKI. Many people know the writer Zand. You only know jockeys. (*Bows*). Brszowski, Boleslav Ivanovich. Graphologist.

SLEEPER (*turns over, mumbles*). Eh...eh...eh...What...

BRSZOWSKI. Sleep, sleep...What's up? Sleep...

ZAND. I've seen you...You define handwriting...In the movie-house...You've got a table.

BRSZOWSKI. Exactly right. The Garibaldi theater. On Sretenka Street.

SOROKINA. He charges a ruble.

BRSZOWSKI. Unfortunately, yours is not among my collection of handwriting. It would be interesting...

ZAND. One day...For sure...(*Pause*). Nadezhda Mikhailovna, give your husband my thanks and regards. I'll go now. Goodbye. (*Takes his leave*).

BRSZOWSKI (*not releasing Zand's hand*). I'm an admirer of yours.

ZAND. Really? Thank you.

BRSZOWSKI. Graphology, palmistry—people regard it with distrust. Isn't that right? Why you, most likely . . .

ZAND. No why should I? Is it a science? An exact sc ;nce?

BRSZOWSKI. Oh no. It's an art. Will you allow me to look at the lines of your hand? Art is remarkable in that it proves that form is the main thing . . .Only form . . .Lines . . .(*Inspects Zand's palm*). Oh . . .very interesting . . .An extraordinary instance . . .You know . . .it seems to me that you have the hand of a murderer and a genius . . .

AFTERWORD

I am attempting to create a dialectical drama. I observe disparate forces and I bring them into collision in order to create drama. The world must be reconstructed on the basis of socialism. The higher mind, the higher intelligence understands that the proletariat is the only creative force and that it will reconstruct the world. As a dramatist I want to prove this thesis as impressively as I can. But drama is an argument, a tournament. In the excerpt here offered, I am expressing only a fragment of the argument. I am convinced that a reactionary work cannot flow from my pen, because my dialectic is in favor of those who are reconstructing the world.